TREATMENT
OF
SEXUAL
DYSFUNCTION

TREATMENT OF SEXUAL DYSFUNCTION

A Bio-Psycho-Social Approach

by WILLIAM E. HARTMAN Ph.D.
and MARILYN A. FITHIAN

WILLIAM E. HARTMAN, Ph.D.
Director, Center for Marital and
Sexual Studies, Professor of
Sociology, California State
University — Long Beach

Published By

CENTER FOR MARITAL AND SEXUAL STUDIES
5199 East Pacific Coast Highway
Long Beach, California 90804

TREATMENT OF SEXUAL DYSFUNCTION:

A Bio-Psycho-Social Approach

MARILYN A. FITHIAN
Associate Director, Center for
Marital and Sexual Studies
Instructor Comparative
Literature, California State
University — Long Beach

Published in the United States of America.

First Edition

International Standard Book No.: 0-9600626-1-0

Library of of Congress Catalog No.: 72-93106

4th Printing

PREFACE

We began conducting one and two-day seminars in "The Treatment of Human Sexual Inadequacy" in 1969. The objectives of the seminars we have been offering during the last four years are primarily three-fold:

1. To present information to the professional so that he can more easily and competently handle emotion-laden material presented to him by his clients or patients, so he will feel freer to discuss openly any sexual problems he may encounter in his practice.

2. To present new information and research findings which will expand the professional's knowledge and awareness.

3. To instruct and present information which will enhance the skills and techniques of working with the sexually dysfunctional.

The participants in our seminars during the past four years have come primarily from the fields of medicine, particularly obstetrics and gynecology, psychiatry, and urology. Other areas also represented have been ministers, psychologists, marriage counselors, and social workers. Many of these professional people and others have requested information about our work. This book is an outline with certain areas explored in more depth. The seminars and the book are complementary yet stand on their own.

We do not feel our form of treatment is the only way sexual therapy can be done. Our initial work involved trying a number of different ways to achieve positive results. The last three years we have fairly well determined how we can obtain optimum results. These are presented here. This does not mean we are inflexible. We are constantly looking for and thinking about—researching ways in which we can obtain even better results. We report briefly on research past, present and future in the last chapter entitled, "Where Do We Go From Here?"

This book is a guide to our method of sexual therapy. We do not elaborate on all of the rationale and theory in relation to our methods. Subsequent publications will detail all of our steps, more extensively with case histories, rationale and theory, and will be published in the next few years. The current publication is presented to fulfill the requests of professionals for written information on our procedures. Not all professionals will be interested in everything we do. The areas which we have developed which are markedly different than found in conventional therapy are presented in more depth, and those which can be found in traditional publications are only superficially covered.

A frequent request from seminar participants has been for a bibliography of human sexual behavior. We acknowledge the help of Dave V. Kusisto in preparing an extensive annotated bibliography of appropriate material which is found in the latter part of this book.

By way of acknowledgement, several significant aspects of our program come from the great pioneers in sexual therapy Dr. William H. Masters and Virginia E. Johnson (Mrs. William H. Masters). Specifically we have included their ideas of Dual Sex Therapy Team, set fee, two-week time-limited program, roundtable, quiet vagina, two of the three non-demand techniques we use, and parts of the sex history.

Edward M. Brecher has become a close and cherished friend during the last four years. He has been responsible for encouraging us to set down in writing just how we do sexual therapy. He has made many helpful comments and suggestions.

Fred Hills is responsible for the line drawings which provide the visual aids in this volume. He is a perceptive behavioral scientist who disclaims any artistic talents. His illustrations, however, demonstrate the maxim "a picture is worth a thousand words."

Mrs. Penny Bassett, secretary, has typed and re-typed the many versions of the manuscript including the final one.

Dr. Berry Campbell, Edward Bassett, Dave Kusisto, Marilyn Fry, and Earl Rugraff have read the manuscript in its entirety, and have made many helpful suggestions.

Our most significant acknowledgement is to our research subjects who did not wait until death to give their bodies to science. Their personal response to feelings and perceptions before, during, and after our experimental work were an even more significant contribution than their bodies per se.

DAILY SCHEDULE
TWO-WEEK INTENSIVE SEXUAL THERAPY PROGRAM

First Day — Monday

M.M.P.I.
T.J.T.A.
Draw-a-Scene   2-2½ hrs.
Luscher Color Test
Sex History   2½ hrs.

Second Day — Tuesday

Follow-up sex history   30 min.
Switch   1½ hr.

Third Day — Wednesday

Physical Exam   2 hrs.
Round Table   1 hr.
(Explain psychological tests if indicated or requested)

Fourth Day — Thursday

Sexological Form   ½ hr.
Draw-a-Person Test   ½ hr.
Sexological Exam   1½ hrs.
Body Imagery   1½ hrs.
Sensitivity   ½ hr.
Kegel Film   ½ hr.
Assignment — Comb Hair

Fifth Day — Friday

Foot Caress   1½ hrs.
Video Tape — Caress   1 hr.
Face Caress   1½ hrs.
Assignment give each other a bath or shower

Sixth Day — Saturday

Body Caress & Breathing Together   2 hrs.
Video Tape — Pleasuring Squeeze Technique   1 hr.
Assignment for Sunday is pleasuring
and clamping successfully several times.
Clamping enough times to go at least 15 minutes.

Seventh Day — Sunday

> Assignment in motel — pleasuring, male and female,
> practice squeeze technique.

Eighth Day — Monday

> Come in and report   1 hr.
> If things are going alright, assignment for more
> pleasuring and quiet vagina.
> See films of coital positions   ½ hr.
> Non-orgasmic woman — audio tape if indicated.   ½ hr.

Ninth Day — Tuesday

> Talk and report   1 hr.
> Intercourse (allowed) if things are going well.
> Video Tape — Intercourse   1 hr.

Tenth Day — Wednesday

> Report   1 hr.
> Video Tape — Intercourse   1 hr.

Eleventh Day — Thursday

> Report   1 hr.
> Video Tape — Intercourse   1 hr.
> Spontaneity assignment

Twelfth Day — Friday

> Report   1 hr.
> Evaluation of progress — if satisfactory, couple
> returns home. If further progress probable by
> seeing another video tape and completing an
> additional assignment or repeating one, couple
> remain another day.

Thirteenth Day — Saturday

> Wrap up   1 hr.
> Schedule for follow-ups, discuss how they will
> be able to implement what they have learned.

The above schedule indicates approximately the way
our time is spent with our clients. Presenting symptoms,
unique individual and couple needs are the final determinants of time allocations.

On the average we spend 35 hours with our couples. In several instances the figure has been close to 50 hours. The second week schedule allows us flexibility to work more intensively with couples who require it.

Hypnosis is not used until the second week, and it is only utilized where indicated—where the individual or couple feels it would be helpful, and we see that it would aid in their progress. The program stands on its own without it, but hypnosis has proved to be helpful with some difficult cases.

The times we see couples is set up in relation to the needs, desires, and wishes of the couples. Our time schedule is such that we can only work with three couples for the first week, but the second week with more free time, we make follow-up calls, and take care of other professional business.

A couple usually sees us in the morning and afternoon unless they prefer to group their appointments together for more free time. If they prefer a certain time, we try to work that time out for them. A typical appointment schedule for couples X, Y, and Z on the busiest day would be:

ROOM A

X	Foot caress	9:00-10:30
Y	Foot caress	10:30-12:00
Z	Foot caress	12:00- 1:30

ROOM B

X	Face caress	1:30- 3:00
Y	Face caress	3:00- 4:30
Z	Face caress	4:30- 6:00

VIDEO ROOM

X	See Video Tape	12:30- 1:30
Y	See Video Tape	2:00- 3:00
Z	See Video Tape	3:30- 4:30

TREATMENT PROCEDURE

The structure of our intensive two-week therapy program as it evolved to date can conveniently be summarized as a series of 34 steps as follows. (The steps are varied, of course, to meet the needs of individual couples. All assignments are carried out in the privacy of the motel room.)

1. Initial referral
2. Socio-psychological testing
3. First sexual history
4. Second sexual history
5. Physical examination
6. Roundtable discussion
7. Developing sensuality
8. Sexological examination
9. Kegel film
10. Body imagery
11. Touching and relating (sensitivity)
12. Assignment: Combing the partner's hair
13. Foot caress
14. Video tape: Foot, face, Body Caress and Breathing Together.
15. Mutual bathing assignment.
16. Face caress
17. Assignment—Wash hair
18. Body caress
19. Breathing Together
20. Sexual caress
21. Video tape — Non-demand techniques — Pleasuring — Squeeze Technique—etc.
22. Assignment: Male-Active/Non-Demand Technique — Female back against male's chest.
23. Assignment: Female-Active/Non-Demand Technique — Squeeze Technique.
24. Assignment: Male-Active/Non-Demand Technique — Female supine-Male pleasuring vagina.
25. Assignment: The "Quiet Vagina"
26. Films of Coital Positions
27. Audio-tape: "How to Become Orgasmic"
28. Video Tape of Coitus — "Effective Sexual Functioning"
29. Hypnosis when indicated
30. "Romantic Tape" of Coitus
31. Play function of sex — "Fun Tape" of coitus
32. Assignment: Spontaneity — How Do You Do Your Thing?
33. Saying Goodbye
34. Follow-up

CONTENTS

TREATMENT OF SEXUAL DYSFUNCTION:
A Bio-Psycho-Social Approach

TABLE OF FIGURES

Chapter **1**

INTRODUCTION

Our program for treatment of human sexual dysfunction includes a series of steps, activities, and exercises moving the individual and the couple toward becoming more intimately in touch with their own feelings and the feelings of the significant other. Since sex is something you do and not something you talk about, we feel it is essential that we have an action-oriented rather than a talk-about sex program.

Our experience indicates that use of action methods with specific steps and techniques to accomplish goals produces the best positive results during a clearly defined time period. We follow a definite programmed procedure flexible enough for any contingencies, taking into account the personalities and problems of the couple we are working with, in order that their unique needs may be met.

We have a bio-psycho-social approach to the treatment of human sexual dysfunction. We believe the physical background and current physical status should be examined; someone with a physical problem should be referred for medical care. This is the biological aspect of our program. We agree with Freud that the image one has about one's self stems from the basic biological image; therefore, it is important that the basic biology be dealt with before the program moves on to consideration of feelings concerning one's self. Self-concept, along with psychological testing forms the psychological portion of the program. It is important this be done before one is put in touch with someone else—this is the sociological step in the program. This process is an interdisciplinary approach to the resolution of sexual dysfunction.

We find a dual-sex therapy team essential in treating a sexually dysfunctional couple. Except for taking the sex histories and the psychological testing, both therapists work together.

Our work as a dual-sex research and therapy team began in 1964. During the past eight years, we began cotherapy with groups, and completed two research projects. One was a major project consisting of six samples and a total N of 2,554 dealing with social nudism[1] as a social-psychological phenomenon. A Non-Orgasmic Women Study[2] ran concurrently the last three years prior to the opening of the Center with an N of 83, including a control sample of seven who were consistently orgasmic.

During this time as a result of our work on the Non-Orgasmic Women Study, we began our observations of intercourse. We found information in the sexual field limited, antiquated, and unsatisfactory. We found few answers to our questions, and the questions grew. We contacted people we knew, and let it be known that we were starting research in the sexual field. We explained the lack of information and the tremendous need. As a result,

---

[1] William E. Hartman, Marilyn A. Fithian, and Donald Johnson, *Nudist Society*, (New York, 1970) Crown Publishers.

[2] Paper presented to the Counseling Section of the National Council on Family Relations, (New Orleans, 1968).

friends, relatives, and colleagues volunteered or told others we were seeking research subjects. It was from our work with these volunteers that our work evolved.

This book is based on our work with a total research and therapy population of 1,167 individuals over the last seven years. The techniques reported evolved from working with individuals and couples in various research projects, our work with dysfunctional couples treated intensively during two-week periods, and work with dysfunctional couples in groups, both at the Center and at various locations in California and the Mid-West. The breakdown on the total research and therapy population will be found in Appendix, page 218.

DUAL-SEX TEAM APPROACH

The team approach as used includes a male and a female therapist working together toward the resolution of problems in human sexual dysfunction. The advantage of the dual-sex approach is that it brings to the situation divergent sexually related viewpoints, and also a greater range of perception is available from the individual who is not currently engaging in the verbal interaction.

The importance of a dual-sex therapy team is evident when one considers the socialization process involved in taking on a sexual identity, male or female. This profound, psychogenic learning conditions men and women to think, feel, and act differently sexually, both coitally, and non-coitally. It is, therefore, essential that representatives of both sexes, with their unique cultural conditioning, be represented in a therapeutic situation involving two individuals with similar cultural experiences.

We have found that two therapists can multiply their observations, especially if the backgrounds of the therapists from socio-economic, cultural, religious, and educational points of view are uniquely different. This was the case in our own research and counseling experience, and it is one of the reasons we have found the dual-sex therapy team approach to sex research and therapy so rewarding and effective.

The team approach minimizes dependency needs, and identification with a single therapist. The chance of sexual involvement is nil, protecting both the client and the therapist. Sexual offers and indication of sexual interests can be easily handled when both sexes are present.

Touch between clients and therapists can take place much more readily and comfortably in such a situation. Touch is the most effective method we have found to get feelings flowing. Superficial touch from one or both professionals in a responsible professional situation is often necessary to get therapeutic clients comfortable with touching. It is often easier to institute superficial touch with a non-significant other before proceeding to touch with a significant other in the client's life.

Referral by authority effectively eliminates inappropriate candidates for our mode of therapy. The two-week intensive program with a two-year follow-up service currently costs $2,400.00. There is no need for such a program if the problem is resolvable in short-term counseling. A referring authority who is aware of the existing problem is best able to determine if the prognosis is favorable with an action-oriented program.

Approximately 50% of our therapy couples have come from medical referrals. Of these, roughly ⅓ came from specialists in obstetrics and gynecology, another ⅓ from psychiatrists, and the final ⅓ from general practitioners and urologists. About ⅓ of our referrals come from psychologists, marriage counselors, and social workers, and the remaining 15% or so are self-referred couples. In the latter category are professional people, such as ministers and lawyers, who could have referred others, but have chosen to refer themselves.

This book is primarily addressed to our intensive two-week therapy program.

Chapter 2

PSYCHOLOGICAL TESTING

A significant portion of the beginning work with clients involves personality and temperament testing. The Minnesota Multiphasic Personality Inventory (M.M.P.I.),[1] the Taylor-Johnson Temperament Analysis (T-JTA),[2] the Draw-a-Person Test, and the Luscher Color Test[3] are administered. The Draw-a-Scene Test is now included and although it appears on our work form, we have insufficient data to discuss it in detail here. We ask an individual to select a color and draw a picture of the partner and self in some activity.

---

[1] Minnesota Multiphasic Personality Inventory, Psychological Corporation, 304 East 45th Street, New York, New York 10017.

[2] Taylor-Johnson Temperament Analysis, Psychological Publications, Inc., 5300 Hollywood Blvd., Los Angeles, California 90027.

[3] Max Luscher, Ph.D., *The Luscher Color Test,* (New York, 1969), translated and edited by Ian Scott.

MINNESOTA MULTIPHASIC PERSONALITY INVENTORY

The Minnesota Multiphasic Personality Inventory is one of a number of contemporary standard objective tests which are used to evaluate personality. It is comprised of 550 true and false statements. The majority of these statements are about the person taking the test: I like (this). I enjoy (that), at times I (do something else). Statements of belief are asked such as Christ performed (such and such), or general statements such as—When a man is with a woman, he is usually (thinking this or that). The test can either be scored by hand or by machine. No specific answer is critical. It is a combination of responses that are important to each scale on the profile. The results are plotted on a graph with scores on fourteen or more scales so that a profile of personality characteristics emerges. The scale consists of scores on groups of items, patterns of true and false answers that have been shown to have particular meanings, and to be consistent in these meanings. Here is an example of how this is scored, a group of sixty items show general differences between people who are unhappy, down-hearted, pessimistic, or dejected people; and those who are normal, gay-hearted, cheerful people. These items are the ones which make up the Depression Scale. The way the individual responds to these sixty questions determines where he will be on the scale. No one answer makes a person one way or the other, it is a constellation of responses that measures the differences. This test is a way of measuring psychological depression.

The test profile is interpreted by the deviations on these scales from scores taken from a group of so-called normal people. Interpretation also can show emergent patterns so that it can be determined if a person who has evaluations on the Depression Scale, is mildly or severely depressed, and if this depression will be expressed by anger, resentment, quiet resignation or attempted suicide.

There is a great deal of knowledge, both published and unpublished, about the characteristics and meanings of the M.M.P.I. The scores themselves can give information about a single personality or a group of individuals, and it is especially valuable to determine deviant characteristics and pathological forms of adjustment.

An M.M.P.I. handbook[4] is useful in evaluating test results, and is easily obtainable.

The test gives objective data about the emotional state and psychological characteristics of each of the clients referred to us for treatment of sexual dysfunction. It is used to supplement our clinical evaluation, not to determine it. Clients are not refused as a result of any of the tests given at this time since we have not encountered a clear indication to do so. We do take emotionally disturbed people if referred by a therapist, since in our Non-Orgasmic Women Study,[5] we found psychotics as measured by T scores above 70 on scales 2, 3, 7, and 8 were as likely to become orgasmic as so-called "normals." Elevations on the clinical scales may be interpreted as evidence of emotional problems or psychopathology. These conditions tend to preclude effective sensate focus during our action-oriented therapy, and require the need for closer supervision of activities.

TAYLOR-JOHNSON TEMPERAMENT ANALYSIS

For the purpose of diagnostic evaluation the Taylor-Johnson Temperament Analysis (T-JTA) is employed.[6] The

---

[4] W. Grant Dahlstrom and George Schlager Welsh, *An M.M.P.I.* Handbook, (1960) The University of Minnesota Press.

[5] Presented in a paper presented to the counseling section of the National Council on Family Relations, (1968) New Orleans, Louisiana.

[6] Robert M. Taylor reviewed our T-JTA material and made helpful suggestions in the presentation and interpretation of the profiles.

T-JTA is a personality test designed for diagnostic, counseling and research purposes. It measures nine important personality traits and their opposites and serves as a convenient and effective method of measuring those characteristics which may significantly influence personal, social or marital adjustment. In addition to its other applications, we have found the T-JTA to be uniquely appropriate for use in our work with couples because it has been developed so that it can be taken by a couple, each on themselves, and also on one another, thus providing a picture of the self-concept of each, as well as a measure of interpersonal perception. The charted results depicting both evaluations is called a "criss-cross" profile.

In general, a high correlation between the "self" and the "other" rating on the various T-JTA traits measured tend to make for greater ease when working with the clients. Where there is a disparity in interpersonal perception, either in the way a spouse sees himself or is seen, in turn, by the other, there is evidence of poor or blocked channels of communication. If there are strong differences in the evaluation of specific personality traits for a spouse, serious misunderstanding is indicated. It is not uncommon to find a spouse who claims to be affectionate, expressive, responsive, and sympathetic, while the partner perceives that same spouse to be cold, indifferent, inhibited, and unresponsive (see Illustration 1). This illustration is an example of the way a spouse sees himself and in turn is seen by the other. The self-concept on the part of the husband is one of an affectionate, demonstrative, sympathetic, kind, understanding and compassionate individual. This husband is seen by his wife as unresponsive, repressed, restrained, unsympathetic, insensitive and unfeeling, as rated by her on the T-JTA Expressive-Responsive/Inhibited and Sympathetic/Indifferent scales.

Actually, both conceptions of this person could be accurate. In his occupational role this person may be all that he says he is, but in his familial role he may function as the wife perceives him. When viewed from their own frames of reference, both individuals may be accurate in their perceptions. This disparity would then be further explored in therapy in an attempt to develop a more realistic understanding of one another.

If we find that the wife is indeed accurate in her perception of her husband, that he is in fact inhibited and unfeeling, we would then work toward helping him learn how to be more demonstrative and understanding. If on the other hand we find that the husband's self-perception is valid, it may be that his wife is unrealistic in her expectations of him and these unrealistic expectations have, in turn, led to his becoming more inhibited and indifferent. In such instances, one of our primary objectives would be to work toward modifying the wife's expectations of her husband which then might allow his warmth and spontaneity to surface and flow more easily.

The most common traits found in sexually dysfunctional couples are the T-JTA traits Quiet, Inhibited and Indifferent; these are indicated by low scores in the opposite traits of Active-Social, Expressive-Responsive, and Sympathetic (see Illustration 2). This profile depicts an individual who has problems in these three areas. Although his wife sees him in a somewhat better light in the areas of quiet and inhibited, a need for improvement is still indicated. It is of interest to note that she sees him as much more sympathetic than he sees himself.

In all of the traits studied in the T-JTA "criss-cross" testing, we find the T-JTA trait Inhibited to be the most important factor related to sexual dysfunction. The most effective method of altering these traits involves action-oriented therapy, including role-training, behavior modification, sex education and counseling.

Husband by Wife _____Husband by Self
Criss-Cross ----------Husband as seen by Wife

TAYLOR-JOHNSON TEMPERAMENT ANALYSIS PROFILE
Profile Revision of 1967

These Answers Describe____#90008_____Age_____Sex_____Date_____

School_____ Grade_____Degree_____Major_____ Occupation_____ Counselor_____

Single____ Years Married____ Years Divorced____ Years Widowed____ Children: M____Ages_____ F____Ages_____

Answers made by: SELF (and/or) husband, wife, father, mother, son, daughter, brother, sister, or_____of the person described.

Norm(s): G.P.C.C.	A		B		C		D		E		F		G		H		I		Attitude (Sten) Score: 7 5
Mids		1		1	2	1		1	1	2	3	1	2		1	1	2	1	Total Mids: 11 9
Raw score	4	5	4	1	32	29	36	17	37	10	9	5	28	34	1	9	26	19	Raw score
Percentile	20	16	34	7	76	66	87	16	87	7	48	20	67	92	6	38	54	33	Percentile
TRAIT	Nervous		Depressive		Active-Social		Expressive-Responsive		Sympathetic		Subjective		Dominant		Hostile		Self-disciplined		TRAIT

| TRAIT OPPOSITE | Composed | Light-hearted | Quiet | Inhibited | Indifferent | Objective | Submissive | Tolerant | Impulsive | TRAIT OPPOSITE |

Excellent   Acceptable   Improvement desirable   Improvement urgent

DEFINITIONS

TRAITS

Nervous — Tense, high-strung, apprehensive.
Depressive — Pessimistic, discouraged, dejected.
Active-Social — Energetic, enthusiastic, socially involved.
Expressive-Responsive — Spontaneous, affectionate, demonstrative.
Sympathetic — Kind, understanding, compassionate.
Subjective — Emotional, illogical, self-absorbed.
Dominant — Confident, assertive, competitive.
Hostile — Critical, argumentative, punitive.
Self-disciplined — Controlled, methodical, persevering.

OPPOSITES

Composed — Calm, relaxed, tranquil.
Light-hearted — Happy, cheerful, optimistic.
Quiet — Socially inactive, lethargic, withdrawn.
Inhibited — Restrained, unresponsive, repressed.
Indifferent — Unsympathetic, insensitive, unfeeling.
Objective — Fair-minded, reasonable, logical.
Submissive — Passive, compliant, dependent.
Tolerant — Accepting, patient, humane.
Impulsive — Uncontrolled, disorganized, changeable.

Note: Important decisions should not be made on the basis of this profile without confirmation of these results by other means.

ILLUSTRATION 1

Husband by Wife _____ Husband by Self
Criss-Cross ----------Husband as seen by Wife

TAYLOR-JOHNSON TEMPERAMENT ANALYSIS PROFILE
Profile Revision of 1967

These Answers Describe ___#9004_____ Age_____ Sex_____ Date_____

School_____ Grade____ Degree____ Major_____ Occupation_____ Counselor_____

Single___ Years Married___ Years Divorced___ Years Widowed___ Children: M___ Ages_____ F___ Ages____

Answers made by: SELF and/or husband, wife, father, mother, son, daughter, brother, sister, or_____ of the person described.

Norms(s)CC GP	A		B		C		D		E		F		G		H		I		Attitude (Sten) Score: 3 7
Mids	1		1		1	1	1	1	1	1	2		1		1				Total Mids: 5 7
Raw score	7	14	11	6	9	17	11	21	23	35	12	16	26	27	14	7	40	40	Raw score
Percentile	35	51	64	32	2	25	4	26	13	79	61	60	55	66	66	30	99	99	Percentile
TRAIT	Nervous		Depressive		Active-Social		Expressive-Responsive		Sympathetic		Subjective		Dominant		Hostile		Self-disciplined		TRAIT

| TRAIT OPPOSITE | Composed | Light-hearted | Quiet | Inhibited | Indifferent | Objective | Submissive | Tolerant | Impulsive | TRAIT OPPOSITE |

■ Excellent ▬ Acceptable ▭ Improvement desirable ☐ Improvement urgent

DEFINITIONS

TRAITS
Nervous — Tense, high-strung, apprehensive.
Depressive — Pessimistic, discouraged, dejected.
Active-Social — Energetic, enthusiastic, socially involved.
Expressive-Responsive — Spontaneous, affectionate, demonstrative.
Sympathetic — Kind, understanding, compassionate.
Subjective — Emotional, illogical, self-absorbed.
Dominant — Confident, assertive, competitive.
Hostile — Critical, argumentative, punitive.
Self-disciplined — Controlled, methodical, persevering.

OPPOSITES
Composed — Calm, relaxed, tranquil.
Light-hearted — Happy, cheerful, optimistic.
Quiet — Socially inactive, lethargic, withdrawn.
Inhibited — Restrained, unresponsive, repressed.
Indifferent — Unsympathetic, insensitive, unfeeling.
Objective — Fair-minded, reasonable, logical.
Submissive — Passive, compliant, dependent.
Tolerant — Accepting, patient, humane.
Impulsive — Uncontrolled, disorganized, changeable.

Note: Important decisions should not be made on the basis of this profile without confirmation of these results by other means.

ILLUSTRATION 2

Figure 1. Draw-A-Person Test. After choosing from 25 available colors, and explaining rationale for that choice, each client draws a front nude view of themselves and then repeats the process doing the same for their partner.

The Draw-a-Person Test is done on 8½ x 11 colored paper. It involves drawing a nude front-view of oneself on one sheet, and a nude front-view of the spouse on a separate sheet. Clients choose from 25 available colors. They are told that it is not an art contest, but to draw the person as best they can. Each client is instructed to select the color that best suits the personality of the one they are drawing, not the color they like best.

Why do they choose this color in relation to their personality? For instance, if they feel that they are a "cool" person, they might choose a blue or a green, and their perception would be in relation to how they perceive these particular colors and themselves. If they see themselves as warm and responsive, they might select something they feel is a warm color such as orange. Indications of personality problems are found in relation to the selection of the color they choose for themselves, and the one they choose for their spouse. Colors often have different meanings for different people. Green is seen as cool, intelligent, vibrant, and peaceful. We cannot simply assume from the color the meaning that it has for them, therefore, it is important that the reasons for choosing the color be written down. In the corner they tell what it is about the personality of the individual that was instrumental in selecting the color. Although separated when taking the test, the same color is often selected by both of them for similar reasons, i.e. Couple both selected a magenta for the female, and she stated it was warm and lively—he stated it was lively and bright.

Future publication will present the relationship we encounter in the Draw-a-Person Test, and its use in our body imagery work. Some of the client's choices of color are revealing, and give quick insights into how they perceive themselves. i.e. A dark brown was used by a 40-year old woman for her 50-year old spouse. Her comment was "Joe's personality is businesslike. I chose this color as a plain, medium, and basic color." For herself, she chose a lighter brown, stating "My personality is not very colorful." She drew both of them as faceless. Her feeling about themselves was that of being sort of non-entities—part of a huge faceless crowd.

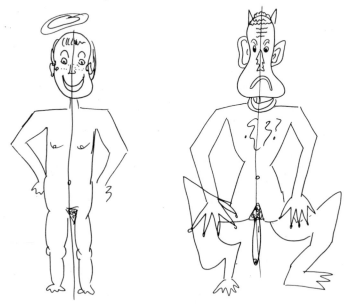

ILLUSTRATION 3

A 40-year old woman choosing a bright yellow for herself said, "I chose yellow to represent me because I am sunny and light, and feel alive and bright. It is a cheerful color, and brings warmth. I associate a spring tartness in my sense of challenge and awareness of the world." She depicted herself in detail holding a flower in her outstretched hand, standing on grass. She is warm, open, and well-based.

A 20-year old male selecting red for himself stated, "I chose this color for myself because I get very angry easily. At certain times the slightest incident is enough to make me want to explode." He drew his 18-year old wife on a magenta sheet stating, "I chose this color because I feel Veronica has feeling in her passion, but I never give her a chance to show it in bed. I feel that this color shows a passion that has never been allowed to come out." He drew both of them without feet, face, or arms, which is quite depictive of them as a couple. They are young, not yet established professionally or identity-wise, and they were very out of touch with each other.

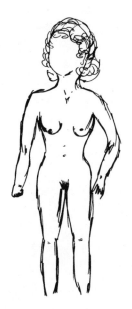

ILLUSTRATION 4

She on the other hand, drew herself on a bright yellow paper with all of her parts, but her hands—she stated, "I picked this color because I feel bright and loving," which she was. Her choice for him was an orange-brown —she stated, "I picked this color because I think Dave has sort of a retired bland personality. He is shy." The description fit him aptly, although his self-perception of violent temper outbursts may also be accurate, since such a suppressed and mild person might tend to build up feelings to an explosion. It apparently is not a problem as far as his partner is concerned. Our work with him would indicate the need to work toward opening him up so that he could easily express both positive and negative emotions so he would not draw upon suppressed feelings which result in major blow-ups.

Occasionally, we encounter a pictorial representation which illustrates clearly the feeling one partner has about their relationship. A 55-year old woman married to a 60-year old man sees herself as an angel, and depicts her partner as a devil. (See Illustration 3) The line through

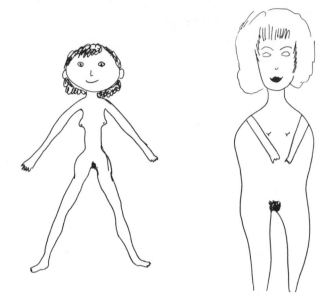

ILLUSTRATION 5

the body is interesting since the body split was evident in our work with her, where her sensate focus span was about two minutes, and her inappropriate comments about what happened 10, 20, or 30 years ago made it difficult to keep them focused in. Continued intensive work enabled us to get positive feelings going for 20 or 30 minutes.

The most significant areas in the drawing, we found, are the face and the feet. The face is the singularly most significant identifying feature of an individual. If it is left completely blank, then symbolically we may be dealing with sort of a faceless creature who has little or no feeling of identity. If they have drawn no feet, we may be working with a very poor and unstable foundation. (Illustration 4) These areas are the ones we find the most likely to be omitted. Some of the drawings depict openness with arms out-stretched as opposed to those where they are closed and tight. (Illustration 5) The size of the drawings are revealing, does a person draw a very small picture of him or herself, but draw their spouse much

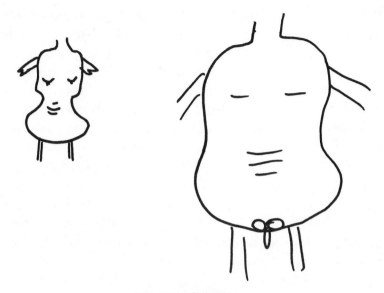

ILLUSTRATION 6

larger? (Illustration 6) Therapeutic efforts to realistically alter perceptions that tend to preclude intimate inter-relating is part of our body image work, and the pictures are used at that time.

We do not find that the drawing of the genitalia is of particular significance. Sometimes a woman will draw an erect penis on her husband. She may only have seen her husband's penis when it was erect. It is more reveal-ing when she has the testicles above the penis, indicating that they have probably had little nude viewing of each other.

Preliminary work is under way with the Luscher Color Test to determine whether it may have some pre-dictive value in terms of personality types, would there be a favorable prognosis for treatment of sexual dysfunc-tion or in specific combinations of colors, would the prognosis be poor for treatment of presenting symptoms of sexual dysfunction.

The psychological testing gives us a preliminary indi-cation of the kind of personalities that are associated with the presenting symptoms of sexual dysfunction. We are able to relate our own subjective evaluation of individual clients and couples with the test data to determine the extent to which there is correlation, and to reveal suggestions of emotional disturbance. Temperament traits may be found which are associated with sexual dysfunction. It is important to see if there may be clues in the use of these materials which help determine specific steps in the therapy program that would best be suited for a couple, i.e. a couple where both are psychotic on the M.M.P.I.—we are aware that people who are psychotic have difficulty with sensate focus, and are only able to stay in focus a brief period of time. We work more closely with them asking for what they are feeling at that moment more frequently, than a so-called "normal" who has no difficulty staying with the feelings of here and now. When they begin having difficulty focusing in on feelings, we stop. We will attempt to increase their sensate focus span with each new exercise, repeating some if the problem is slow in being resolved.

Chapter 3

SEX HISTORY

The taking of a sex history is one of the most significant diagnostic and therapeutic aspects of our program in treatment of human sexual dysfunction. It is not only a sex history, but a time when learning can take place. Often it is reassuring to a person to learn that his or her sexual behavior is similar to that of the majority of his fellow Americans, based on reputable scientific data. Useless guilt feelings frequently result from a lack of knowledge. If, for example, a husband says, "I must be a homosexual because I enjoy oral-genital sex with my wife"; then the client can be assured that there is no known relationship between oral-genital sex and homosexuality, and that according to Kinsey, the majority of married people have engaged at some time in oral-genital contact, and it is a perfectly normal mode of expression in a heterosexual relationship as long as both are agreeable. Reassurance and support for the person in therapy is helpful when realistic. Pursuing the possibility of homosexual interest would come later in the history.

We find many people have never discussed their sexual life, activities, or fantasies with anyone, and the sex history gives them an opportunity to verbalize openly their behavior, and most significantly, their feelings about that behavior. Once these feelings come out and have been discussed, they become less threatening. It helps them to be freer in their sexual thinking and attitudes, opening communication between the partners.

Our history is a combination of the Kinsey[1] and Masters and Johnson[2] sex histories, with massive inclusion of our own items. We like the Kinsey format of going from emotionless material to emotion-laden material, and back to neutral material. This is helpful in eliciting responses from the individual where they are hesitant to talk about topics such as homosexuality or masturbation. After we approach an emotion-laden area several times and they become more comfortable with us, clients become freer in opening up and discussing all aspects of their sexual experience. Also the one, two, or three word reminder of topics allows us to phrase our questions in the language of the individual.

Forcing denial of involvement in areas by using assumptive questions, rather than asking "did you ever," will make admission of behavior easier. For example, "When did you first masturbate?" rather than "Did you ever masturbate?"

Another technique which Charles W. Wahl, M.D.[3] finds helpful and one we also employ deals with the universality of experience, i.e. "I find males frequently had

---

[1] Alfred C. Kinsey, Wardell B. Pomeroy, and Clyde E. Martin, *Sexual Behavior in the Human Male* (Philadelphia, 1948), pp. 63–70.

[2] William H. Masters and Virginia E. Johnson, *Human Sexual Inadequacy,* (Boston, 1970), pp. 35–51.

[3] Ortho Panel 7, "The Art of Taking the Sexual History," by Charles W. Wahl, M.D., pp. 2–6.

their first exposure to sex through 'Tijuana' comic books —did this play any part in your sex education?" If they have had such exposure, it may help pinpoint for them when they first learned about sexual material.

Often clients need to be asked questions which will be helpful in recalling sex education. For instance, when asking about knowledge of pregnancy, we ask about pregnancies of mother, relatives or friends, and were they aware before then of conception, fertilization, etc.

Clients often have difficulty recalling early sexuality. Leaving home for instance, going into the armed services or away to college, frequently exposes people to a broader and more liberal background. Through these experiences, there may be a developing awareness of sexuality that prior to that time seemingly did not exist. Contraception, abortion, prostitution, menstruation, venereal disease were unknown to a few of our clients until that time. Sex histories have been taken of people in their 30's who have grown to adulthood with little or no information in these areas.

From our experience, even the younger so-called liberated generation, although more sexually permissive, are limited in actual sexual knowledge. Typical responses of both young and old couples are, "I didn't realize there was so much I didn't know," or "If I had only learned all of this 20 years ago, we would not have had to suffer all these years."

We ask each client to define their goal in treatment by responding to the question, "If we are successful in helping you, what will you be able to do that you cannot do now?" This gives us information on how realistic their goals may be. Resolution of sexual problems does not resolve all problems in a relationship, and if they perceive good sexual functioning to be the major hope in resolving personality problems and conflicts, then success will be limited. On the other hand, if sex becomes good, the relationship may improve greatly, but "good sex" is certainly not the panacea for all problems.

By design, the sex history is taken heterosexually so that the intimate details of the client's past and present sexual life have been discussed with a member of the opposite sex. The history taker understands more readily the position of that individual.

The therapeutic foursome (dual-sex therapy team and dysfunctional couple) are not composed of two men against two women, but interact with understanding toward the opposite sex and at the same time are easily able to point out same sex general point of view on certain matters. For example: If the male complains that his partner will not let him touch her, and she points out that he always grabs for her breasts, then the female therapist can point out that women generally do not like to be grabbed at, especially on the breasts. At the same time it is essential that he is supported by the female therapist who informs the wife that he should be able to touch her. The female therapist then asks the wife how she would like to be touched. This may be the first time in the relationship that she has any say in how she wants to be touched. If the man is only interested in being able to touch her, then both are satisfied if she indicates the kind of touch she would like. If he follows her suggestions, then she has no reason to complain.

Our experience has shown that we get better results through taking histories heterosexually. Other dual-sex therapy teams may have good results taking same sex first, and it may be that the personalities of the therapists will determine which procedure will be most effective. A 15-30 minute follow-up for afterthoughts and remarks takes place when the client returns the following day.

A switch in therapists then occurs, where the same sex client and therapist have a chance to discuss the history in a one-hour review of the points both feel are most significant. The initial sex history usually requires from two to three hours, although there have been exceptional instances where as many as five hours were required. Our scheduling is such that when we are involved in work that is undeterminable in time, we use flexible scheduling so that appointments are not consecutively booked. We take the sex history sitting beside the client or across from the client without anything obstructing the dyadic interaction such as a desk or table. The sex histories are audio-taped and transcribed and become part of the case history, which can be referred to as needed.

It is important in treating human sexual dysfunction for us to have a complete picture of our clients. Place of birth, rural or urban socialization, racial and ethnic background, religious and emotional climate of the home, emotional relationship of clients with each of their parents and each of their siblings, their school and work history, and then specific heterosexual and homosexual experiences, learning of sexual material, sexual functioning past and present. All of these are important to know so that the presenting symptoms of dysfunction may be seen in their relationship to the general life and specific sexual history of each client.

The sex history gives us information about other sexual involvements which may have been successful, and what happened in those which is not happening in their present relationship. We may learn that the pattern of sexual dysfunction started early, and that repeated encounters have simply compounded the problem so that we are working with an individual where there has been a long succession of "failures."

A pattern of life-long sexual failure is usually different than a recently developing failure pattern, and though the symptoms are similar, we may be dealing with two different phenomena. The learning pattern of the first requires a relearning, whereas the inability on the second case after years of function, may have entirely different etiology. It is important to determine if they function well in extramarital relationships but not in the marital relationship. If this is the case, what do they perceive to be the difference.

It is important to determine when dysfunction started and what was going on, both sexually and non-sexually with the individual, and their partner, such as the birth of a child, loss of job, illness, medication, drinking, etc.

Most of the individual counseling that transpires during the two weeks of therapy takes place during the taking of the sex history. This is one of the reasons for time discrepancy, since any material which has caused any emotional problems for the individual is discussed during this period. It is easy for some people to be open about their sexuality, others need to become comfortable with us before they can freely open up and discuss it. Some people we work with have had wide and varied sexual experience. Many have had very limited sexual experiences both in terms of number of partners and quality and quantity of coital experiences.

We have frequently found that later on, in the therapeutic foursome, the client often looks for answers from that therapist to whom he has originally given his sex history. Moreover, when that therapist is of the opposite sex the client is more readily disposed to accept therapist's observations about the client's partner regarding differences in sexual perception or relating. i.e. Female client says, "He never shows any emotion or tells me he loves me." The male therapist points out that the male socialization process in our culture directs a male away from showing emotion. As a child, he is taught not to cry when hurt—be mother's "little man." The discussion can go into how does the husband show emotion. The sex history has already indicated to the female therapist the things he does, and this can be brought out and reinforced by her. If the female is realistic—that in no way does he express or show emotion—then the action methods we use are ideal in developing the ability to show his wife through touch that he does feel warmth and love for her.

The following outline indicates how we proceed with taking the sex history. In general, the approach is to move from non-threatening identifying data to the material dealing with overt sexual functioning. The ten major categories in the sex history outline are found in Table 1 below.

Table 1
MAJOR CATEGORIES-SEX HISTORY

1. Identification and Background
2. Sex Education
3. Masturbation—Fantasy—Dreams
4. Contraception
5. Heterosexuality
6. Homosexuality
7. Group Sex Activities
8. Erotic Responses
9. Spouses History
10. Presenting Symptoms
11. Expectations
12. Summarize Client's History

It would seem that taking the sex history is self-explanatory, however, we found that we needed to take it several times with research subjects to be able to take it easily. Remembering the 10 main categories facilitates taking the history. Some of the questions are repetitious, but that usually is to elicit further or different information, since it is in another sequence of questions which may produce different recall. Our experience has been that people are very open about their history, but they cannot always remember. As we go along they may recall something they could not remember earlier.

The same sex history is used for both males and females, except where it is listed specifically male or female. We each have our own sex history outline from which we work; however, the two were combined here, to conserve space.

We ask the questions in the language of the clients which is quickly determined as we proceed through the early part of the sex history.

The sex history goes about like this—"How old are you? What is your date of birth? Do you know the time of your birth? What is your astrological sign?" We feel that the astrological sign is significant only if it is important to the client. If so, we pursue it. This is an outline, meaning that we may elaborate on questions if we receive responses which indicate the need for further exploration.

"What sign is your partner? Are your signs compatible?" Once we pursue an area to our satisfaction, we return to the outline. By following the lead of the client, we often gain important knowledge about the way they think or what they feel. It also tends to break up the canned feeling of reading off of an outline. When we diverge from it, we have a chance to look the client in the eye and develop closer rapport with him.

Back to the outline, and asking about parents. "How old were your parents when you were born? Were your parents ever divorced or separated? Are they both living? Were you still at home when your (father-mother) died? Who raised you? How long did you live with your aunt? Where else did you live? Before your mother died, did you live in the city or country? Did you live in the city or country when you went to live with your aunt? How old when you left there? Where did you go?

How tall are you? Your weight? What is the most you have ever weighed? Are you right or left handed? Any chronic illness or handicaps? Have you ever had venereal disease? Have you ever had diabetes? Has any member of your family ever had diabetes? What major illness have you had? We find that all of the questions need not be asked. Often segments are not applicable and are omitted so the length of the history is not formidable.

SEX HISTORY

I. IDENTIFICATION AND BACKGROUND
  A. Social and Economic Data
      1. Age
      2. Date of Birth
      3. Place of Birth
      4. Time of Birth
      5. Astrological sign
      6. Attach any significance
      7. Parents age at birth
      8. Home broken by death, divorce, separation, other
      9. Who raised?
          (a.) How long?
      10. Rural-urban background
  B. Physical Data
      1. General development and health
          (a.) Height
          (b.) Weight, and maximum ever reached
          (c.) Handedness
          (d.) History of chronic illnesses and handicaps
          (e.) History of venereal disease
          (f.) History of diabetes—self
          (g.) History of diabetes—family
          (h.) Any major illness
      2A. Male genital characteristics
          (a.) Testes
          (b.) History of injury-surgery
          (c.) History of circumcision
          (d.) Age involved
          (e.) Extent of foreskin
          (f.) Pre-coital mucous secretion
          (g.) Erection

(h.) Speed
(i.) Extent
(j.) Presence of pulsation
(k.) Pleasurable genital feelings
    (1) Thoughts
    (2) Activities
    (3) Situations
    (4) Reaction to
(l.) Morning erection, frequency
(m.) Night erections, frequency

2B. Female genital characteristics
  (a.) Breasts—development
  (b.) History of injury-surgery
  (c.) Clitoris
    (1) Adherence of foreskin
  (d.) Labia
    (1) Size
  (e.) Pre-coital mucous secretion
  (f.) First menstruation
    (1) Problems with
    (2) Duration of flow
    (3) Cycle-variations in
    (4) Age at menarche
    (5) Prepared beforehand for—by whom
    (6) Discussed with friends
    (7) Looked forward to or dreaded
    (8) Intercourse during menstruation
    (9) Vaginal odor
  (g.) Hymen
    (1) Status
    (2) Rupture
  (h.) Vaginal mucous secretions
  (i.) Orgasmic
    (1) Under what circumstances
    (2) Physical feelings
  (j.) Age at first childbirth
  (k.) Delivery
    (1) Length of time
    (2) Difficulty
    (3) Response to
    (4) Desire for more children
      (a) Partner's response to

      (l.) Menopause
          (1) Symptoms
          (2) Degree of distress
          (3) Sex hormone replacement
              (a) Describe
      (m.) Abortions
          (1) Spontaneous
          (2) Induced
3A. Male concerning wife
    (a.) Clitoris
    (b.) Vaginal secretions
    (c.) Vaginal odors
    (d.) Length of menstrual flow
    (e.) Intercourse during cycle
    (f.) Hymen
        (1) Status
        (2) History of rupture
    (g.) Desire for more children
        (1) Your response to
3B. Female concerning husband
    (a.) Testicles
    (b.) Penis
        (1) Foreskin
    (c.) Speed of erection
    (d.) Degree of erection
        (1) Pulsation
    (e.) Ejaculation
    (f.) Pre-coital mucous secretion
    (g.) Morning erections, frequency
    (h.) Night erections, frequency
C. Sociologic and Psychologic Data
   1. Most memorable event in life
     (a.) Who was responsible
     (b.) Your response to
   2. Most tragic event in life
     (a.) Who was responsible
     (b.) Your response to
   3. Attitudinal influence on sexual values
     (a.) Church
     (b.) Home
     (c.) Peer group
     (d.) Ethnic background

        (e.) National origin or ancestory
    4. Counseling or therapy
        (a.) Self
        (b.) Spouse
        (c.) Family
        (d.) Parents

D. Self-concept
    1. Attractiveness
        (a.) Now
        (b.) As child
    2. Change if could
    3. Attractive to partner
    4. Greatest attribute
        (a.) a person
        (b.) To partner
        (c.) To children
        (d.) In social situations
    5. Describe sexual identity
        (a.) Comfortable with
        (b.) Please you

E. Parental and Family Information
    1. Mother and father living
        (a.) Age
        (b.) Health
    2. Relationship with parents
        (a.) Frequency of contact
        (b.) Place of birth
        (c.) Rural-urban background
        (d.) Ethnic background
        (e.) Status
        (f.) Marital history
        (g.) Happiness—adjustment
        (h.) First memories
        (i.) Separation—divorce—death
        (j.) If remarried, age of present partner
        (k.) Grandparents ever divorced or separated
        (l.) As sexual beings
        (m.) Attitudes toward sex
            (1) Mother
            (2) Father
        (n.) Discuss sex topics
        (o.) Ask questions

3. Describe atmosphere and home environment
4. Parents relationship in retrospect
   (a.) In high school
      (1) Mother
      (2) Father
   (b.) In college
      (1) Mother
      (2) Father
   (c.) Prior to marriage
      (1) Mother
      (2) Father
   (d.) Currently
      (1) Mother
      (2) Father
5. Emotional climate of the home through teenage years
6. How were summers spent
   (a.) High school years
   (b.) College years
7. Father's job
   (a.) Effect on you
8. Mother's job
   (a.) Effect on you
9. Educational background
   (a.) Mother
   (b.) Father
10. Child relationship
   (a.) Attachment to father
   (b.) Attachment to mother
11. Involvement with youth groups
   (a.) Your reaction to
12. Whom did you take your problems to
   (a.) Why
13. Shared important events with
   (a.) Why
14. Brother—Sisters
   (a.) Number
   (b.) Ages
   (c.) Others raised in home
      (1) Age
      (2) Sex
      (3) Origin
   (d.) Relationship with siblings

           (1) Closest relationship
           (2) Dislike or conflict with
    15. Atmosphere at home
    16. Show of affection
        (a.) To each other
        (b.) To you
        (c.) To siblings
    17. Relationship with close relatives
        (a.) Aunts
        (b.) Uncles
        (c.) Grandparents
        (d.) Cousins
    18. Companions at:
        (a.) 10-13
        (b.) 14-18
        (c.) Parent's reaction to
    19. Friends from childhood
    20. Friends now
        (a.) Male
        (b.) Female
    21. Popular with schoolmates
        (a.) Comparison
    22. Started Dating
        (a.) Age
        (b.) Group
        (c.) Couple
F. Religious Background
    1. Denominations involved
        (a.) Mother's
        (b.) Father's
       (c.) Yours
    2. Degree of adherence
        (a.) Parents
        (b.) Yours
    3. Church involvement
        (a.) Parents
        (b.) Yours
           (1) Alone
           (2) Partner
    4. Present religious practice or adherence
        (a.) Affiliation
        (b.) Church involvement

      (c.) Change in religious views
G. Educational History
    1. Co-education or segregated (male-female)
    2. Years of schooling
    3. Vocational school
    4. Colleges attended
    5. College majors
    6. Post graduate or professional
    7. Age upon leaving school
    8. Age while in high school
    9. Ability as student
H. Institutional History
    1. Private schools
    2. Orphanage
    3. Prison, etc.
    4. Armed service experience
       (a.) Conflict with authority
I. Occupational History
    1. First job for pay through current job
       (a.) Work for relative
       (b.) Money as child
    2. Part-time
    3. Full-time
    4. Enjoy work
       (a.) Feel trapped
       (b.) Consider changing
       (c.) Other professional interests
    5. Work capable of
J. Economic Status
    1. Comfortable
    2. Enjoyable to both
K. Recreational Interests
    1. Extracurricular activities
       (a.) High school
       (b.) College
    2. Athletic experience
       (a.) Little League
       (b.) Sand lot
    3. On high school and college organized teams
       (a.) Describe
    4. Fraternity membership in college
       (a.) Describe

    (b.) Offices

    (c.) Participation

5. Fraternal or other organizations

    (a.) Office held

    (b.) Attendance at meetings

    (c.) Partner involved

6. Moving pictures

    (a.) Kind

    (b.) Alone

    (c.) Partner

7. Dancing

    (a.) Kind

    (b.) Partner

8. Cards

    (a.) Partner

    (b.) Friends

9. Gambling

    (a.) Alone

    (b.) Partner

    (c.) Friends

10. Smoking

    (a.) Ever stopped

    (b.) Difference in sexual function

11. Use of alcohol

    (a.) Alone

    (b.) Friends

    (c.) Situational

    (d.) Sexual function problem

    (e.) Effects on sexual function

12. Use of narcotics

    (a.) Alone

    (b.) Friends

    (c.) Situational

    (d.) Effect on sexual function

    (e.) Any problem

13. Use of marijuana

    (a.) Alone

    (b.) Friends

    (c.) Situational

    (d.) Effect on sexual function

    (e.) Any problem

14. Hunting
    (a.) Alone
    (b.) Friends
15. Reading
    (a.) Shared
    (b.) Kind
16. Flying
17. Special interest in music
    (a.) Shared
    (b.) Alone
18. Boating—Sailing
    (a.) Shared
    (b.) Alone
19. Sports
    (a.) Spectator—Extent
        (1) Alone
        (2) Shared
        (3) Partner
    Male
    (b.) Participant—Extent in:
    Shared with whom
        (1) Football
        (2) Baseball
        (3) Hockey
        (4) Golf
        (5) Tennis
        (6) Softball
    Female
    (b.) Participant—Extent in:
    Shared with whom
        (1) Golf
        (2) Tennis
        (3) Softball
20. Hobbies
21. Leisure time activities
L. Mobility
    1. Times moved—reason and adjustment
        (a.) Up to 5
        (b.) 5-10
        (c.) 11-13
        (d.) 14-left home
        (e.) How old then

       (f.) Moved where—why
- 2. Countries, states of residence for one year or more
- 3. Moved last five years—why
- 4. Length current residence
- 5. Moved since marriage
- 6. Own or rent
  - (a.) For how long
  - (b.) Problems with neighbors

M. Emotional Response
- 1. How do you feel about:
  - (a.) Current state of marriage
  - (b.) Partner
  - (c.) Children
  - (d.) Parents
  - (e.) In-laws
  - (f.) Neighbors
  - (g.) Friends
  - (h.) Partner's response to you
- 2. Mutual interests in marriage
  - (a.) Social
  - (b.) Recreational
  - (c.) Leisure time
- 3. Who does the:
  - (a.) Yard work
  - (b.) House repair
  - (c.) Budgeting
  - (d.) Conflict over
- 4. Feel about:
  - (a.) Children's school work
  - (b.) Children's social activities
  - (c.) Partner going to school
  - (d.) Partner's social activities
- 5. What do you resent most in your relationship with your partner?
- 6. Present attitude changes:
  - (a.) Self
  - (b.) Partner's
  - (c.) Friends

N. Social and Educational Differences
- 1. Social Background
- 2. Educational Background
- 3. Any religious conflicts

(a.) Each other
(b.) Children

II. SEX EDUCATION
  A. What did you think about sexual matters before you knew the truth about making babies, where they come from, etc.
  B. Sources of knowledge, ages when learned:
   1. Pregnancy
   2. Coitus
   3. Fertilization
   4. Menstruation
   5. Venereal diseases
   6. Prostitution
   7. Contraception
   8. Abortions
   9. Male erection
   10. First sexual experimentation
     (a.) Age
     (b.) Alone or others
     (c.) Situation—same or opposite sex
       (1) Describe
       (2) Reaction
     (d.) Play Doctor
       (1) Caught
       (2) Results
       (3) Feelings
     (e.) Play House
       (1) Caught
       (2) Results
       (3) Feelings
     (f.) Exploration
       (1) Same sex
       (2) Opposite
       (3) Feelings
     (g.) Comparison
       (1) Same sex
       (2) Opposite
       (3) Feelings about
     (h.) Games with sexual connotation
       (1) Nudity
       (2) Tying up others
       (3) Being tied up

   (4) Feelings about
  (i.) See animals
   (1) In coitus
   (2) Giving birth
   (3) Response
  (j.) Circle Jerk
   (1) Caught .
   (2) Results
   (3) Feelings
 11. Parental contributions to sex education
  (a.) What sources
 12. Friends, peer group
 13. Experience with graphic depictions of sexual activity
 14. Formal sex education in school and college
 15. Reading
  (a.) What
 16. Ever see anyone in intercourse
  (a.) Circumstances
  (b.) Age
  (c.) Reaction
 17. Attitudes on nudity
  (a.) Of parents
  (b.) Of subject
  (c.) Partner
 18. When did you put everything together

III. MASTURBATION—FANTASY—DREAMS
 A. Masturbation
  1. First genital feelings
  2. Ages involved—pre and post adolescent
  3. Sources of learning
   (a.) Conversation
   (b.) Reading
   (c.) Observation
   (d.) Participation—hetero or homosexual
   (e.) Self-discovery
   (f.) Frequencies
    (1) Maximum per week
    (2) Means at each age
   Male
   (g.) Techniques
    (1) Penis other

        (2) Manual
        (3) Frictional
        (4) Oral
        (5) Special devices
        (6) Urethral insertions
        (7) Vibrator
    Female
    (g.) Techniques
        (1) Clitoral
            (a) around
            (b) direct
        (2) Vaginal
        (3) Manual
        (4) Frictional
        (5) Oral
        (6) Special devices
        (7) Urethral insertions
    (h.) Always have orgasm
        (1) Frequency without
    (i.) Time required for orgasm
    (j.) Current frequency
    (k.) Subject's evaluation
        (1) Period involving fear or conflict
        (2) Sources of resolution of conflict
        (3) Rejection: period involved, reasons for
        (4) Estimate of moral, psychic, physical consequences

B. Fantasy
    1. Importance of fantasy in life
      (a.) As child
      (b.) As adult
      (c.) Non-coitally
        (1) Describe
      (d.) Coitally
        (1) Describe
      (e.) Masturbate
        (1) Describe
            (a) Homosexual
            (b) Heterosexual
            (c) Zoo-erotic
            (d) Masochistic—Sadistic
        (2) Feel about
            (a) Adolescent

(b) Adult
C. Nocturnal Sex Dreams
    1. Ages involved
    2. Frequencies of dreams with orgasm
        (a.) Your reaction
        (b.) Parents
    3. Frequencies of dreams without orgasm
    4. Content of dreams
        (a.) Homo-erotic
        (b.) Hetero-erotic
        (c.) Zoo-erotic
    5. Dreams currently
        (a.) Content
        (b.) Feelings
        (c.) Result in masturbation

IV. CONTRACEPTION
A. Condom
    1. Source
    2. Testing
    3. Lubrication
    4. Breakage
B. Diaphragm or cap
    1. Source
    2. Type
C. Withdrawal
D. Douche alone
    1. Materials employed
E. Jelly alone
F. Foam
G. Pill
    1. Kind
    2. Hamper sexual satisfaction
    3. Side effects
    4. Enlarge breasts
    5. Emotional problems
    6. Nervousness
    7. Weight gain
H. Safe Period
I. IUD
J. Vasectomy
K. Tubal ligation

L. Hysterectomy

M. Did any of foregoing hamper sexual interest.

V. HETEROSEXUALITY

A. Pre-adolescent sex play
    1. Ages involved
       (a.) Frequencies
    2. Companions
       (a.) Ages
       (b.) Number
       (c.) Sex
    3. Techniques
       (a.) Exhibition
       (b.) Physical exploration
       (c.) Vaginal insertion
       (d.) Urethral insertion
       (e.) Mouth-genital contact
       (f.)   Coitus

B. Involvement with kin
    1. Overt or covert involvement with kin at pre-adolescent—
       adolescent level.
       (a.) Father
       (b.) Mother
       (c.) Brothers
       (d.) Sisters
       (e.) Cousins
       (f.)   Uncles
       (g.) Aunts
    2. Reaction to:
       (a.) Fear
       (b.) Found out
    3. Problems related to
       (a.) Fear of
       (b.) Desire for
       (c.) Response to

C. Adolescence
    1. Age of onset puberty
       (a.) Feeling about
       (b.) Pre-knowledge about
       (c.) Erotic responsiveness
       (d.) First orgasm
          (1) Source

(2) How would you describe it
(e.) Pubic hair growth
(f.) Breast knots in adolescence
(g.) Onset of rapid growth
(h.) Voice change
(i.) Completion of growth
(j.) Feeling about sex
(k.) Sexual experience
D. Dating
  1. Age at first date
    (a.) Frequency
    (b.) Number before first sex encounter
      (1) What occurred
      (2) Techniques
        (a) Pre-play
          (1) Duration
          (2) Lip Kissing
          (3) Tongue kissing
          (4) Breast manipulation—Manual
          (5) Breast manipulation—Oral
          (6) Genital manipulation: with partner
              Manual
              Oral
          (7) Frequency of orgasm
      (3) Nudity
        (a) Frequency
        (b) Attitudes
      (4) Result
        (a) Nervous disturbance
        (b) Genital cramps
        (c) Masturbation
      (5) Attitudes on premarital coitus
        (a) Sources of restraint
          (1) Moral
          (2) Lack of opportunity
          (3) Lack of interest
          (4) Fear of pregnancy
          (5) Fear of venereal disease
          (6) Fear of social disapproval
          (7) Desire for virginity in fiancee
E. Premarital sexual relationships
  1. Age

2. Number
3. Ethnic or racial background
4. Age range
5. Marital status
6. Companions
7. Prostitutes
8. First sexual encounter
    (a.) Under what circumstances
        (1) Pleasure
        (2) Freedom from concern
    (b.) Subsequent circumstances
        (1) Pleasure
        (2) Freedom from concern
9. Frequency of contact
10. Techniques
    (a.) Lip kissing
    (b.) Tongue kissing
    (c.) Breast manipulation
        (1) Manual
        (2) Oral
    (d.) Frequency of orgasm
    (e.) Coital activities
        (1) Frequency
        (2) Duration
        (3) Erection
            Difficulties
        (4) Ejaculation
            Difficulties
    (f.) Effect of marriage
    (g.) Frequency of intercourse—premarital
        (1) Satisfaction
        (2) Length of coitus
        (3) Erections
        (4) Ejaculations
        (5) Any sexual problems
            Self
            Partner
        (6) Where
        (7) Time
        (8) Possibility of conception
        (9) Ever caught
        (10) Contraception

11. Engagements—number
    (a.) Duration
    (b.) Reason for terminating
    (c.) Age and nature of partner
    (d.) Virginity of partner
    (e.) Speed of orgasm
    (f.) Physical satisfaction
12. Frequencies of coitus
13. Partners
    (a.) Total number
    (b.) Prostitutes or companions
    (c.) Age range
    (d.) Youngest since subject was eighteen
    (e.) Age preference
    (f.) Marital status
    (g.) Consanguinity
    (h.) Virginity
    (i.) Rape—force
        (1) Who
        (2) Describe
14. Resulting pregnancies, births, abortions
    (a.) Ages involved
    (b.) Legal aspects
    (c.) Financial aspects
    (d.) Emotional aspects
15. Arrangements
    (a.) Places utilized for coitus
    (b.) Opportunity and desire for nudity
16. Coital positions: relative frequencies and preferences
    (a.) Male superior
    (b.) Female superior
    (c.) Side
    (d.) Sitting
    (e.) Standing
    (f.) Rear entry
17. Preference for light or darkness during coitus
18. Evaluation of coital experience
F. Marital histories for each marriage
    1. Marital status
    2. Number of marriages
    3. Ethnic or racial background
    4. Age of each spouse

5. Widowed
6. Divorced
7. Separated
8. Lapse between marriage and first coitus
9. Years married
10. Age each spouse at marriage
11. Sexual satisfaction in previous marriage
    (a.) Length of coitus
    (b.) Erections
    (c.) Ejaculations
    (d.) Any sexual problems
        (1) Self
        (2) Partner
    (e.) Children
        (1) Number
        (2) Ages
        (3) Where are they
        (4) Problems
12. Current Partner
    (a.) Where met
    (b.) How long
    (c.) Why attracted to partner
    (d.) Present attraction
    (e.) Subsequent dating activities
    (f.) Desire for marriage
    (g.) Desire for children
        (1) number desired
        (2) number have
        (3) conflict over number
    (h.) Type of wedding
        (1) Where
        (2) Describe
    (i.) Honeymoon
        (1) Where
        (2) How long
    (j.) Wedding night
    (k.) Intercourse
        (1) Reaction
        (2) Satisfaction
            Self
            Spouse
        (3) Difference before/after marriage

        (4) Difficulties
        (5) Length of intercourse
        (6) Erection
        (7) Ejaculation—orgasm
        (8) Sexual problems
        (9) Response of partner
    (l.) Frequency of intercourse
        (1) First month
        (2) First year
        (3) Five years
        (4) Current
        (5) Maximum ever
        (6) How frequently would you like to have intercourse
        (7) If withdrawal from intercourse—frequency prior
        (8) Diminished sex drive result of partner's
            (a) Traits
            (b) Habits
            (c) Behavior patterns
  (m.) Influence on frequency
        (1) Who initiates
        (2) Lovemaking always lead to intercourse
        (3) Touch other than intercourse
        (4) Coitus spontaneous or scheduled
        (5) Is intercourse habit or duty
        (6) Intercourse usually takes place (time)
        (7) Is this satisfactory
   (n.) Express sexual drives freely
        (1) Partner's reaction
   (o.) Partner express
        (1) desire—your reaction
   (p.) Partner orgasms
        (1) If not, ever achieve
        (2) Under what conditions
   (q.) Role as husband
   (r.) Role as wife
   (s.) Separation—3 months or more
   (t.) Sexual satisfaction to overall satisfaction
   (u.) Get along with partner's family

G. Sexual Adjustment in Marriage
    1. Rating
    2. Sources of conflict
    3. Sex relationships

4. Frequency of intercourse
5. Present sexual compatability
6. Raise partner's status
7. Enhance partner's sexuality
8. Raise your status
9. Enhance your sexuality
10. Partner involved
    (a.) Intimate
    (b.) Warm responsive
    (c.) Empathetic
11. Are you
    (a.) Intimate
    (b.) Warm responsive
    (c.) Empathetic
12. First noticed sexual difficulties
13. Situation or occurrence at time
    (a.) Any illness
    (b.) Change of medication
    (c.) Pregnancy
    (d.) Operation
14. Effect spouses sexual function
15. Effect your sexual function
    (a.) Response to this
    (b.) How attempted to resolve
    (c.) Effectiveness
    (d.) How do you feel about it
    (e.) Interest in resolution
    (f.) Does your spouse have orgasm
        (1) Describe
    (g.) Erective difficulties
        (1) Describe
    (h.) Ejaculatory difficulties
        (1) Describe
    (i.) Orgasm difficulties
        (1) Describe
    (j.) In what other ways beside intercourse have you
        brought pleasure to your relationship
    (k.) Pleasure besides sexual
    (l.) What has partner done to bring you sexual pleasure
        besides intercourse
    (m.) Pleasure besides sexual
16. Describe activities

(a.) Foreplay
  (1) Length of time
(b.) Activities
  (1) Caress
    (a) Hair
    (b) Face
    (c) Body
    (d) Breasts
  (2) Stimulate
    (a) Clitoral area
    (b) Mons
    (c) Vagina
  (3) Lip kissing
  (4) Tongue kissing
  (5) Breast manipulation
    (a) Manual
    (b) Oral
  (6) Genital manipulation
    (a) Partner
       Manual
       Oral
    (b) Of you
       Manual
       Oral
  (7) Frequency of orgasm
  (8) Evaluation of coital experience
  (9) Preference for light or darkness during coitus
  (10) Fantasies during coitus
  (11) Do you show
    (a) skill
    (b) agility
    (c) technique
    (d) uniqueness
  (12) Does partner show
    (a) skill
    (b) agility
    (c) technique
    (d) uniqueness
17. Partner's recent sexual attitude
  (a.) Frequency of intercourse
  (b.) Difficulty in intercourse
  (c.) Response of partner in intercourse

(d.) Self-response in intercourse
18. Social attitudinal changes
    (a.) Double standard
    (b.) Your views
    (c.) Partner's social views
19. Vacations away from children
20. Children-vacation away from parents
21. Babysitter
    (a.) Parents exchange
    (b.) Motels together or away
22. Marital activities together
    (a.) Activities apart—problems with
23. Average time spent together a week
24. No. of times out per week
25. Frequency of intercourse per week
    (a.) Satisfaction
    (b.) What influences having intercourse
    (c.) What influences not having intercourse
    (d.) Initiates sex
        (1) Satisfactory
        (2) If not, percent of time
            (a) Male
            (b) Female
26. Sexual behavior in marriage
    (a.) Sex scheduled
    (b.) Grows out of warm relationship
    (c.) Habit
    (d.) Sense of duty
27. Warmth of partner response
28. Warmth of your response
29. Situation most desirable
    (a.) Most stimulating
30. Tell partner what you like, dislike, would like
    (a.) Accepts their likes and dislikes
31. Specifically why are you here
32. What do you expect to accomplish
33. Who instituted coming
34. What changes would successful treatment make in relationship
35. Changes in personality
    (a.) Self
    (b.) Spouse

H. Sex Outside of Marriage
  1. Extramarital relationships
    (a.) Self
      (1) Number
      (2) Age
      (3) Marital status
      (4) Companion
      (5) Prostitute
      (6) Extramarital
        (a) Petting
        (b) Coitus
        (c) Frequency
      (7) Partner aware
      (8) Effect on marriage
      (9) Desire for further experiences
      (10) Length of foreplay
      (11) Activities
        (a) Caress
          (1) Hair
          (2) Face
          (3) Body
          (4) Breasts
        (b) Stimulate
          (1) Clitoral area
          (2) Mons
          (3) Vagina
        (c) Lip kissing
        (d) Tongue kissing
        (e) Breast manipulation
          (1) Manual
          (2) Oral
        (f) Genital manipulation
          (1) Partner
            (a) Manual
            (b) Oral
          (2) Of you
            (a) Manual
            (b) Oral
        (g) Frequency of orgasm
        (h) Evaluation of coital experience
      (12) Intercourse
        (a) Ejaculation

        (b) Erections
    (b.) Spouse
        (1) Any known extramarital activity
        (2) Number
        (3) Frequency
        (4) Effect on marriage
2. Post-marital relationships
    (a.) Number
    (b.) Age
    (c.) Marital status
    (d.) Frequency
    (e.) Length of foreplay
    (f.) Activities
        (1) Caress
           (a) Hair
           (b) Face
           (c) Body
           (d) Breasts
        (2) Stimulate
           (a) Clitoral area
           (b) Mons
           (c) Vagina
        (3) Lip kissing
        (4) Tongue kissing
        (5) Breast manipulation
           (a) Manual
           (b) Oral
        (6) Genital manipulation
           (a) Partner
               (1) Manual
               (2) Oral
           (b) Of you
               (1) Manual
               (2) Oral
        (7) Frequency of orgasm
        (8) Intercourse
           (a) Ejaculation
           (b) Erections
        (9) Evaluation of coital experiences
3. Intercourse with prostitutes
    (a.) Ages involved
    (b.) Number

(c.) Frequency

VI. HOMOSEXUAL HISTORY

A. First homosexual opportunity occurred
 1. Describe

B. Pre-adolescent play
 1. Ages involved
 2. Frequencies
 3. Companions
  (a.) Ages
  (b.) Number
  (c.) Techniques
   (1) Exhibition
   (2) Manual manipulation
   (3) Vaginal or urethral insertion
   (4) Mouth-genital contact
   (5) Anal

C. Post-Adolescent experience
 1. Ages involved
 2. First experience
  (a.) Age
  (b.) Race
  (c.) Relation to subject
 3. Circumstances
  (a.) Place of contact
  (b.) Initiation of approach
  (c.) Techniques employed
   (1) Passive
   (2) Active
   (3) Mutual
  (d.) Financial arrangements
  (e.) Satisfaction for subject
  (f.) Age of first experience with each technique—
   passive and active
   (1) Manual
   (2) Oral
   (3) Anal
   (4) Full body contact
  (g.) Frequency
   (1) During first year
   (2) Maximum, ever, per day

      (3) Maximum, ever, per week
      (4) Average per week during each year
      (5) Total number of contacts
(h.) Partners
      (1) Total number
      (2) Age range
      (3) Comparisons with age of subject
      (4) Age preferences
      (5) Reason for age preferences
      (6) Social position
         (a) Students in grade school
         (b) Students in high school
         (c) Students in college
         (d) Clergy
         (e) Teachers
         (f) Art groups
         (g) Professional persons
         (h) Business groups
         (i) Armed forces
         (j) Laboring groups
         (k) Law enforcement officers
      (7) Highest position held
      (8) Number Married
      (9) Number without previous homosexual experience
     (10) Number of oncers
     (11) Duration of longest affairs
     (12) Relations involving love and affection
     (13) Percentage of approaches which are rejected
     (14) Races involved
         (a) Caucasion
         (b) Negro
         (c) Others
     (15) Techniques
         (a) Petting, passive and active
         (b) Lip kissing
         (c) Tongue kissing
         (d) Body kissing
         (e) Breast manipulation, manual
         (f) Breast manipulation, oral
         (g) Genital manipulation

manual
oral
(h) Flagellation on back, buttocks, genitalia
(i) Urethral insertions
(j) Anilinctus
(k) Nudity
(l) Positions involved (including 69)
(m) Preference for light or dark
(n) Places involved
(o) Subject's orgasm
(p) Frequency by each technique or by spontaneous ejaculation
(q) Psychic reactions
(r) Preferences for masculine or feminine type of partner
(s) Satisfaction
(t) Problems
  (1) Erection
  (2) Ejaculation
(u) How attempt to resolve

VII. GROUP SEX ACTIVITY
A. Participation in strip poker
B. Fraternal and other group initiation activities
C. Observation of coitus
  1. Of parents
  2. Of friends
  3. Of professional exhibitionists
D. Communes
E. Swinging activities
F. Group marriage

VIII. EROTIC RESPONSES
A. Sensory Information
  1. Touch
    (a.) How do you feel about touch
      (1) By self
      (2) By partner
      (3) By others
      (4) Children
      (5) Others
      (6) Fabrics

(7) Textures
(8) Animals
(9) Feel various surfaces
(b.) Partner's response to:
   (1) Your touch
   (2) Others
(c.) Touch between spouses
   (1) What form
   (2) Where
   (3) Without sex
(d.) Reason for body contact:
   (1) Affection
   (2) Desire for affection
   (3) Identification
   (4) Recognition
   (5) Reassurance
   (6) To be reassure
   (7) Comfort
   (8) Sexual desire
   (9) Gratification
(e.) Touch initiated by
   (1) Self
   (2) Partner
   (3) Both
(f.) What most desirous of
   (1) Self
   (2) Partner
(g.) Touch irritating
   (1) To you
      (a) Circumstances
   (2) Partner
      (a) Circumstances
(h.) Touch dislike intensely
   (1) Self
      (a) Describe
   (2) Spouse
      (a) Describe
(i.) Touch embarrassing
   (1) To you
      (a) Circumstances
   (2) Partner
      (a) Circumstances

      (j.) Meet people
          (1) Partner
          (2) Family members
          (3) Friends
          (4) Casual acquaintances
          (5) Strangers
      (k.) Embarrassed in public by
          (1) Being kissed or hugged
             (a) By male
             (b) By female
      (l.) Seeing others kissed or hugged
      (m.) Most exciting touch
          (1) To you
             (a) Describe
             (b) Partner's reaction
          (2) To Partner
             (a) Describe
             (b) Your reaction
      (n.) Do you and partner
          (1) Exchange caressing
          (2) Exchange back rubs
      (o.) Body contact
          (1) Relaxing
          (2) Stimulating
          (3) Depressing
      (p.) Need for physical closeness
          (1) After intercourse
      (q.) Reaction of contact
          (1) Rebuffed
          (2) Ignored
      (r.) More pleasurable
          (1) Intercourse
          (2) Touch and body contact
      (s.) Walk with partner
          (1) Agreeable to her
      (t.) Most pleasing body contact
          (1) As a child
             (a) Who responsible
          (2) As an adult
             (a) Who responsible
  2. Sight
      (a.) Partner's attractiveness

       (1) Presently

       (2) Choice as partner

       (3) In social situations

       (4) At home

       (5) During lovemaking

       (6) When well-groomed or excitingly dressed

    (b.) Enjoy watching partner

       (1) Absorbed in interest

       (2) Talking to others

       (3) Undressing   .

       (4) Nude

    (c.) Observing self in mirror

       (1) Face

       (2) Body

    (d.) Observing genitalia

       (1) Face

       (2) Body

    (e.) Exhibitionism

3. Smells

    (a.) Awareness of specific odors

       (1) Kinds

       (2) Response to

    (b.) Response to following odors

       (1) Food-related odors

       (2) Outdoor odors

           (a) Smoke

           (b) Grass

           (c) Hay

           (d) Sea

           (e) Flowers

           (f) Fresh Air

           (g) Earth

       (3) Perfumed products

       (4) Other

    (c.) Odors related to specific events in childhood

       (1) Pleasant

       (2) Unpleasant

    (d.) Recall any odor connected with the most pleasurable experience in life

    (e.) Odors related to most unpleasant event

       (1) Describe

    (f.) Odors

        (1) Growing up
        (2) Teen years
        (3) Dating
        (4) Related to this courtship
        (5) Marriage
    (g.) Change in odor of spouse
        (1) Since marriage
        (2) When angry
    (h.) Do you wear
        (1) After shave lotion
           (a) Kind
        (1) Perfume-cologne
           (a) Kind
        (2) Other scented products
    (i.) Some fragrances
        (1) Masculine
        (2) Feminine
    (j.) Does partner use scented products
        (1) Reaction to
        (2) What kind
        (3) Preference for
    (k.) Odor from home
        (1) Most pleasing
        (2) Least pleasing
    (l.) Body odor of
        (1) Self
        (2) Partner
        (3) Friends
        (4) Strangers
        (5) People disliked
    (m.) Odor change in partner under
        (1) Stress
        (2) Anger
4. Sound
    (a.) Disturbing noises
        (1) Children
           (a) Response to
        (2) Neighbors
           (a) Response to
        (3) Music
           (a) Response to
        (4) TV or Radio

(a) Response to
(5) Spouse
  (a) Response to
(b.) Music important to
  (1) Self
  (2) Spouse
  (3) Children
(c.) Do you play an instrument
  (1) Kind
(d.) Spouse
  (1) Your response
(e.) Children
  (1) Your response
  (2) Partner's response
(f.) Music used for
  (1) Relaxation
  (2) Social
  (3) Escape
  (4) To work by
(g.) Response to voice
  (1) Partner's
  (2) Children

5. Homo-erotic responses
  (a.) Thinking of own sex
  (b.) Observing own sex
  (c.) Observing erect genitalia
  (d.) Observing buttocks

6. Hetero-erotic responses
  (a.) Thinking of other sex
  (b.) Observing other sex
  (c.) Nude art
  (d.) Burlesque shows
  (e.) Erotic pictures
  (f.) Obscene stories
  (g.) Erotic literature
  (h.) Moving pictures
  (i.) Dancing
  (j.) Physical contacts
  (k.) Biting
  (l.) Being bitten

7. Zoo-erotic responses
  (a.) Observing animal in coitus

      (b.) Give birth
      (c.) Physical contact with animals
      (d.) Have any pets
      (e.) Sexual stimulation
      (f.) Sexual involvement
         (1) Age
   8. Non-sexual stimuli
     (a.) Other
       (1) Music
       (2) Alcohol
       (3) Motion
         (a) Automobiles
         (b) Airplanes
         (c) Motorcycles
       (4) Pain
       (5) Sadistic situations
       (6) Masochistic situations
       (7) Other emotional situations

IX. SPOUSE'S HISTORY
  A. Age
  B. Previous Marriage
    1. Number
    2. Children
    3. Duration of marriage
    4. Reason for divorce
  C. Length of previous acquaintance
  D. Length of engagement
  E. Religious affiliations
  F. Educational history
  G. Occupation and other interests
    1. Percent of time in home
    2. Spouse's occupation
      (a.) Money
    3. Goes to school
    4. Enjoy work or school
    5. Club Activities
    6. Affect on marriage
  H. Premarital sex
  I. Vaginal infections
  J. Unpleasant or unusual body odors
  K. Call menstruation

    1. Self
    2. Partner
L. Sex satisfaction
M. Sexual incompatibility
N. Reason for divorce
    1. No. of children
O. Common-law marriages
    1. Children
    2. Separation
P. Offspring
    1. No. of children
    2. Planned or unplanned
    3. Sterility
    4. Adopted
    5. Step-children
    6. Sex
    7. Ages
    8. Children living with you
Q. Affiliation with youth groups
    1. Children's reaction
R. Time spent with children
    1. Types of activities
    2. Partner's involvement
    3. Source of conflict
S. Spouse's involvement with children
    1. Your reaction
    2. Types of activities
    3. Source of conflict
T. What do you and spouse disagree most about
U. Spare time
    1. Together
    2. Separate
V. Amount of time together
W. Confide in
    1. Mate
    2. Friends
    3. Relatives
X. Sense of humor
    1. Partner
    2. Self
    3. How used
        (a.) In sex

         (b.) When things go wrong

         (c.) Escape

  Y. Spouse's age at first childbirth

     1. Delivery

         (a.) Length of time

         (b.) Difficulty with

  Z. Affect of children on relationship

A-1. Affect of response to you

B-1. Demonstrate affection in front of children

C-1. Concern about coital noise

D-1. Pleasure besides intercourse

     1. Self

     2. Partner

E-1. Abortions

     1. Spontaneous

     2. Induced

X. PRESENTING SYMPTOMS

  A. Problem as you see it

     1. Spouse

  B. Chronology

  C. Affect on partner

  D. How handled in past

  E. If you resolve this problem, what are you going to be able to do sexually you cannot do now?

XI. EXPECTATIONS

  A. Of opposite sex generally

  B. Of spouse

  C. How do these differ

  D. How realistic

  E. Relationship between expectations and dysfunction

  F. Of opposite sex sexually

  G. Of partner sexually

  H. How do these differ

  I. How realistic

  J. Relationship between expectation and dysfunction

  K. Your concept of effective sexual function

     1. Self

     2. Partner

  L. Expectations in

     1. Relation to home

      (a.) How close
2. In marital bed
      (a.) How close
3. In other aspects of marriage
      (a.) How close
M. Expectations before marriage of
  1. Sex
  2. Love
  3. Marriage
      (a.) Anytime fulfilled first year
      (b.) How closely met
  4. Want most, not provided now
      (a.) Attitude
      (b.) Behavior
  5. From Partner
      (a.) Attitude
      (b.) Behavior
  6. Positive reaction to you
  7. Negative reaction to you
N. How do you think your spouse would answer these questions?
O. Are there any other aspects of your sexual life that I should know about and that would help me to understand you or the situation better?
P. Is there anything that you would like to ask me?
Q. How do you feel about my taking your sex history?
R. Would you have preferred giving it to a member of your sex?

XII. SUMMARIZE CLIENT'S HISTORY

We must be able to handle all sexual material objectively and matter of factly without value judgment. A cultural expectation seems to be that married persons do not masturbate. Typically we find they do, and that they often feel guilty about it. Often the wife feels guilty about her husband's masturbation because it infers that she is not doing her "wifely duty" in meeting his sexual needs. Masturbation and intercourse are not the same thing, for the response feels much different. As long as masturbation is not devisive in the relationship, there is no need to discourage it. Homosexuality, oral-genital, animal contacts, group sex, and extramarital involvements when encountered are handled as objectively as is age, education, and place of birth. The Kinsey work on male and female[4] responses is excellent, showing the incidence of various types of behavior in our society. We feel that understanding the normalcy of all sexual behavior is important because needless guilt may effectively be removed by providing evidence of commonness of forbidden sexual behavior.

We agree that it is important for a doctor or therapist to have a sexual value system of his own, however, under no circumstances, either directly or indirectly, should they force that on another individual.

If a therapist wishes not to masturbate, that is their option, but to force others or condemn other's behavior because it varies from their own functioning, is beyond the realm of the counselor. We try to accept someone's statement of masturbation and make necessary inquiries about it, determining how they feel about it. If they feel guilty, we point out the statistical evidence indicating the commonality of such behavior. We try to alleviate guilt. We do not have to tell the person he must masturbate. If we feel it would be helpful in learning to go longer before ejaculation, we may suggest it to retard orgasm, if a pattern of masturbation already exists. This can easily be done within the couple's value system. Female masturbation, when not contrary to her sexual value system, is the most direct route for a non-orgasmic female to experience orgasm. If strong feelings exist against masturbation and it has never been engaged in, it is still wise to mention the normalcy of such behavior, but unwise to suggest the client must masturbate. We work within the sexual value system of each individual and couple.

We find there is no basic conflict between conserva-

---

[4] Alfred C. Kinsey, Wardell B. Pomeroy, Clyde E. Martin, and Paul H. Gebhard, *Sexual Behavior in the Human Female*, (Philadelphia, 1953), W. B. Saunders Company.

tive sexual value systems and effective sexual functioning. Mutually enjoyable penile-vaginal intercourse is the
stated goal our clients usually bring to therapy.

Chapter 4

PHYSICAL EXAMINATION

A physical examination is given by a medical doctor in our presence. To save time, an extensive two-page medical check list is completed by the individual prior to the examination. Half an hour is spent discussing this form and checking information related to sexual functioning. Determination of any use of medication or drugs is important, since some of these products may produce sexual dysfunction. Our experience indicates few sexual problems are physical in origin, however, it is still important to attempt detection of any sex-oriented medical problem. Any physical dysfunction should be ruled out prior to proceeding with intensive sexual therapy, and if necessary, the client is referred back to their physician if there is a physical dysfunction. Therapy would not be needed unless the physical problem has affected the psychic area to the extent that intensive sexual therapy is indicated beyond the correction of the physical problem.

Laboratory work is ordered where indicated. Blood sugar tests are taken in the office in order to get an immediate indication of diabetes. This often manifests itself through the inability to get an erection.

A routine physical examination is given both the male and the female with emphasis placed on those areas considered sexual or sex-related.

A swivel-handled mirror held by the woman is used in the physical and sexological examination. This allows the woman to look at her clitoris while the doctor checks for clitoral adhesions. If the adhesions are present, it is suggested that these be freed. Clitoral adhesions refer to the skin covering the clitoris being stuck to the glans. Adhesion of the inner surface of the foreskin and the glans is the normal finding in infant girls (the comparable situation existing also in boys). The normal freeing of these adhesions in the first few months of life does not occur in some individuals. Consequently, some girls enter puberty and even adulthood with tightly adhered foreskins in which hard grains of smegma may be embedded. LeMon Clark, M.D., first alerted us to the fact that freeing up the clitoris often is significant for the non-orgasmic female.[1] In several instances women with clitoral adhesions have become orgasmic in the immediate subsequent coital opportunity following removal of these adhesions. The best overall explanation for the results are contained in a book by Mary Jane Sherfey, M.D.,[2] and her attempt to reconcile Freud with Masters and Johnson. Dr. Sherfey maintains that the clitoris withdraws and does a 180° turn about one minute before orgasm. Several medi-

---

[1] LeMon Clark, M.D., "Adhesions Between Clitoris and Prepuce," *"Advances in Sex Research,* Harper & Row Publishers, New York, 1963, pp. 233–235.

[2] Mary Jane Sherfey, M.D., "The Evolution and Nature of Female Sexuality in Relation to Psychoanalytic Theory," *American Psychoanalytic Association Journal,* 1966, 14 (1) pp. 28–128, and *The Nature and Evolution of Female Sexuality,* Random House, Inc., 1972, p. 84.

cal doctors have pointed out that the clitoris is hinged in the same manner as the tongue, providing a certain latitude of movement. Clinical evidence with research subjects clearly reflects the withdrawal of the clitoris as sexual arousal heightens, but the exact extent of movement has not been observed. In our study of 83 non-orgasmic women, approximately ⅓ had clitoral adhesions, and about ⅓ of those women who had clitoral adhesions removed as part of the physical examination became orgasimic within a few weeks after the removal of the adhesions.

Reference to clitoral adhesions can be found in the work of Robert L. Dickinson, M.D.,[3] where he shows the medical approach to their removal. This is accomplished by inserting a dull probe in the 12:00 o'clock position and flicking down and away on each side of the glans of the clitoris. Our physicians have found an anesthetic to be unnecessary in this procedure, which takes only a few seconds to accomplish during the physical examination.

Kinsey was aware of the significance of clitoral adhesions in the 30's. Dr. Wardell Pomeroy recalled in his biography of Dr. Kinsey[4] the suggestions Kinsey made to a non-orgasmic woman asking for help. A woman who had taken Kinsey's Marriage Course at Indiana wrote saying she was now married, but was unable to reach orgasm. Kinsey responded telling her it was a common problem especially among the newly married without prior coital experience. He explained that clitoral adhesions might be the problem, stating "If the foreskin of the clitoris was adhering, he said, a not uncommon problem, she might have difficulty in finding a doctor who knows this, though a clever surgeon could perform the operation with a

---

[3] Robert L. Dickinson, *Atlas of Human Sex Anatomy* (Baltimore, 1949), Figure 77-A.

[4] Wardell Pomeroy, *Dr. Kinsey and the Institute For Sex Research* (New York, 1972), Harper and Row, p. 56.

minimum of time and expense. We have gotten the co-operation of one of the best physicians in this town, and he performs the operation for something like $3.00 for our girls, and it has been a material factor in correcting difficulties of several of our married women."

It seems incredible that knowledge of clitoral adhesions clearly available to scientists of the stature of Dickinson and Kinsey is no more widespread today than it was 50 years ago. What Kinsey calls "operation" is really not cutting of any tissue. Rather it consists of separating prepuce adhered to the glans clitoris.

As the physical examination proceeds, the doctor next inserts a lighted speculum in the vagina not only so he is able to see into the vagina, but so that the woman may also look into her vagina by using the mirror.

A measurement of the vaginal muscles in an unstimulated state is taken by the doctor with a perineometer.[5] The perineometer is a simple pressure gauge (Figure 2). Our concern is not limited to the amount of pressure she can exert upon the perineometer, rather the desire of developing a base reading of approximately 20. Flexibility, good tone, and perception in the muscles is essential to penile-vaginal orgasmic response.

The physician gives the male a complete physical examination with special attention to the penis, prostate, and testicles. As with the female, anything that may be encountered in the physical history is checked to see if a problem exists which would preclude success in our program.

The doctor verbally states what he is examining and

---

[5] The perineometer is a pressure chamber. It is used to measure vaginal muscle contractions, and is a biofeedback instrument for female muscle training. It was invented by the late Arnold H. Kegel, M.D. Information about the perineometer can be obtained from: Perineometer Clinic, Post Office Box 57070, Foy Station, Los Angeles, California 90057.

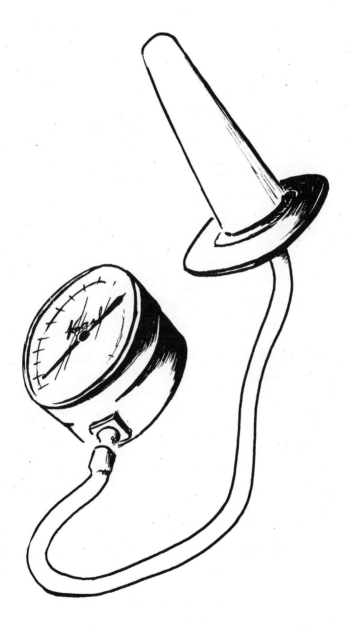

Figure 2.   The Perineometer.

what he finds during the physical examination. It is transcribed by a therapist for further reference. The doctor then briefly chats with the patient and answers questions. Our experience indicates that many people have had physical examinations where nothing has been communicated about the findings except that they are healthy. People are concerned about how they compare with other people. If the person is normal, then this should be stated to the individual at the time; it can be quite reassuring to be told that they are "normal."

ROUNDTABLE

The roundtable discussion takes place on the third day of the program following the physical examination. By this time each of the therapists have taken and reviewed each client's sex history. The couple has completed their psychological testing, and the physical examination. The physician has indicated to them in our presence that there is no physical reason why they should not obtain results in the program, since he can find no physical base for their sexual problems. In rare instances, laboratory tests are ordered, but this has never precluded continuation of the therapy program.

The first item of business in the roundtable is for the couple individually to have an opportunity to indicate their desire to continue or withdraw. Since motivation is such a basic factor to success in sexual therapy, we feel that each person should be strongly motivated in order for the program to continue. Needless to say, couples who come from a distance have arranged a two-week vacation with babysitters, and have reservations in a motel, and have typically planned the visit at least several months in advance, seldom show any signs of the desire to withdraw during the third day of a two-week intensive therapy program. They are asked about their commitment and desire to continue. A verbal statement is given with the four of us sitting together (Figure 3).

We then proceed to briefly review the results of the psychological tests, and to indicate to them whether we feel they will profit by their two weeks with us. No couple has requested to withdraw from the program at this time. We have yet to see a situation in which we felt that it would be wisdom for the couple not to continue. One couple did ask not to continue in the program several years ago after their sex history was taken, and one couple was terminated toward the end of the program. Extensive psychiatric problems precluded effective sensate focus, and we felt resolution of these problems was indicated before we could effectively help the sexual relationship. Other than that, there have been no drop-outs or terminations, and the ones we have experienced have not come at the time of the roundtable.

Figure 3.   Roundtable.

Chapter 5

SEXOLOGICAL EXAMINATION

A unique aspect of our program deals with the sexological examination which evolved during our Non-Orgasmic Women Study with Kenneth Morgan, M.D. We feel it is important for several reasons. It gives us a clearer understanding of the sexual response pattern of the person with whom we are working. We realize that verbal information is based on their personal subjective knowledge about themselves without having someone they can compare with. Women frequently discuss female problems such as menstruation, childbirth, and menopause with friends, but only occasionally will they discuss things of a sexual nature. Usually they have read articles in women's magazines or books dealing with sex-related material. Their personal knowledge, however, about their own body is very limited. The sexological allows her to know, understand, and more readily accept her own body.

A woman may discuss in the sex history the fact that she does not lubricate well when she is having sexual relations. In giving a sexological examination, we can determine not only that lubrication does take place, but that vasocongestion occurs, and that there are areas in the vaginal vault that feel good to her. We frequently discover that what a woman tells us in the sex history session is not supported in fact by what we find by doing the sexological examination. Then, and right then, we can reassure her that there is lubrication, and that it should be sufficient for easy intercourse, provided there is enough foreplay. If she is not getting enough lubrication for penetration, the probability is that foreplay has been inadequate either in duration or method. To become aware that there are areas that do feel pleasurable in the vagina and that an orgasmic platform physically does occur, can be reassuring to the woman. If there are tears and lesions in the vaginal walls which have caused pain in intercourse, we can reassure her they are all right, and vaginal exercises should fill in the muscle so that intercourse is no longer painful. We have encountered many women whose doctor has said that there is nothing wrong. Many have gone to doctors for the pain only to be treated, they say, as if they were mentally unbalanced or rushed out of the office as though they had expressed a dirty word. We can show them that their pain is not a figment of their imagination, and that a penis thrusting into a separation in the muscle of the wall can be a very painful experience. If they understand why they have the pain and can be told how they can correct the situation, this eliminates fears of cancer or other terrifying thoughts about what is happening physically "in there," or concern that they are a "kooky," or "hysterical female." If they understand they are normal, working with them is easier, and achieving results more likely.

Two of the great bugaboos of our culture is fear and lack of knowledge in the area of sexual function and behavior. To reassure a woman that she is normal, normal,

normal, realistically right down the line can be a tremendous boost to her morale and self-confidence. Giving her assignments she can specifically do for herself to help her own sexual functioning, makes her an involved participant in our work.

Her complaints about little or no vaginal perception may be realistic. She may have blamed her partner for her lack of vaginal feelings where it may be due to her insensitive or unconditioned vaginal muscles. She will have to decide if she wants to do the vaginal exercises we discuss later. She no longer blames her partner if she does not do them. Her goal may have shifted; she may no longer really be interested in spending the time and effort to resolve the problem, but she is aware that the problem can be resolved if she wishes to make the effort. This means she is going to be more satisfied and content in the relationship since she is aware of the responsibility on her part in alleviating the problem. The initial complaint may become acceptable rather than going through the effort needed to change the situation. This is one of the reasons that results are difficult to evaluate.

A one-page questionnaire (Appendix pg. 219) is filled out prior to the examination which gives us briefly some information from the sex history, as well as more specific sexual information. We usually are working with several couples at one time, and it is important to be able to recall at a glance key information that will bring into recall the essentials of a specific sex history. We feel it is important to possess information about a couple, rather than ask them constantly to refresh our memory about something we already have learned.

Each client independently fills out the sexological form. It asks how many people they have had intercourse with, the coital positions they prefer, the one they get the most satisfaction from, the one most often used, when they last had intercourse, orgasmic response, if any, prematurity problem, if any, and the length of time the male is able to go in intercourse. (Appendix pg. 000)

The female sexological examination is usually first, since her genitalia, for the most part, are internal, therefore taking longer for the examination.

The typical drape employed in the physical examination is not used although a robe is provided which prepares them for later work, and comfort with their own nudity.

In the sexological examination we are checking for sexual response. We are interested, for example, in whether the breast becomes engorged or the nipple erects during stimulation. The breast is lightly touched and the nipple gently squeezed to determine physiological response, as well as eliciting any feeling or response in the vagina. When nipple erection starts to develop, it is pointed out to the woman and she is asked if this happens in response to her partner's foreplay. We ask if she has feelings in her breasts at any time such as cold or fright. Does stimulation of the breasts by her partner produce pleasurable feelings in the vagina? We are interested in knowing if she has nursed her children or not, and if she nursed her children, did she have orgasm at any time or develop any sexual arousal or feelings, and if she did, how did she feel about it. We stress to her the normalcy of this, since we have encountered women who have terminated nursing their infants because of sexual arousal or orgasmic response and the feeling that there must be something wrong with them. If there is little breast response and she dislikes her breasts, we suggest she focus on pleasurable feelings in her breasts as her partner caresses or fondles her, developing a more positive response. We also suggest she use her breasts to caress her partner to bring pleasure to herself.

The clitoris is again checked. If it has been freed of clitoral adhesions, we want to see that the prepuce is being pulled back and the glans cleaned. This is part of the instructions given a woman to maintain cleanliness of the genitalia. If there is smegma present, we show it to her and explain the importance of washing the genitalia with mild soap and water. Douching and the use of vaginal deodorants is discouraged and the possible negative effects explained.

We then evaluate vaginal sensitivity, looking for possible scarring, fibrosity, pain, and separation of muscle in the wall of the vagina. We have found that some women have a tight muscle, but it is fibrous and causes pain with penetration. When encountered, the woman can usually be reassured that these conditions can be corrected by vaginal exercises. Vaginal surgery is rarely required, but if found to be the case, referral is made.

It is important to determine whether there is any sensation or awareness in the vagina. Some women are unaware if the examining finger or if the speculum is in or out. What we attempt to do is get her to focus on the feelings in the vagina, with an examining finger in the vagina. We find that often nothing has ever been in the vagina long enough for her to have developed any perception, and that because of this, she may describe any movement as pain. This is easily determined if the pain is inconsistent in location. Both of us spend time stimulating the vaginal area to develop a more comfortable and relaxed feeling with something in her vagina. We have her focus on what we are doing, as well as direct her in specific exercises she can do. We find by asking her if it feels good and reassuring her that it is all right to let it feel good that she becomes comfortable in telling us what does or does not feel good. If sex flush develops as it does on occasion, we use a mirror and show it to her. Whenever there are positive sexual feelings we re-enforce the acceptability of pleasurable sexual feelings. She is in a position where two opposite sex people in authority say "it is all right to have positive sexual feelings," and "it is all right to have positive sexual response."

Even the most inhibited woman is pleased to find that they are "normal" and are able to develop nipple response, vasocongestion, lubrication, and sex flush even in a clinical situation which would be much less conducive to sex response than the pleasuring done by the partner in the privacy of their motel.

This may be the first time the woman has ever focused on sexual feelings.

Inappropriate response patterns are encountered frequently, i.e. a woman while being examined complains of being cold, although both therapists are quite warm and the heater is on in the room to eliminate possibility of coldness. If we ask her about her feelings of cold, she may state that her nipples feel like they always do when she is cold, (nipple erection) and she has goose bumps (often encountered with sexual arousal).

Since some people are not aware of what happens in sexual arousal, they do not know when sexual arousal is physiologically occurring. They have to be made to focus in on what they are feeling when these physical changes are taking place.

How many women have missed their own orgasmic response by looking for the block-buster their best friend talked about? Orgasmic response is a unique individualistic response. Not all women achieve orgasm in the same way nor are all orgasmic releases the same. Recordings show differences from woman to woman, but a consistency in her pattern. If she learns to have orgasm in a different way, then her orgasmic pattern changes in response to what she does.

Some women believe fallaciously that orgasmic response is so intense and fantastic that you cannot miss it. Our research with both orgasmic and non-orgasmic women has shown us that like pain, there are different responses and thresholds. Some women when they become orgasmic are disappointed stating, "It is not all that great, and not what I expected at all." For other women it is described as a fantastic experience while some may experience pain due to physiological problems. It is important during the sexological to talk to the woman about her orgasm, and her expectations concerning it.

VAGINAL EXERCISES

A series of vaginal exercises are then taught to the female while the examining finger of the therapist is in the vagina to determine if they are being done correctly.

About one out of ten women that we see are not able to move their vaginal muscles at all. In these women the vagina is often gapping and open, and they usually have some problem with urinary stress-incontinence. In such cases we have difficulty in getting them to move the muscle enough to identify it so that they can do vaginal exercises. However, if they can learn to do the exercises and will do them, remarkable changes can take place in the physiology of the vaginal barrel, even where there has been extensive trauma in childbirth.

The most instructive educational film on the vagina as a female sex organ is the one produced by the late Arnold H. Kegel, M.D., "Pathologic Physiology of the Pubococcygeus Muscle in Women."[1] In this film Dr. Kegel indicates something of the physiologic make-up of the vagina, and how it functions as a female sex organ. His major contribution is the location of the centers of sexual sensory perception at the 4:00 and 8:00 o'clock areas. We pay special attention to these areas which are about two finger joints in depth in the vagina. (Figure 4) Neurologically nature has provided areas in the vagina that if

---

[1] Rented and sold by Morgan Camera Shop, 6262 Sunset Blvd., Hollywood, California 90028.

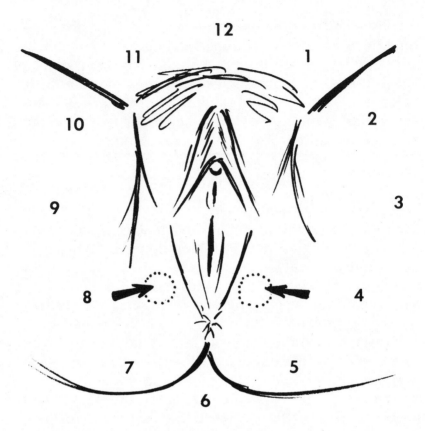

Figure 4.   Location of areas of sexual sensory perception in female vagina—1-2 finger joints in depth at 4:00 and 8:00 o'clock.

stimulated, will produce positive sexual response. Vaginal exercises not only contribute to sensory perception, elimination of pain during intercourse, but also toward better bladder control, and easier expression of fecal material in the female. Both areas are important since we encounter women who are embarrassed by loss of urine during coital activities, (this is differentiated from profuse vaginal lubrication which some women experience), and the problem of constipation where the penis hits the fecal material in the lower bowel often causing discomfort for both partners as well as forcing the penis to ride high in the vagina away from any contact with the sexual segments at 4:00 and 8:00 o'clock.

ILLUSTRATION 1

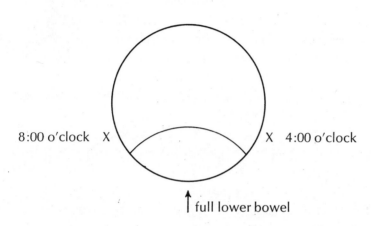

8:00 o'clock X   X   4:00 o'clock

↑ full lower bowel

The pubococcygeus muscle, which is the master sphincter of the pelvis, extends from the os pubis in front to the coccyx in the rear. It is associated not only with bowel and bladder function, but also with positive female vaginal perception and response during penile-vaginal intercourse. Since many clients already orgasmic by clitoral stimulation desire to become orgasmic by penile-vaginal stimulation, the use and training of this and other muscles is one of the most significant individual techniques known to produce the therapeutic results desired.

It is important to state at this point that orgasm is orgasm and one is not superior, better, or more mature than another; but since many of the people we work with desire to achieve orgasm in intercourse with their partners, we move them toward that goal.

Our own experience has been that about 75% of those we examined have reported definite vaginal response in these areas. We also encounter women who have no feeling in this area. Often we find that this particular area has a degree of fibrosity, and there is some discomfort when examined. If there is a tear or lesion in the wall of the vagina and we insert a finger in that area or we flick the bands where there is any fibrosity, this can often be painful and the woman frequently responds by saying, "What is that? That is exactly what happens in intercourse, but I have never been able to find out what it is." We can assure the woman that it is simply a fibrous band or a separation in the vaginal wall, and can easily be filled in or corrected by her doing the suggested vaginal exercises.

We want all the women we work with to learn to contract and hold the pubococcygeus muscle for three seconds and then relax. They are to do anywhere from 25 to 50 of these exercises a day depending on the condition of the muscle. If the muscle is fibrous, but tight, it may be that we would only have her do about 30 contractions per day. But if it is a good tight muscle with no fibrosity, 25 contractions and hold for a count of three would be sufficient. If the vagina is open and gapping, then at least 50 should be done per day. We have had a few exceptions where more have been recommended. We suggest that they do them at different times during the day so that they will not become tired. They must also be told that they may have to work up to that number gradually over a period of many days, since, like other muscles which have not been exercised, this one will become sore if there is too much exercise at a time. Soreness is temporary and is often helped by the gentle massage given later on by the partner.

Exercises are best done routinely at some consistent time during the day. i.e. driving to and from work, doing dishes, preparing meal, changing diapers, or talking on the telephone. This tends to serve as a useful reminder. Once exercises are learned, they can be done easily at any time or any place. Doing some in bed before getting up, are helpful before the weight of all the internal organs are placed on the muscle.

Dr. Kegel recommended that exercises be done three times a day, 20 minutes each time.[2] He also taught women to clearly identify this muscle by sitting on the toilet, legs spread as widely apart as possible, and starting and stopping the flow of urine. (see Figure 5) It is the only way of stopping urine under this circumstance. He suggested muscle training as part of everyday toilet activities.

Another exercise we would like them to do is a flicking of the pubococcygeus muscle where they contract and relax very rapidly, 25 to 50 times a day, depending upon muscular condition and whether the female is orgasmic or not. This exercise approximates what the major sphincter muscle does involuntarily at orgasm. No research subject, faking orgasm, has ever been able to flick the muscle as rapidly as it involuntarily contracts at orgasm.

A breathing exercise which is taught involves taking a deep breath, pulling up from the vagina at the same time tightening up of the genital muscles then relaxing the whole pelvic region as air is exhaled. We like to have them do about 10 of those a day.

The last exercise we teach is that of bearing down as though they are going to expell something from the vagina, then tightening up the muscle after ceasing to bear down. The bearing down simulates childbirth. Grantly Dick Reed's natural childbirth compared by Niles Newton[3] with Kinsey's summary of orgasmic response,

---

[2] J. P. Greenhill, *Office Gynecology*, (Chicago, 1965), "Genital Relaxation, Urinary Stress Incontinence and Sexual Dysfunction," p. 279.

[3] See Edward M. Brecher, *The Sex Researchers*, (Boston, 1969), Little, Brown and Company, pp. 176–177, and article in *Psychology Today*, "Trebly Sensuous Woman," Niles Newton, (July, 1971).

Figure 5. Identifying female pubococcygeus muscle. "Sit on the toilet. Spread your legs as far apart as possible. Start and stop the flow of urine. The pubococcygeus is the only muscle that can stop the flow of urine in this position."

shows that the steps are markedly similar. We find that with this exercise more vasocongestion develops in the vagina with resultant increase in lubrication of the area. We can then check to see how much lubrication and vasocongestion is developing. The perineometer is again utilized (see Chapter 4, Fig. 2), and a measurement is taken in the congested state to determine the degree of vasocongestion. This is usually 5 mm. Hg. higher than the unstimulated state. A form is filled out in relation to findings (Appendix pg. 221).

The woman is given the perineometer so that she can look at the gauge as she contracts. The feedback she gets from the reading results in an ability to increase vaginal pressure, and is a positive re-enforcer in doing vaginal exercises to increase readings.

We emphasize the importance of the vaginal exercises, especially where there is a loose and gapping vagina, not only for the woman's pleasure, but the satisfaction of the male. If the vaginal vault is loose, the penis going in and out of the vagina may have little friction on the walls. We encounter males who lose their erection during intercourse because of this problem. Some women have asked their partner if they are in, which has been in the past considered a put down of the male, and has been defined as the cause of some impotence problems for their partner. Actually the woman was probably not feeling anything herself, and was not sure whether he was in or out due to an unconditioned muscle with no perception or because the vagina was loose and gapping, and there was little or no friction. The woman has the organ of accommodation and can develop a tight vaginal vault where she can receive much more friction and feeling through vaginal exercises. This is not only positive for her in the vagina, but also a tight vagina will cause more movement of the foreskin over the clitoral shaft which will increase her satisfaction and pleasure.

We feel that it is to the advantage of both the female and male for the woman to do these exercises. A sheet is given the woman listing number and exercises indicated from the examination (Appendix pg. 222).

Vaginal exercises also force the woman to focus on an area that has always been that "other place" or "that place she really does not consider part of her body," "that place down there," etc. If she can focus on the vaginal muscles and vagina, and her feelings from doing vaginal exercises, and the movement in the vagina; she will develop sensations and feelings that may have been blocked over a number of years, and a person in authority has told her that it is proper.

We have found some women who report themselves to be non-orgasmic are in fact orgasmic, but have completely cut themselves off from their own sexual feelings. The biological response they are getting have not filtered into consciousness. Unless a woman can respond both physiologically and psychologically, she typically does not report an enjoyable orgasmic response.

A form is filled out during the sexological examination (see Illustration 2), which covers those things discussed in the examination.

Our forms all have an identifying number and if a name is used, only the first name is listed.

Suggested positions are listed which would maximize contact with areas of receptivity, and minimize contact with areas of discomfort.

The boxes in the illustration give us a visual idea of the vagina. You will notice that at first examination the vagina was loose and gapping as exemplified by the opening of the lines at the bottom of the squares. The start of the lines outward from the top indicated a V-shaped vagina. This means a penis would not have contact with vaginal walls at the area of the sexual segments. Another pattern we encounter is a bottle-shaped

ILLUSTRATION 2

ILLUSTRATION #2

71060

NAME *Jane*

PERINEOMETER

Reading Unstimulated State *10-17*

Date *1-7-71*

Dr. comments from physical form:

Good physical condition

Physical response good.

Breast Response *Breast surgery 7 yrs. ago-plastic inserts-important to ego.*

Erection during stimulation: *yes* Cold *yes* Other ———

Nurse Babies: *Couldn't* Vaginal Feelings ——— Orgasm ———

Diastasis *none* Platform *thin*

Episiotomy *medialateral*

Identify Sexual Segments at 4: *yes* at 8: *yes*

Sensory perception in vagina at: Suggested Positions *Female*

12 *pleasurable* 6 *good*   *superior - legs together*
1 *fine* 7 *not so great*   *when possible.*
2 *fine* 8 *fine*   *Positions where thrusts*
3 *fine* 9 *not too good*   *hit top half vagina.*
4 *hurts* 10 *all right*
5 *fine* 11 *fine*

Other Comments: *Finger in vagina feels pressure. Fibrosity feels dis-*
Comfort. Muscle pulled away on right side. V-shaped vagina. Unaware
of vaginal contractions. Husband resists them during intercourse. Husband used
lighted
speculum

DATE *1-8-71*   DATE *6-16-71*   DATE *1-10-72*
READING *15-17*   READING *16-30*   READING *24-60*
COMMENTS *Stimulated* COMMENTS *Unstimulated* COMMENTS *Unstimulated*
state   *hold at 55*

vagina where it is tight at the opening, but almost immediately goes in (see Illustration 3).

ILLUSTRATION 3

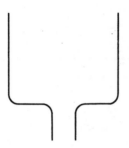

A well-conditioned vagina is long and narrow. It should be remembered that a vagina is not an actual space, but a potential. It is by inserting a finger and moving it against the wall, and in pressing against the wall we ascertain the contour, since the fleshy part of the vagina meets the resistance of the vaginal muscles when palpated with a finger.

If you notice again Illustration 2, you will see that the bottom left-hand boxes which are divided into thirds identify the vaginal barrel right and left by lower, middle, and upper third which have different markings in them. The top third of that illustration indicates no observable muscle. It is in poor condition with a lot of fibrosity indicated by the X. The lower third has a circle with an X which indicates there is some muscle response there, but there is fibrosity or lesions in the muscle. The lower part indicates the muscle is in better shape having less fibrosity on the right side, but still not too good. If you look at the last set of boxes, you see that in a year's time the muscle has markedly changed. There is some fibrosity in the upper third, but lower and middle third are now in good tone, and the V-shape and gapping are gone. The readings at rest are also markedly improved.

We always check for diastasis to see if there is any separation in the abdominal muscles. The client is asked to lift her head up off of the examining table, and the lower abdomen is checked to see if there is any separation in the muscle. A diastasis is often accompanied by a separation in the vaginal muscles causing a gapping and open vagina.

Episiotomies are checked to see that a medialateral episiotomy has not cut through vaginal muscles which preclude much feeling or sensation on that side. If we encounter this situation, we suggest positions which direct the penis toward the intact side.

Occasionally we encounter a woman whose vaginal muscles have been badly torn in childbirth—sometimes completely pulling loose from one side or the other. Vaginal exercises are suggested, and our experience has been if faithfully followed, marked changes occur in the vagina and surgery is unnecessary. Surgical repair can be done, but exercises are suggested first to see if surgery is necessary, but if so, the exercises will be helpful in building tone and flexibility in the muscle whereby recovery from surgery will be much more rapid. Surgery never precludes the need for vaginal exercises.

We have encountered old episiotomy scars which are still giving pain in intercourse. The vaginal exercises are given to soften the scar tissue and flatten it out so there is no longer pain.

HUSBAND'S PARTICIPATION

We feel it is important to have the husband be a part of the sexological examination, and it is at this point he comes into the examining room. The wife's permission is always requested by us and is almost always given by her. Some question—"will it destroy the mystery?" and the answer is "we hope so"—he is much more likely to function if it is not quite so mysterious. We have him insert a lighted plastic speculum into his wife's vagina. This allows him to look into the vagina and see the vaginal walls and the cervix and its opening, and he is able to see the area that has been forbidden for so long in our culture. The wife usually likes to have another look at her vagina and see her cervix again using the mirror. Frequently they will ask questions about the cervix and vaginal walls. Spouses consider incredulous the fact that a baby is able to come through the small cervical opening. This gives us an opportunity to give some good on-the-spot sex education, and point out different areas and functions. We can explain to her that with muscular exercises the vagina can get an 8 to 1 stretch during childbirth as opposed to a 4 to 1 stretch of the unconditioned vagina. If she is ever planning to have a baby, it would be a much easier labor for her if her vagina was flexible so that it could stretch readily in having the baby, and with less likelihood of the need for an episiotomy. The sexually responsive and functional reproductive vaginas appear to be physiologically synonymous.

We then have the husband insert his index finger into the vagina and starting at the top with the fleshy side against the pubic bone, moving very slowly in and out. We ask the woman if her husband's penis was in that position during coitus, would that feel good to her? We instruct the husband to go around the vagina as he would a clock, and stimulate the vaginal walls at every hour (see Fig. 4, page 84), and we repeatedly ask the same question—if your husband's penis was **there,** how would that feel to you? In some women one area may feel quite good, but the area right next to it may be painful or uncomfortable. As vaginal exploration proceeds, the husband is able to determine the areas which feel best to his wife, and can then be encouraged to utilize coital positions which maximize stimulation at the preferred areas.

It helps him become comfortable with the vagina, and touching the genital area. Some men are very apprehensive about any genital contact with their partner. Their participation helps work through their fears in a situation where they can be helped. Their feelings are reported on the response sheet (see illustration 2, page 91).

The husband is shown the clitoris, and one man stated "I have been married for 29 years, and I always wondered where the darn thing was." Any questions that are asked, are responded to.

MALE SEXOLOGICAL

A male sexological form (Appendix pg. 220) is filled out and includes information similar to that contained on the form for the female. Including information on prematurity, and how long he is able to function in penile-vaginal intercourse. Often we find a male states he has no prematurity problem, but in the following question states he goes 2 or 3 minutes in intercourse, which to us, is a problem in prematurity if his wife is non-orgasmic. Our Non-Orgasmic Woman Study plus research here at the Center has indicated that it takes approximately 15 or 20 minutes of penile-vaginal thrusting to develop female orgasmic response through intercourse.

The male sexological examination is not as complex, but does involve checking the penis to see that the foreskin is loose, and movable. The frenum is examined and the client asked whether there has ever been bleeding during intercourse or any discomfort of any kind. We ask if there is ever any breaking out of the skin of the penis. Certain mouth washes used by the female prior to oral-genital contact may act as an irritant to the penis, and sometimes, apprehensions concerning intercourse may cause a breaking out.

The woman comes into the examining room, and tactually and visually examines the husband's penis. We point out where the frenulum is and the very sensitive part of the underside of the penis. The wife is encouraged to have a close look at the penis and to move the foreskin back and forth. The female therapist helps her in examining and feeling the testicles, being told to be gentle with them and that sometimes they can be very sensitive, determining at that point how much sensitivity there is so that later on she will be able to know how careful she will need to be.

It is important to ascertain if there is particular penile sensitivity after ejaculation. This varies from male to male, and where one male finds his penis super-sensitive, another notices little or no difference. This is important to discuss in the presence of the woman, since she may have an expectation that he will continue thrusting, whereas the sensitivity of the penis precludes going on. Erections may subside immediately or the penis may remain erect for many minutes.

At this time the female is taught how to hold the penis in the squeeze exercise they will be doing later on. We note whether she is able to touch her husband's penis and testicles. Some women have never touched the genitalia of their spouse, and are quite uncomfortable about it and need to have help in learning how to do this.

Since the female therapist demonstrates how to do the squeeze with the statement "now you do it," she may be helped over a hurdle by demonstration of what would have been difficult to bridge on her own.

We go from the sexological examination to individual body imagery work. When the sexological and body imagery work is done, both of us are in the room with the individual. The spouse is usually in the adjoining room where they can be reading from the sex library, but immediately available when needed. We feel it is important that the partner be close by to reduce anxiety in the client we are working with, but far enough away that negative self-perceptions are discussed only in our presence.

Chapter 6

BODY IMAGERY

The fourth day of the program involves body imagery work. This unique aspect of our therapy protocol evolved from a combination of our nudist research and the perceptive insight supposedly attributable to Freud to the effect that all the images one has about one's self come from the basic biological image. How one literally feels about one's self seems to be a very important concept in all relationships, including those sexual. In our nudist research, the nude marathons in particular, we felt that the removal of clothing tended to expose a person to the more basic feelings they have about the self. The therapeutic possibilities of this procedure were observed by the humanistic psychologist Dr. Abraham Maslow when he wrote, "I still think that nudism, simply going naked before a lot of other people, is itself a kind of therapy, especially if we can be conscious of it, that is, if there's a skilled person around to direct what's going on, to bring things to consciousness."[1]

---

[1] Abraham H. Maslow, *Eupsychian Management* (Homewood, Illinois, 1965) Irwin-Dorsey Press, p. 160.

We found the use of mirrors and patterned color slides to be beneficial in marathons, developing an acceptance of one's nude body. We added the dimension of self-touch and feeling during the body imagery work here at the office as well as a fantasy trip to the interior of the body.

We noticed in the Non-Orgasmic Women Study that self-concept was closely related to non-orgasmic response. If she felt she was so totally unworthy of achieving orgasm, it was improbable that we could do much for her without some change in her self-concept. We also encountered the phenomena where a woman pointed out that she had never been successful in any walk of life—including sex. Therefore, it seemed important to us when we started our work at the Center that we evolve some type of method or technique which would be effective in dealing with this particular self-image.

Touch through physical and sexological examination and self-touch through body imagery work, proved to be the most effective techniques in realistically raising the self-concept of the non-orgasmic female to enable her to function sexually.

An example from our Non-Orgasmic Women Study involved a woman who had no qualms in taking her clothes off for an examination, but absolutely refused to take off her shoes, contending "I have the ugliest feet in the world." Marked progress was made once shoes were removed, but several sessions were required before she could take this step.

The body imagery work is done individually, in front of a traditional three-way tailor's mirror which allows clients to have a complete nude view of themselves. Some people we work with have never seen themselves completely nude before, some individuals appear very self-conscious holding their arms close to their body while maintaining a rigidity of stance. As work progresses, they tend to become relaxed. This is important since the more comfortable we can get them with their body and with nudity, the easier other work will be. Individuals who are uncomfortable being seen nude by the spouse, can learn to feel more relaxed in such a situation.

A curious phenomenon often makes its appearance during the body imagery work. A person who is uncomfortable with his or her own nudity faces a problem when standing in front of the mirror with therapists present— should they shield their bodies from the view of the therapist? Should they shield their bodies from their own view? Faced with these conflicts, a high proportion of individuals give priority to protecting themselves from themselves; they will turn to examine their backs in the mirror and look over their shoulders at themselves in a gingerly fashion—ignoring the fact that they are standing full-front toward the therapists, when turning the opposite way would hide their front and genitalia from view.

We find it is important to have the person make a realistic appraisal of themselves during body examination in our presence. This tends to keep them honest with their feelings, and at the same time, they cannot be to unrealistic about what they see.

When a 90-pound, well distributed woman tells us she is fat, we need to find her frame of reference as well as have her compare herself to people in general. The definition of self as fat may not be related to other people at all.

We can be objective and realistically reassuring with individuals. We have never encountered anyone whom we felt was hopeless nor about whom we did not find a number of positive attributes. Where they have realistically had reason to feel negative about some aspects of their body, typically the majority of other attributes were positive and could be emphasized. We find individuals

tend to look towards the negative rather than the positive. We feel it is important to focus on the positive,
otherwise one negative coital session per week becomes
more important than three positive ones. Being able to
accept negative things realistically is worth strong emphasis, when viewed within a total context, these negative
elements may prove insignificant.

Occasionally we have people with a physical handicap who have suppressed negative feelings. Negative
feelings when internalized, can be self-destructive. It is
ridiculous for a handicapped person to tell us he likes
the deformity. He can accept that as the way it is, but he
does not have to like it. In our nudist research, we encountered a number of handicapped people and quite a
few with surgically scarred bodies. These people talked
about how, through social contact, nudity had helped
them accept themselves and their bodies. They were accepted even with the handicap or scars.

Negative feelings often come from people who are
good physical specimens with attractive bodies. At some-
time in their life they were fatter or thinner or in some
way less attractive, and while their perception of that self
was realistically unflattering, their current self-concept
has remained unrealistically in the past and needs to be
up-dated.

People want to play the numbers game. Few females
are satisfied with their breasts, feeling they are too big,
too small or too flabby. Men are hung-up on size or
erectibility of the penis. Some men can give us an exact
percentage of erection. We initially encounter some discussion of this during the sex history. In the body imagery
sessions we can have a look at the "problem", and openly
discuss it. This is feasible in a dyadic counseling situation.
We have never encountered a penis which was not adequate for effective sexual functioning. Size is of little consequence since the woman has the organ of accommo-

dation. The disparity between erect and flacid state is marked in the small penis and minor in the large. Weight is by far the biggest complaint we encounter other than penis and breast size. The desire for a "perfect figure," as typified by Madison Avenue seems to be the wish.

A beautiful, well-built physique may pose a problem. A person's whole self-concept may be tied up in their physiology. They could be completely destroyed by an incapacitating illness or physical disfigurement. In this instance we have asked them to fantasy such an occurrance, they are now present in front of this mirror completely helpless in a wheel chair. This forces them to find positives other than the physical body. Going inside in fantasy also forces acknowledgement of intelligence and feelings.

We start by instructing the subject to place both hands on the top of their head. (Figure 6). Then we ask them to work down to the bottom of their feet, while on a tactile and emotional level tell us how they feel and perceive all parts of their body, both positive and negative. For instance, do they like or dislike the texture and color of their hair, how do they relate to the way it feels as they touch it, and what do they feel emotionally about these things.

As they examine their body, we notice exclusions. Often they have negative feelings about these excluded and overlooked parts, and it is the responsibility of the therapist to direct them back to these areas. Genitalia is rarely skipped. Areas such as hands, feet, chin, stomach, buttocks, chest, etc. have all been areas people have felt negative about and avoided. Occasionally an area is genuinely missed. More commonly, the areas have some negative meaning for them.

The most important and significant body parts encountered in body imagery are the hands and feet. They are as important to self-concept as the body. Feet repre-

Figure 6.   Body Imagery—"Place your hands on your head, touch every part of your body from the top of your head to the bottom of your feet, and tell us how you feel about each part of your body tactually and emotionally."

sent foundation and base. They carry us around all day. They symbolically represent the foundation of who we are as individuals. In drawing the nude front view of self and partner, one of the couples drew the female complete, neither drew "him" with feet or face. She was working and financing him through graduate school; both felt insecure about the future and where they were going in life. They both perceived the wife as having arrived. He had not as yet found his identity and base in life.

Stance often is an indication of comfort with one's self-concept. Arms across the body in a protective stance, generally indicates some sort of fears about the acceptability of one's own body to one's self; since our position and the client's position precluded our getting a good view of the subject unless they turned directly toward us, he could hardly be protecting himself from us.

Once a realistic self-concept is obtained, we enclose the client in the mirrors observing how he likes his own company. We ask them: "Do you feel good about the person in there with you?"—"Would you like to spend more time with that individual?" etc. People who feel negative about themselves get upset viewing these images in close proximity. We then ask if they have seen a place, part, or view of their body that they have never seen before, and how they feel about it. Frequently an unattractive feature viewed from another angle looks good. "How many separate images of themself can they count?" Is this symbolic of a broad or narrow view of self or life in general?

Looking full-length in the mirror they give themselves an overall rating of 0 to 100 with 0 being the least worthwhile and 100 being the most positive. People who like themselves, give themselves a high rating (85-100). People with a poor self-concept, give a rating below 50. Often it is a personal feeling of self-worth that they are really evaluating. They have to look into their own eyes and express how they feel and what they think of themselves. Neither high nor low ratings are accepted by the therapists as realistic unless it "adds up" in terms of the individual touching areas just completed.

After they have completely examined the exterior, the lights are dimmed and they are asked to close their eyes and explore the interior of their body in fantasy. In fantasy they are to enter their body anyway they desire. We give them direction if they need it. We suggest going inside through an opening in their body or by osmosis, typically the mouth is used. Once inside, we have them look around. They inform us once inside, where they are, and how they got there. They are asked to travel to various parts of the body such as seat of emotions, sexuality, intelligence, and let us know where each is and what is observed, plus positive and negative feelings about what is observed. The seat of emotions is often somewhere they have a physical problem, i.e. a man who says "It's crazy, but I feel that the colon is the seat of my emotion," we recall his medical history indicates he has colitis. Another example is the woman who went to her stomach—we were aware she had ulcers.

The genitals are not always where they go when asked about the seat of their sexuality. Frequently it is the brain. These people often function on an intellectual level and want to intellectualize sex rather than deal with it on an emotional level.

Some people have difficulty fantasizing, especially those who are in an occupation of absolutes. For instance engineers or people who work in solid sciences frequently have a great deal of difficulty fantasizing. Their travel through the body generally sounds like a physiology or anatomy lesson. It is more scenic than feeling. We have become aware that this may be part of the problem in the sexual relationship. Those whose feelings are open, talk about beauty, color, and emotions connected with areas visited.

The brain is checked to see if it is functioning to capacity and whether it is a useful brain, an intelligent brain, what it looks like and how they feel about it. Lungs are checked (especially if the individual smokes), the heart, the stomach, and the intestines to see if it is full of fecal material (shit), and whether this is symbolic of them as a person. They are asked if they are full of crappy material—how do they get rid of it? Especially if it is fouling up themselves and their relationships with other people.

The symbolism concerning what they encounter and what it means to the individual is important. The genital region is important. A male goes to the testicles and the penis to see if they can see out the penis, and if so, what do they see? "Is the penis erect or flacid?" This is particularly significant for the impotent male. He either sees no physical reason for lack of function or if one is found, he is asked what can be done to correct it while still on the fantasy trip.

The orgasmic woman often sees the vagina as a beautiful, colorful place of reds and pinks, and sometimes with streamers and butterflies.

The fantasy is often a re-run of the view with the mirror and lighted speculum of the previous day. Women tell us that looking at the vagina is significant for them. The ability to see out and what she sees may be significant in predicting prognosis in the case, such as the perception of her husband's erect penis coming toward her and her desire for it to do so. Before concluding the fantasy trip, an opportunity is given the client to visit any other area in his body he desires. Frequently clients have led us to significant places, and resolved important internal problems and blocks.

Once through, the client is asked to come out informing us how this is accomplished. Once out he is asked to open his eyes and to discuss his feelings.

Fantasy trips are often described as "fantastic."

We feel people should have a realistic perception and feeling for "self" before they can relate deeply to another. We find that many couples sleep nude together, but are uncomfortable being seen nude by their spouse, feeling that they are really an unattractive person. It is only when you can have positive and pleasant feelings about yourself that you can relate to another person. If you feel negative about yourself and your body, you cannot understand why someone would find you and your body pleasing, attractive, or desirable.

We find in treating human sexual dysfunction that it is important for each individual to have a realistically high self-appraisal before they are put in meaningful touch with the spouse. This idea comes from the ideal biblical injunction, "Love thy neighbor as thy self," suggesting that self-love must precede any meaningful neighborly love. Josh Leibman, the Rabbi who wrote a best selling book[2] before his untimely death, spelled out the important details of this perceptive insight.

Out of self-acceptance we are trying to get self-appreciation, trying to get clients to realistically upgrade their own self-perception.

The body imagery work takes from one and one-half to two hours. It is quite intensive and quite detailed, but many of our former clients have informed us of its unusual and personal significance to them.

MALE BODY IMAGERY

The following is a body imagery of a 30-year old male who functions well with casual relationships, but has difficulty with the significant other in his life.

This client was verbal and able to carry on quite well

---

[2] Josh Leibman, *Peace of Mind*.

on his own, but it is a good presentation of how we use body imagery therapeutically to work through blocks.

T=Female Therapist   S=Subject   R=Male Therapist

T   Please remove your robe, and place it on the table. Stand here and look at yourself in the mirrors. Place your hands on top of your head, and give us verbal feedback on a tactile and emotional level about your feelings concerning each part of your body from the top of your head to the bottom of your feet. (He places hands on head and says:)[3]

S   I like the shape of my head. My hair feels good. It feels a lot better than it did really short. Emotionally I like it a lot of the time except when I feel that my emotions are blocked, and then I am not really happy with it. It is sort of 50-50. I like what it can do, but when the blocking occurs, that is when I feel uncomfortable about my head. I like the shape of it. In the back my hair is a little bit too long, and does not feel too good. I like it when there is feelings, good positive feelings going through it of love and affection. I feel uncomfortable at times when there are feelings of anger and hostility.

(Going to the forehead he stated:)

S   Boy, it feels good. The smoothness feels nice. I do not like the wrinkles in it, but it is nice to touch. It is nice to have it touched. It sort of evokes a feeling of pleasantness to people I do not know. I like the shape of it. It feels smooth. It feels nice.

My eyebrows feel good. They are a little bit too thick. I do not have as good a feeling about my eyebrows as I did when I was touching my forehead.

My eyes feel good. It feels nice to touch them. I like the color of them. The smoothness of the skin

---

[3] We acknowledge the assistance of Charldene Sato in the transcription of this material.

around them feels good. It feels uncomfortable if the hands of someone else touch right around the eyes. I like it when my eyes look at people better than not looking at them. I like it when they are very expressive, and do not like it when they are expressionless.

I like my nose very much. I like the shape of it.

It feels good to be a pair of eyes. I am pretty happy with that. Here again, I like it when the expression in them is very expressive, not boring.

(Talking about his lips he says:)

It really feels nice touching someone else's. I like it when they smile at you rather than get mad. I like my lips. As far as touching them, I think they are a little thin—I would like it if they were a little larger. I like it for the emotions they express when kissing somebody. The warmth that they show though, is really nice. They are also nice for the negative feelings that can be expressed by them. They are a little too dry. It feels nicer when they are more moist.

I like the top row of my teeth. It gives me a nice look. The bottom row—I am not crazy about. They are crooked. They are not as nicely shaped as the top layer. Here again, it is a nice feeling of a combination of parts turning the negative feelings that are expressed through them to positive.

My chin I am not too crazy about. It is a little bit too small. I would like it just a little bit larger. It has a nice shape, and a nice feel to it, but I would like it if it were a little prominent. My jaws I always liked, the feeling in my jaws. It seems to imply a feeling of experience. I do not like it when I hold back. I like the closeness that comes from using them in expressing myself.

My neck I used to like a lot, until about six months ago. I hurt it in an auto accident. I like it better now because it feels better. I like the shape of it.

The smoothness feels good. I like it when it is pretty straight. It holds my head pretty straight rather than slouched over. I like it when someone rubs my head. It is sort of a feeling of closeness. It is also nice because a feeling of anger can be expressed.

I like my shoulders. I would like them to be a little larger, but I am still satisfied with them. I like the shape of them. There is a feeling of power and strength associated with them, as well as a capacity for expressing tender emotions. They feel nice and warm.

I also like my arms. I would like them to be a little bit larger, but I am pretty satisfied with them. I would like my biceps to be a little larger. I am not that satisfied with them. Here again, I am happy with the negative feelings that can be expressed with them. My arms and hands, I like the amount of hair on them. It feels good. It is nice and soft. Mainly the thing that comes to mind is the strength associated with them. I like my elbows too. I do not really have much feeling about them, except that I like the shape of them. I feel good about the quickness with which they can move. My forearms I really like. I like the color of the hair on them. I like the blondness in the hair. Here again, I like them for similar reasons. I like the upper part of my arms, because it can be expressive. I like the feel because they feel nice and warm. They do not feel oily.

My hands, there are a lot of things I like about them. I like them because they are a nice size. They are somewhat delicate but they are still fairly strong, and they can be very expressive, both in a positive and a negative way. I like the shape of my fingers. I do not like the veins in the back of my hands. I think that they are kind of ugly, when they stand out. I like the shape of my hands.

I like my chest pretty much. There again, like my shoulders, I wish they were just a little bit wider. I like the hair distribution. I think it is nice. My chest feels good to me too. Here again, part of the strength that goes with my arms seems to also be passed over to my chest. It feels good when I rub my chest. It feels even better when someone else rubs it. It is even more a sense of closeness than associated with my forehead. I like my nipples. I like the size of them. They feel good when they stick out. And they are very sensitive when someone else touches them. That always feels good. It is sort of a feeling of affection and warmth that goes with them.

My stomach I do not like right now. It is too fat. I do not like the contour of it. I sure would like it better if I would lose weight. Right now it is just too heavy. I do not like the feeling of fat. I like the hair distribution. I feel very conscious of it because it has an odd shape right now. It is still possible to have a feeling of closeness with my wife touching it even though it is still fat.

My thighs I like very much. I like the shape of them. I like them because they are not fat. I do not like it because very frequently there is a lot of tension and anxiety that extends from my thighs, especially in a sexual situation there is an uncomfortable feeling. I do not like it because they are not as responsive as they used to be as far as my wife touching them. I like the feel of them. Again, I like the hair distribution on them. The warmth on them feels good. It is a sense of power and this also feels good. The thing that seems to be missing from them right now is the feeling of closeness to someone else, physical closeness to someone else, sort of a warmth associated with them.

My buttocks I like. I am pretty happy with them. They are just a little bit too heavy right now but for the most I am happy with their size, shape . . .

T   Turn around, look . . . Turn around and look at them. Touch them.

S   They are a little bit too fat. I do not like the blemishes on them. For the most part, I am pretty happy with them. They feel good. They just feel a little bit too fat.

I am pretty happy with my testicles. I like the shape of them and they feel nice to touch. It also feels nice when someone else touches them. I like the hair distribution and the color of the hair, and the warmth of them feels good. I am pretty happy with them.

My penis I am not very happy with right now because it does not function. The other thing is that it seems a little too short. I like the shape of it. It feels good. The shortness I am not particularly happy about.

My knees, I am pretty happy with. I like the shape of them.

T   Can you touch them?

S   I like to touch them. It is more fun to touch them when I am not standing straight because it is fun to play with the kneecaps, at times. That feels good and I am really happy with my knees. My kneecaps feel good too. There is also a sense of power in my knees which is also comfortable.

My calves and lower legs, I am very happy with. I like the shape of them. They feel good and they feel very strong. I like the hair distribution and the color of the hair on them. My ankles I like. I like the shape of them. I do not really have too much feeling about my ankles. I do like the appearance.

My feet I do not like. I think they are ugly. My feet are cold a lot too. That is another reason I do not like them.

T   Then touch them.

S   Yeah, they are cold right now. That is what I do not like about them. I think they are the ugliest part of my body. My toes I like. I like the shape of them.

T   Which part of your foot do you feel is ugly?

S   I think this part right here, where all the veins stand out. See, on both feet. I like the shape of the bottoms of my feet. I like my toes but I am not so crazy about the rest of my foot.

T   How about the heel?

S   The heel I like.

R   Do you feel that your feet provide a solid foundation for you?

S   More solid than before, but not as solid as I really would want it to be.

R   They are becoming more solid as time goes on?

S   Yes.

R   That may be symbolic of a movement toward becoming a more solidly based person.

S   They feel a lot better than they used to.

T   Do you like your arches?

S   Yes, I like the arch.

T   Then actually the only place you really do not like is right across the top of them?

S   Yes, right.

T   Yes, then most of the foot you do like?

S   Yes, it is just this part over here. The base of it I did not used to like, but I like it now. It feels stronger. It just needed more strength.

I forgot my ears. My ears I like. I like the feel of them. I like the shape of them. I like the shape of them, and they are a nice size. I am pretty happy with my ears.

My belly button, I think, is an average run-of-the-mill belly button. I really do not have such strong feelings about it.

T   What about your back?

S   My back?

T   Right. Can you feel your backbone?

S   Yes, I really like the shape of my back.

Can you feel your spine at all? Are you a spineless creature?

No, I feel a lot better than I used to. It seems to be getting stronger. The same as my feet—I have a better feeling about them. I do not like all the hair on it. It is just a little bit ugly. I think that it looks good on the front, but not on the back. I like these muscles through here because they are really strong. Right up here too, because it feels really strong. It is also neat when my wife rubs against there. It feels really good.

Do you want to stand and face the mirror again? Look at that person in the mirror. Take a good look. Give that person an overall rating. If 0 was the least worthwhile and 100 was the most worthwhile, looking at that person from the top of his head to the tip of his toes, what kind of a rating would you give him?

70-75.

Okay, now taking a look at him again, from the top of his head to the tip of his toes, what kind of a masculinity rating would you give him? As a man? Zero to 100?

About 50.

Did those two ratings change in the last six months? What would you have given in terms of those same figures six months ago?

The first one would have been about 50.

All right. Now it is gone 50 per cent. The second one? The second one would have been 40.

Then it has gone up 10 percent . . . 20 per cent.

(The female therapist encloses the client in mirrors.) Put your shoulder area against the mirror again. It will be a little cold, I am afraid. Move a little bit. How do you like being in there?

I do not really like it.

Are you with someone you would like to spend some time with? That you feel good about?

S Not yet. No.

T Or somebody maybe of being someone you would like that has the potential?

S Yes.

R What do not you like about being in there?

S The fact that it is too controlled and does not allow expression at all. Just makes for uncomfortableness.

T Okay, how many you's can you count if you start at your left and moving just your head and not your feet, going all the way around?

S 24.

T See any view of yourself that you have never seen before?

S Yes. The ones in the back.

T How does it look?

S I like it.

T Any other view?

S I like the front view. The side view I like, but not as much as the others.

T Does the person look any different close up than he does far apart?

S He looks warmer close up than far away.

T Is the warmer individual more friendly and more open?

S Yes, I think so.

T When you looked into his eyes close up does he look very, very warm?

S He looks like he can be very warm.
(The mirrors are opened.)

T Come out now.
(Inside fantasy trip)

T Look toward the mirror but close your eyes. The light will be turned out, and a dim one will be turned on. What we want you to do is to take a fantasy trip. Go inside your body any way you want. You can go right through your skin or any opening. This is a fantasy trip so we want you to get inside your body and let us have a look inside. When you are inside let us know.

S Okay, I am inside now.

T Okay, where are you?

S Right between my heart and my lungs.

T How did you get in?

S Going through the esophagus.

T I see, opened your mouth and came in that way?

S Yes.

T All right now, while you are there let us go first to the seat of your emotions, and have a look. Go to the seat of your emotions, and tell me where you are?

S I am here right now.

T Okay, where are you?

S I am half way. I am looking at the parts of emotions on one side directing the healthy emotions, but there is even a stronger attraction to the aggressive and hostile emotions on the other side.

T Where is this?

S Right at the back of my head.

T Up in your brain?

S Yes.

T But you see both your healthy emotions and your hostile emotions right there side by side? How do you feel about those?

S I feel that both types are somewhat limited right now. I mean, I think that I limit them. I think they come out and that I am still re-training them.

T What do you see in what you are saying? What do you see when you look out? Do you see them limited?

S Yes. I do not see them limited. I see them limited in getting out.

T What do you see blocking them getting out? Do you see any kind of block there in the back?

S Yes, there is a definite block.

T What kind of block is this like? Is it something you can move, or do something about?

S Yes, I think so. It feels like it is going to be removed.

T How do you feel that you are going to do that? Do you have any feelings as to how it is going to be removed?

S I think that the best way it is going to be removed is to be more honest with people, and express both sides of emotions instead of having just one side come out.

T Do you like to be able to express more and do you see the potential there to express more, it is just a matter of moving some of the blocks that are in there and letting them come out. Is there anything you can do about the blocks when you are in there now? Is there anything you can do about moving them, pushing them, or getting rid of them while you are in there?

S I can figuratively take the blocks off but, it seems that it is rather tedious now that it is done, and I can see myself removing the blocks. I can actually, there is a wall between the positive and the negative sides and in the fantasy I can see myself removing that.

T Do you want to do some moving while you are in there?

S Yes, that sounds nice. In the fantasy it seems like both sides are attracted to each other, and they sort of want to mix a little. It really feels good to remove the blocks between them. As I remove more of the blocks, the feeling inside of me really becomes good. It feels more like being human. It is almost a release phenomenon that they are with. When the blocks were all there, it was rather a stifling feeling. There is resistance removing a lot of the blocks, not like they can not be moved. With a lot of effort they can be pushed aside.

T Have you moved all of the blocks that you want to move right now?

S Not all that I want; all that I can.

T   All that you can right now?

S   Yes.

T   You can always go back in there any time you want and move some more. Isn't that possible?

S   Yes.

T   And you think you will be able to do that?

S   I think I will.

T   All right, while we are in the brain we might take a look around there. Is that an intelligent brain?

S   Yes, it is.

T   It functions well?

S   Once I allow it to.

T   What seems to be holding it back from functioning well?

S   The same type of blocking that was in the seat of emotions.

T   Okay, then where do you see that? In the back?

S   Yes, it covers most of the brain.

T   All right, can you remove some of that blockage?

S   It is very intimately tied up to the other blockage. It seems to fall away as the other falls away. It almost drops away by itself. There is a sense of relief as the falling off occurs—not that much effort required really to get rid of it.

T   How about going to the seat of your sexuality. And tell me where that is.

S   It is in my penis.

T   Let us have a look down in your penis. What do you see in there? What does it look like on the inside?

S   In the inside it is just like a huge rubber band holding it back. There seems to be a lot of fear inside of that rubber band.

T   Fear of what?

S   Fear of aggression. Fear of power.

T   Does your penis symbolize power to you?

S   Yes.

T Can you look out your penis? What do you see when you look out?

S There is a really good feeling looking out. It is a sense of power and the fear is gone when I look out through it.

T What do you see?

S Actually, I see Sally's pelvis opposite it, but it is at a distance. (Sally is the client's wife. He has trouble functioning sexually with her. He cannot get and maintain erections.)

T Is your penis flacid or erect?

S It is flacid.

T Can you imagine it being erect?

S As her pelvis comes closer it seems to be getting half erect.

T How does it feel about it coming closer? Is it any more erect as it gets closer to you?

S Yes, it feels good.

T All right, does it get more and more erect as it gets closer?

S Yes, right now there is no sense of fear dictating when it is getting erect.

T Now as you get closer to her pelvis can you put the penis in her vagina?

S The fear is coming back a little now.

T Move back a little bit from the vagina now. As we get closer what seems to be the big fear? What does the penis fear? As we get a little bit closer to the pelvis we will see what happens again? Move in a little bit closer and then when we get to the point where the fear begins to start let us see what we can see.

S There is a definite point where it begins to get really close inside her. There is a feeling of potential castration.

T Does she cut it off?

S Yes, figuratively.

T As though you withdraw, or you pull back and lose your erection as though it cannot function?

S Yes, that is what happens.

T How about taking your finger and putting it into her pelvis and examining her vagina with your finger to see if there is anything your penis should legitimately fear in there?

S No, it feels good.

R It feels nice and warm?

S Yes.

R Spongy?

S It is a little spongy. It feels nice and warm and a little moist.

R Can we get the penis right up to the opening?

S Yes.

T It feels okay there?

S Yes, it is still erect.

T All right, then let us slowly move it in. Let us move it in barely an eighth of an inch, so that it is barely in. How does that feel?

S That feels good.

T Is that all right? How about a little more, maybe half an inch? Is that all right?

S That still feels good.

T Still erect? How about moving it an inch? That feels good still?

S It is erect and feels good but there is a sense of a threat coming back.

T Then we will come back out again. Bring it out. Okay, let us see if we can move it in a little bit again. Get it in about an eighth of an inch? Okay there?

S Yes, it is fine there.

T Okay, how about half an inch?

S It is still fine.

T Bring it in an inch now. Can you get it in an inch?

S It is still okay.

T All right, an inch and a half?

S It is still okay.

T Two inches?

S Now there is a little . . .

T Okay, let us take it out very slowly. Now do you still have an erection?

S Yes.

T Okay, let us try it again. Half an inch? An inch?

S It still feels nice.

T An inch and a half?

S It still feels good.

T A couple of inches now?

S It feels a lot better.

T Two and a half inches?

S It still feels good.

T Three inches?

S It still feels good.

T Three and a half inches?

S It still feels good.

T Four inches?

S It feels a lot better now.

T Four and a half inches now.

S It feels very good.

T Five inches?

S It still feels good.

T Can you put it in all the way now? Can you see how it feels?

S It feels really neat.

T Okay, now let us just hold it there now and see how it feels in there. Just relax and put it in there and just flow with the rest of it. Feel okay?

S It feels good. The closeness feels good.

T Feels really good and now you are inside of your penis in there and you can really feel it. It really feels good and it does not have a giant in it. It feels warm and comfortable and you really like it. Now can you move gradually back and forth drawing it out and putting it back in. Move it half an inch first, just half an inch, back and forth. That feels okay?

S   That feels really good.

T   Okay, let us move it a little more than half an inch. Let us move it an inch.

S   It feels even better.

T   Okay, let us move it a couple of inches.

S   It is a combination of closeness and power associated with it really feels nice.

T   Now is it bringing lots of pleasure to you and to your wife, lots of power in your penis?

S   It feels that way, yes.

T   Okay, now you can thrust, continue to thrust back and forth. Feel the power of the thrust? How do you feel?

S   It feels really nice.

T   It feels very, very powerful?

S   Yes, powerful.

T   Very, very powerful?

S   It feels affection . . .

T   Very, very potent?

S   Yes.

T   Very, very masculine?

S   Yes.

T   Very, very fulfilling?

S   It does feel that, yes.

T   All right. Okay, shall we take the penis out now?

R   Is there anything else you would like to do with it in the vagina now? Would you like to do any more thrusting? Or are you ready to bring it out since you have now clearly worked through your fear and you have got power. Is there anything else you would like to do with it in there?

S I think this power is far-out though.

T Why do you think it is far-out with your penis in there?

R Why don't you give us the feedback of what you get in your explorations with your penis in the vagina?

S Okay, the head of my penis feels, right above her cervix, it really feels like a nice feeling, a sort of smooth, soothing feeling. In the next exploration it bumps up against her cervix. It really feels nice. It almost feels like a cohesiveness between the two of us, especially when they both meet in the center.

T Do you feel the walls of the vagina?

S Not at this point, not too well, just sort of on the surface. Now my penis is exploring along the wall and it is going back and forth and exploring the walls and that feels really nice. It is really not just the power of the cervix up there. There is a sense of love for her too, associated with it. There is no sense of graphic error for the area associated with it at this point, just a sense of warmth and togetherness associated, especially as she acts and comes up against her vagina.

T Is that penis bringing you pleasure?

S Yes.

T Is it bringing your wife pleasure?

S Yes, bringing her a lot of pleasure.

T How do you feel about that?

S I think I feel very worthwhile to be in there but it is also equally gratifying to myself to be getting pleasure from her. And the fact that she seems to be enjoying the fact that I am getting pleasure. There is no sense of castration right at this moment.

T Do you see anything in there that suggests castration?

S No.

T A nice, warm vagina? It feels very good?

S Yes, very good.

T A responsive penis? Feels very, very positive in that nice, warm vagina?

S   Yes.

T   Is there anything more you want to explore in there?

S   Yeah, right along the side walls. That really feels good, going along the muscles of the side walls. It feels good from the response she gets too. It is an equal satisfaction and an equal flow of positive feelings between us as I do that.

T   Can you feel her have orgasm?

S   No, not yet.

T   How do you feel about her having orgasm?

S   I think it would be nice but it is not really a prime concern at the moment. As a matter of fact, neither of us has had an orgasm.

T   Would you be concerned if she did have an orgasm? Would that affect you?

S   If she did?

T   Yes.

S   No, I think it would be neat.

T   Would it be all right if her muscles contracted on your penis?

S   I think it would be great.

T   That would not be a threat to you at all?

S   No.

T   That would feel good?

S   Yes.

T   You would not perceive it as being castrated at all?

S   Not at all.

T   But something you would both like?

S   Yes.

T   With a little more thrusting, is she likely to have orgasm?

S   She is getting very close to it.

T   Do you want to pursue that now and have her have orgasm?

S   Yes.

T   All right, why don't you continue with your thrusting and as soon as there is any fear or anything negative or as soon as she has orgasm give us some feedback. Meanwhile you will be all tied up with your feelings with her and what is happening.

S   We are getting closer and closer with the thrusting and it is really a very closing feeling. It is a really good feeling and it is the closest we have been in a long time. Her excitement and her affection is starting to go up. She is starting, she is working closer to an orgasm. And, the most prominent feature is the sense of attraction that seems to be flowing between us as she gets closer to orgasm. As it gets more intense we both get close to orgasm. And we are both having orgasm right now. There is almost a feeling like we are almost wanting to consume each other and still hold on to each other. And it is really a nice, it is the closest feeling we have ever had.

T   And you are having your orgasm?

S   Yes, just about the same time.

T   Okay, does it feel good?

S   It feels good physically but even more, emotionally it feels even better.

T   It is a positive experience for you?

S   Yes, very.

T   Is the orgasm still going on?

S   Yes, on the down side now. The feelings though, are not really on the down side.

T   You feel exhilarated?

S   Yes.

T   Is it a positive experience for both of you?

S   Very positive for both.

T   Tell us as soon as the orgasm is over and what the feelings are.

S   The orgasm is over. The feeling of closeness and affection between us has lasted. And we are still holding each other. And the degree of closeness and having given to each other is more intense than it has been in a long time. And we are both enjoying the closeness and neither of us gets the usual feeling that is associated with the closeness. We are both extremely happy. And we just do not want to let go of each other. We are still holding each other and we are sort of snuggling up and sort of relaxing, half dozing and half holding each other and half enjoying the closeness of it. The closeness is lasting and we are sort of drowsing off beside each other but still holding each other very closely. The whole experience seems rather positive.

T Is there any negative aspect of it?

S Not that I am aware of.

T All we heard were overwhelming positive feelings. Since you said rather positive it made us wonder.

S I am not aware of any negative feelings.

T Okay. Go down to your testicles and have a look at those. They seem to be very functional?

S Yes, very. They seem to be normal.

T And healthy?

S Yes.

T Okay, does it feel as good on the inside as it does on the outside?

S Yes.

T Let us go down and look at your feet? How do your feet look on the inside? You do not feel so good about them on the outside. How do they feel on the inside?

S They feel good on the inside. They feel well-structured and they feel capable of strength.

T They look pretty good in there? Look healthy?

S They look healthy but the muscles could be larger. They do not seem to be exercised too much. They are good looking muscles but they do not seem to be as thick as they should be.

T But you can do something about that if you wanted to, couldn't you?

S Yes.

T Okay, let us come back up the leg now. The legs look good to you?

S Yes, they look very good.

T Healthy, strong?

S Yes.

T How about the buttocks? Do they feel good?

S The buttocks look good, yes.

T Let us go to the anus. Can you see out your anus at all?

S Yes.

T Is it nice and clear?

S It is pretty clear. It could be clearer.

T Still a little shitty in there?

S Yes.

T Okay, do you want to get rid of that? Is it moving or is it blocked?

S No, it has been moving.

T Okay, you are getting rid of it. You are getting a good perspective and a good view out there from the anus. It looks pretty good out there.

S Yes.

T How about coming up to the stomach? What does it look like in there? Healthy inside?

S It is healthy, but it is too big.

T Too big! How about the lungs? You looked at them before but you did not really have a look at them. Do they look nice and clear?

S They look a little smokey.

T A little smokey? Take a deep breath and let the air out and see what it looks like in there. Let the air out. How does that look when you look at it?

S It looks better. It gets rid of the smoke.

T Now let us go to the heart. What kind of heart do you see over there?

S The heart looks really warm and really healthy looking.

T Do you mean having a capacity for warmth and a lot of things going good for it?

S Yes, a capacity for a lot of warmth.

T How about your arms and down to your hands? What do they look like in the inside? Do they look like they are strong enough to hold somebody very close?

S Yes, I like the looks of the arms inside.

T The hands look like they could be gentle and caressing and strong at the same time?

S They look like they can be both, yes.

T Then they look pretty good on the inside?

S Yes.

T All right, is there any other place in the body you would like to go, and have a look?

S Yes, I would like to go into my eyes.

T Go into your eyes and have a look. Are your eyes closed or can you see out?

S Yes, there seem to be cloud formations in front of my eyes. A lot of times it is really easy to see clearly. When the clouds come over however, perceptions seem to get fogged up.

T How do we get the clouds out of the way?

S I am doing it now, going to a higher altitude.

T All right?

S It is a lot clearer there.

T Do you see much better?

S Yes.

T Much more in perspective?

S Yes.

T What do you see when you look out?

S I see a lot of my friends standing out there. I can see them better than I can at a lower altitude. They seem more in perspective. I have a better feeling about myself which makes it easier to feel better about them.

T How do they feel about you as you perceive them looking towards you?

R Smiling?

S Some of them are, yes, not all of them.

T Do they have their arms out toward you?

S Yes, a lot of them do but a lot of them are beckoning to come over. And there is less of a wall in the lower altitude. There is still a little bit of a wall.

T Let us see if you can try to remove that wall?

S Sure. I am going towards them, well actually we are going towards each other.

T Do you want them to help you remove the wall?

S Yes, I think it would be neat.

T Then maybe you can work together in terms of re-moving it.

S They are coming over. A lot of them are trying to tear down the wall. They are working on one side and I am working on the other. Parts of the wall are really strong. There is a really thin part. About 50 per cent of it is really thin that we removed really quickly. And there is sort of a steel structure that we are having trouble getting down. But we are still working at it.

T Is it possible that with cooperative effort that you are going to remove it faster than if you tried to do it by yourself?

S Yes, it is much easier. There is a part that they are showing me that I have to remove.

T Think that it will be able to be removed?

S I think that I will be able to remove it. It is really tough right now.

T Have you figured out how you are going to do it? Is it possible to move?

S Yes, it is possible. I am not sure quite how yet.

T Will be able to figure it out?

S I think eventually, yes.

T Do you feel that it will be a help?

S I think that it could, yes. I think that I will be able to.

T Will you remove as much as you can now?

S   Yes.

T   Is there anything else that you want to look at while you are there?

S   I would like to know what the walls are made of. It is really hard to tell.

T   You might like to get closer to it. Can you pick up a piece of it? Touch it?

S   Yes.

T   What does it feel like?

S   It feels very similar to the shell of the center of emotions.

T   You were able to remove some of that? Are you able to remove some of this?

S   It seemed like I removed the same proportions as I did that time.

T   If you are able to remove some of it, maybe you can remove more?

S   It is getting a lot weaker.

T   Is it possible that you can work on it and remove all of it?

S   I think that it will all come down.

T   Is there anything more you want to look at now?

S   No, I don't think so.

T   Have you pretty well looked around at the inside of your body and you feel pretty good inside there?

S   I want to look at my mouth.

T   Go down to your mouth. Open your mouth and look out. Do you see out?

S   Yes, very clearly. There is a very good feeling associated with looking out through my mouth. Mostly the feeling associated with that are really warm, affectionate feelings. There is a potential for aggressive feelings, but they are not right there at this moment. But there is no block to them like there used to be.

T   Do you want to rate your entire body on the inside? From 0 to 100 what would you give the rating on the inside, as an overall rating of that individual.

S   75.

T   How about that rating as a sexual individual? Now we are talking about the penis and that area of sexuality and so forth and have been able to function in the fantasy very effectually sexually. What would you give that rating?

S   80-85.

T   Now what we would like you to do is to come out of your body in any way that you would like to, the same way you went in or any other way. And then when you are out, tell us.

S   I am out. I came out through my penis!

T   Was your trip out good?

S   Yes, it was great.

T   How did you feel about that trip inside your body?

S   It felt better than the trip outside. The outside felt good, but this felt better.

T   No negative feelings about it?

S   Very few.

T   Any you want to talk about?

S   The steady experience of going through my penis really felt good. It felt that there were a lot less inhibitions than the external trip. It was much easier to get in touch with emotions and feelings that I was feeling going through the inside. And like the whole rubber band thing seemed to dissolve and go away in the inside which didn't happen when I was going on the outside. It was nice in that respect.

T   Quite a fantastic trip in every way. You know that?

S   Yes, that was good.

T   Now, close your eyes for a minute. I will switch the light on, and it will be bright for a minute.

After the psychological aspects of body imagery work have been completed for both, we bring the couple in together. The biological and psychological aspects of our work behind us, we are ready to begin the sociological. We ask each spouse to touch that part of their partner's anatomy they like best, and almost invariably it will be a part the individual feels negative about. (Figure 7) This can be reassuring and reaffirming to the individual, especially since they know their spouse is unaware of their negative reactions to this particular area.

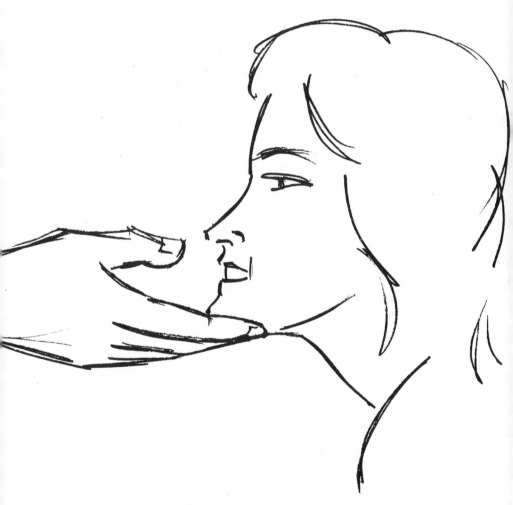

Figure 7.   Sensitivity—"John touch the part of Anne's body you like best."

SENSITIVITY

The next portion of our program involves sensitivity exercises. We have the couple stand facing each other in front of the mirror showing us how they physically touch and relate to each other.

Figure 8.   Sensitivity—"Show us how you like to hold and be held by your partner."

We ask them to show how they like to be kissed by their partner, how they would like to be held by their partner, giving them both an opportunity to demonstrate and show us how they like to be touched, held, and kissed so that the woman cannot say he is doing something that she does not want or like. (Figure 8). At this point, she has the opportunity of showing us what it is she does like and wishes to have him do. This is quite important when we are dealing with a couple who have been separated for a long period, especially if the woman is very apprehensive or she simply does not wish him to touch her. If we ask her to show us how she would like to have him touch her, she has some control over the touching situation and she is more comfortable. Our experience has been that she can always show us some way she would like to be touched. In other cases the woman has never had an opportunity to express her likes or feelings about kissing. One very surprised man after a passionate kiss by his wife said, "Gee, I didn't know you liked to be kissed that way." Sometimes we can see that by the way the male holds the woman she looks uncomfortable or looks as though she is being smothered. Often we find that the reason the woman has rejected her partner's attentions is due to her feeling of being smothered. If the therapist asks about any feelings of smothering and this is a problem, then new ways of holding and kissing are mutually worked out. We then make the suggestion that when he is touching her that he try to follow her suggestions in relation to how she wishes to be touched. It is equally important to find out how he desires to be touched so that the woman also has a chance to discover what he finds pleasing and stimulating. While initially to get touch going, it is important how one is caressed. We find that after the problems have worked themselves out, really neither partner cares how they are touched. This is especially true for couples who have not touched for a long time.

At first our clients hold each other's hands, then they are directed through a series of exercises using only hands. We want to know how they feel about each other; how they express positive emotions, negative emotions; how they fight with each other in a non-hurtful way. We can tell a lot about their feelings for each other by the way they deal with each other's hands—overpoweringly, withdrawing, a give and take in the fighting situation. A person who withdraws may also withdraw sexually and become a spectator in intercourse.

A way of measuring commitment to and feeling about a relationship is to ask the couple to imagine that something unexpected has come up, and they are to say goodbye to each other for the last time using only their hands. We ask them to "imagine that you are never going to get to touch these hands again. You are to say goodbye for the last time expecting never to touch these hands again, and to then drop your hands to your side." After dropping the hands to the side, we ask them to "imagine that just as unexpectedly following a long period of time you are going to get to touch these hands again." We ask them to "show us with your eyes closed how you will reach out and greet the hands you never expected to touch again." At this point some of the deeper feelings of involvement in a relationship are brought to the surface, and the usual response is for both partners to feel a greater commitment to their relationship than either had previously been aware of or willing to express. It is a positive factor in moving them toward warmer and more intimate touch.

It is common to find a good deal of warmth expressed between couples despite years of hostility, bickering, and struggling for supremacy in the relationship. The role of the therapist is to encourage the continued expression of the warmth present and to capitalize on the warm, positive feelings spouses have for each other, while teaching them new or different techniques for expressing their feelings.

Chapter 7

CARESS EXERCISES

We attach significance to the terminology used in our
work. For the first few years at the Center, we utilized
the term "massage" when teaching couples touching and
pleasuring techniques. In February, 1972, when we were
running a weekend workshop in Chicago, a very perceptive participant pointed out to us that the term "caress"
was much more appropriate. We could not agree more,
and since that time have consistently used this expression. Originally when getting people in touch both
physically and emotionally, a more structured way of
caressing was used, but as we worked with couples and
saw that they could be comfortable with intimacy in
front of others, we directed them to be as warm and
emotionally aware as possible. This change in procedure
paralleled the change in terminology from "massage" to
"caress." Webster's definition of caress is: "An act of
endearment; a tender or loving embrace, touch. To touch,
stroke, pat; tenderly, lovingly, or softly." This is in distinct contrast to massage which is defined as "A method

of treating the body for remedial or hygenic purposes, consisting in rubbing, stroking, kneading, tapping with the hand or instrument." From the inception of our work, we were not running a massage parlor, but massage seemed to be the most appropriate term.

Beyond the term "caress," which certainly emphasizes tender, loving touch, we could consider occasional use of the term fondle defined by Webster as: "To coddle; to handle tenderly or lovingly; to caress. To manifest fondness, especially by caresses." Webster thus defines "caress" to be synonymous with "fondle" and to manifest fondness especially by caresses as the basic definition of the term "fondle." Our culture has emphasized fondling to be associated with genitalia. Certainly we would emphasize the importance of fondling genitalia, but since we want a broader frame of reference, namely the entire human organism, we have chosen to stay with the terminology caress. We thus emphasize a warm intimate, non-verbal dialogue as our primary frame of reference.

By the fifth day we are at the stage where our therapeutic couple are on a seeing and doing basis. When we are working intensively with a couple for two weeks, it is amazing how the exercises can become tiring, particularly those assignments that are very time-consuming. We break up the action partly with a program of visual aids, and by suggesting that they spend some time away from sexual material all together, by being involved in some of the available local activities such as swimming, tennis, golf, sailing, theatre, and sightseeing so that saturation with the sexual area is less likely to occur. Frequently we need to give them a day off without any assignments whatsoever.

There are several moments of truth in an intensive two-week treatment program for sexual dysfunction. One is when the couple is first placed in touch with each other in the presence of the therapists. We start with the foot caress, the goal of which is providing a warm and stable, feeling-foundation for a loving relationship. We proceed to the face to be certain of a clarity of feeling identity. Identity without foundation is useless, foundation without identity equally paradoxical. We connect foundation and identity with overall body feeling, and finally we seek a spiritual communication beyond the world of physical and verbal communication, with sexual caress setting the stage for that most significant and unique human experience—coitus.

The foot, face, and body caress are done in our offices so that we may observe if there is warmth and feeling or hostility and rejection. Our experience with having the first caress exercises done at the motel has been unsatisfactory, the couple often ended up bickering or fighting, or unable for some other reason to complete the assignment. If we have them do it in the office, we can see how they touch and relate to each other. We have them do it without words, explaining that we want to see as much warmth and positive feelings expressed in the caressing activities as possible.

We want to know that they can touch and relate well with each other, and that they are pleasing each other. We ask them from time to time about their feelings. We ask simple questions: What do you feel? Do you like this? Would you like it heavier or lighter, faster or slower? Do you find this pleasurable? We try to elicit as much feedback as possible so that the individual who is doing the pleasuring will have some cues to his partner's responses without interruption of the caress. Responses would be elicited at any point where there is a change of breathing, expression or movement. Typically interruptions occur about four times in an hour body caress.

FOOT CARESS

The foot caress takes place in our offices with the couple clothed except for shoes and stockings. They decide who is to give and who is to receive first. They have been informed that this procedure will be reversed the next day so that the one receiving foot caress today will give the face caress tomorrow. The receiver is seated in a comfortable, upholstered, high-back chair. He is instructed to close his eyes with the head resting against the back of the chair, and to have hands, feet, and total body posture reflective of an open and receptive position.

We usually express no preference for who is to give and receive the foot caress first. Both are expected to learn to give and to receive. It is just as important to be able to receive in situations involving caressing as it is to give. If a client only wants to give, he does not allow someone else to give. If he only wants to take, he does not give the other an opportunity to receive feelings for self. Hence, sexual problems of impotence and non-orgasmic function often result. We have clients who are unable to receive and who do not allow people to give to them. They must learn to become comfortable with receiving. We are interested in sensate focus so we must keep them in the here and now, and deal with their feelings in that context. If they have difficulty focusing in on their feelings, we must find a way to help them focus. A man who has a difficult time in getting an erection typically is so concerned with the other person that he does not allow himself to share in the good feelings. i.e. We ask him what he is feeling while being caressed, he responds "I don't think she likes doing this." We point out to him, "that is her problem and all we are concerned about at this point is what you are feeling. We will check with her to see how **she** feels when the time comes." He cannot feel for her. We then ask her what she is feeling,

if she is uncomfortable or does not like what she is doing, she can then say so, but he is not to decide for her
what it is she feels. Later on he can ask her if he wants
to know what she is feeling, but initially he is just to take
in feelings for himself.

Too often one or the other partner in a relationship
decides for the other how they feel without asking, often
because they are unable to accept an honest feeling from
anyone else. They are so fearful of being rejected that
they will not take the chance. They have to learn to allow
people to have and express feelings without interpreting
this as rejection. Feelings are not necessarily rational and
may be either positive or negative, but are generally not
a rejection of the other. As their self-concept improves,
(Chapter 6) they learn to accept negative remarks without internalizing it to mean "I am no good as a person."

We give them both an opportunity to express their
feelings verbally from time to time, while working with
them. If we see any change in breathing, body movement
or expression which may indicate that feelings are being
aroused or changed, we ask what is being felt.

Many sexually dysfunctional people mis-read each
other. Frequently the woman is enjoying what she is doing, whereas he is defining her feeling as negative. This
is often the case if he feels rejecting about a particular
part of his body. If he does not like his chest or the size
of his penis, he then cannot understand how she can enjoy touching these areas. If a woman has negative feelings about her genitalia or breasts, she cannot understand
how anyone else could like them, let alone touch them.
We encounter women who do not like their breasts for
some reason and as a consequence, do not like their partner to fondle them. We have to help couples accept those
bodily parts they do not like, and teach these individuals
to take pleasure in their partner caressing or fondling
them. It is important to be able to both receive and to

give,[1] and to stay focused on what one is feeling as well as to express feelings when asked. We get clues about how the couple touch and relate with each other by what they do.

The caressing and bathing of the feet is undirected. A tub of warm water, soap, towels, and baby oil are provided. The clients are allowed to do what they wish. We can see whether they rapidly move through the caressing or whether they go slowly and gently, varying the pressure from time to time, while paying attention to what they are doing, and where their partner is. At the same time, they must learn to take in feelings for themselves.

One of the first clues the therapists observe in the foot caress is how rapidly the hands are moved during the caress. (Figure 9) We perceive a close positive correlation between the premature ejaculator and the fast foot caress. SLOW—SLOW—SLOW is one of the main suggestions we must make when working with sexually dysfunctional people. In our culture great premium seems to be placed on speed of all kinds—in working, social situations, recreation, even including lovemaking and intercourse. Slowing couples down to warm, sensual expression of feelings and establishment of a sensual dimension, of a personality and a relationship, are basic to success in sexual therapy. **If it feels good, take time to enjoy it.**

The foot caress is the beginning of non-verbal communication. Its primary purpose is to begin to capitalize on existent warmth and positive expression between the sexually dysfunctional couple. In addition, it is the beginning of establishing the sensual dimension of human

---

[1] The reversal in wording of old phraseology "it is more blessed to give than to receive" lends itself to an awkward sentence. However, if breaking the stereotype is to occur, changes have to take place.

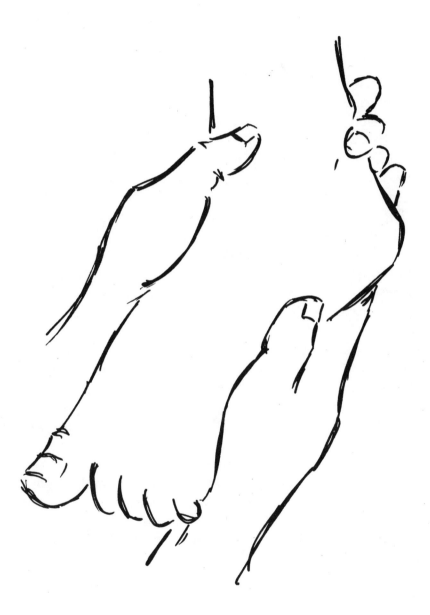

Figure 9.   Foot Caress.

personality. It stresses touching in a warm, loving, and caring way. Ideally it helps to establish a very positive beginning to other caressing techniques, the successful development of which are positively correlated with establishment of effective sexual functioning.

It generally takes from an hour to an hour and a half to complete the foot caress exercise; some couples have been out of touch for long periods of time and if the touch is agreeable to them and if they both seem to be feeling positive about it, we let them go longer. Clients are often left emotionally enervated. It is not unusual to have one or both a bit teary at this point, especially where touch between them has been taboo for a period of months or years.

Since touch is often related to a sexual advance and intercourse and since there is often apprehension about caressing when the couple have not touched for a long period of time or touch has only been used as a preliminary to intercourse, beginning work in the office seems essential for us.

We are working toward eliminating a sexual problem of some kind, but we find that frequently this is simply a symptom of a poor relationship. Sex has developed within a context of little warmth, love, or affection. One or both of them in the situation have come to feel that they are being used in a sexual way, it is necessary for us to develop a good emotional climate so that sexual intercourse makes sense in the context of a good overall relationship containing warm, positive feelings. We ask them not to have coitus during the first week of the program. Our goal at this time is to establish a warm intimate non-coital framework into which coitus will later be integrated.

We would like to have our clients do a good deal of touching and caressing in our office where intercourse is not likely to take place. We do not stay in the room longer than necessary once we see that positive feelings exist. We feel that the more the couple does on their own, the better off they are. With some couples, however, it is important that we stay and spend time with them to see that things go smoothly, especially if one partner is fearful of what the other may do or needs the support of the therapists.

After the foot caress, we make another appointment for later on in the day when more work can be done. We always try to have an opportunity to do some talking with the clients when they first come into the office for each appointment. We discuss and observe where they are emotionally, what they are feeling, and how they are relating. Little time is spent in talking, since we feel that our program achieves its best results through action methods. If traditional talk therapy could have resolved their problem, this would have been accomplished in the typical therapy situation that most of our clients have been through elsewhere. Anything of a non-sexual nature can best be handled by their referring therapist.

On their second visit that day they see a video tape of a research couple going through what they have just experienced, showing how they did the foot caress as well as the caressing of the face and body, which will be future assignments for the couple. We usually do not deal directly with the presenting sexual problems at this stage. We are interested in prevention as well as cure, therefore, we like to show people how to resolve the usual kinds of sexual problems that they may encounter in their lifetime. Even though they may not remember exactly what to do, they will be aware of the fact that something can be done to resolve the situation if a new problem arises later on. Simply knowing there is a solution reduces the likelihood of future problems developing.

FACIAL CARESS

After viewing the video tape presentation (details found in Chapter 9, p. 172) of foot, face, body, and sexual caress, we alternate the previous giver and receiver for the facial caress, hoping to establish, through effective role-training, a giving and receiving spontaneity in all caressing and pleasuring activities. The receiver lies on a bed. This exercise is designed to establish warm, positive, non-verbal communication in the traditional lovemaking setting. Face cream is used to minimize any abrasive affect of skin against skin. The giver is instructed to close his or her eyes and focus on the feelings as he explores and caresses his partner's face. (Figure 10)

About half-way through this exercise, a very important procedural learning device is introduced. This is the point at which the receiver places both their hands on the giver's hands and shows the giver how they would like to have their face explored or caressed. This principle is then carried over to all other exercises with strong encouragement given to clients to express non-verbally by using their hands to show their partner what they would like to have done in caressing, fondling, and lovemaking activities. Once they become comfortable in letting their partner know what they like or dislike, this frees them to experiment and try out new things with each other. This idea was pioneered by Helena Wright[2] in her work several decades ago.

Care must be taken not to suggest to a dysfunctional client that by showing a partner what they wish, they will obtain control of lovemaking activities. Dysfunctional spouses are hurt more than helped when either gets the idea that to show is to take over control of all such experiences. It is equally important to have them accept

---

[2] Helena Wright, *More About the Sex Factor in Marriage*, (London, 1959) 2nd ed.

Figure 10.   Face Caress.

without qualification that which is given by the spouse as an important part of the loving and caressing. Many couples are referred for therapy because of the insistence on the part of one of the dysfunctional spouses that only certain techniques, positions, or lovemaking activities are to be engaged in, of which they personally approve.

An important aspect of our work during the caressing activities is in giving permission to experiment by suggesting quietly that the giver try nibbling on the partner's ear, big toe or whatever seems to be indicated at the moment, suggesting that the giver may want to try some things in our presence where we can ask for feedback. The fact that we are there, seems to make experimentation less threatening. It is also re-enforced by us for suggested non-coital activities in the motel.

BODY CARESS

The body caress is accomplished with special lotions provided by us, with the couple deciding which one wishes to give and to receive first. It should be recalled that in the foot and face caress there was alternating between who gives and receives first. This is significant because clients typically wished to be caressed the way they caress their partner. This gives the passive partner distinct clues as to how the other would like to be caressed when roles are reversed.

The back of the body is always caressed first, since it is less threatening and less connected with sexuality and sex organs (Figure 11). We have encountered people who have made a body split, and the front and back of their bodies were not connected psychologically. A back touch was fine—there were no problems, but frontal caressing caused fear and apprehension. Several couples have indicated how glad they were to become a totality, learning to be as comfortable with their front as their back.

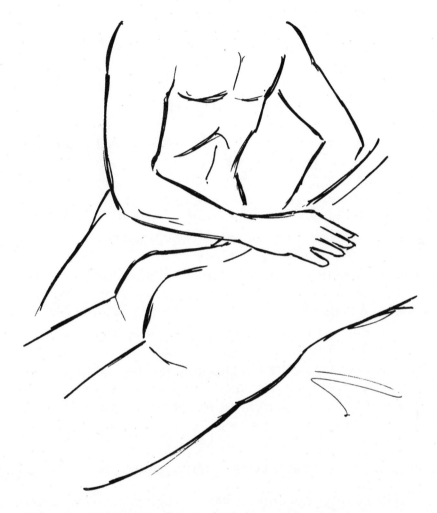

Figure 11.   Body Caress.

Warm lotion is provided to the person giving the body caress, and the receiver is asked at appropriate times about their feelings. Both giver and receiver are encouraged to focus on and stay with their feelings, which is a continued emphasis on the concept of sensate focus. How they have touched or caressed in the past is not important; what is important is how they are learning to touch and caress more warmly, enjoyably, and sensually at the time of the exercise.

After the back of the body is caressed, the giver is instructed to lie down and breath in rhythm with the one who has received the caress. Instructions include attempting to follow the inhaling and exhaling of the partner and to see how close they can emotionally feel while breathing. There is a synchronizing of the heartbeat, and often a feeling of oneness during the exercise. After breathing toegther for two or three minutes, the giver asks the receiver to roll over on his back so that the front part of the body can be caressed. At this time no preference should be encouraged between caressing genitalia and breasts, over caressing any other part of the body. The goal is to establish sensuality and feeling and not sexual arousal. If sexual arousal takes place during any caressing activity, this can be interpreted as a physiological response, but it should be clear that this is not the goal or purpose of the exercise; awareness is. After the front of the body has been caressed, the couple again breathes together for two or three minutes. Once positive feelings are experienced and focus is made on these feelings, this part of the exercise is completed.

BREATHING TOGETHER

The breathing-together exercise is first presented to the couple on video tape. The tape shows a woman lying on her side with a man pressed up against her back. He places his hand on her abdomen to gauge her breathing, and then adjusts his breathing to match hers. Later the roles are reversed (Figure 12). Typically, the exercise is engaged in between the two halves of the body caress, as a pause or rest period.

The purpose of this device is to help lovers pay attention to the responses of their partner. While there

Figure 12.   Breathing together. Female following male.

was some advantage to following the breathing exactly, the main purpose of the device is a perception training technique so that a greater degree of attention is paid to the partner during all lovemaking activities.

SEXUAL CARESS

The sexual caress emanates from body caress; the couple is asked to demonstrate what they have seen previously on video tape, where in addition to body caress the back of the neck at the hairline, and the spine about three inches up from the coccyx is caressed. The latter is particularly significant in non-orgasmic females because of the nerve innervation to the pelvis. Spreading the thighs while the client is lying on his stomach and caressing the inside of the thighs, starting at the knees, moving up the inside of the thighs slowly with the use of forearms and hands up over the buttocks and into the small of the back are techniques suggested at the beginning of the sexual caress.

The same procedure is followed on the front of the body with emphasis again on the inside of the thighs, up over the mons and genitalia to about the level of the navel, and with specifically light touch applied to nipples, areola, and breast tissues, but with the caress emphasizing a greater sensual and sexual feeling than was present during the body caress.

Special lotion, Physicians Formula Emollient Oil[3] which is non-allergenic is used on the genitalia so that there is no reaction to lotion. (Figure 13). Clients who are allergic to any body lotions should, of course, use only non-allergenic lotions on all parts of the body. Emollient oil has never elicited any rash or uncomfortable response on the genitalia of either male or female subjects.

The last phase of sexual caress is for the male to use his index finger and the emollient oil to massage the female vagina, particularly in the areas found to be more responsive in the sexological examination. Conclusion of the sexual caress of the male involves the female putting lotion on her breasts and caressing the male from his collarbone down to and including his genitalia using only her breasts. This gives the therapists definite clues as to how the female moves in the female superior coital position. (Figure 14). Although intercourse is not observed, the female superior position is recommended as the most singularly important therapeutic coital position for dys-

---

[3] Physicians Formula Cosmetics, 4623 San Fernando Road, Glendale, California 91204.

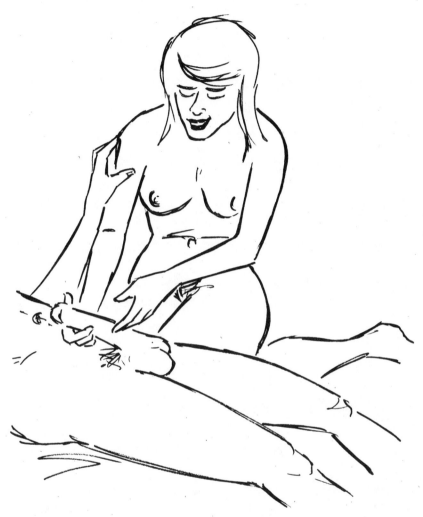

Figure 13. Sexual Caress—Use of special non-allergenic oil on genitalia.

functional couples, once the point of coitus as part of the therapy is reached. The woman knows where the penis feels good in her vagina, and she can direct penile-vaginal thrusting into areas that are pleasurable in order to maximize her own response and arousal.

We point out to our clients that they should never

*Figure 14.   Breast Caress and suggestion about how the woman
will function in the female superior coital position.*

go directly to sexual caress, but that the body caress
should precede it. Also it is important that it does not
inevitably result in intercourse. If touch activity always
and inevitably results in coitus, any touch will be avoided.
Coitus will more readily take place in a relationship where
there is a lot of non-coital touching.

Once the body and sexual caress have been completed, all other touching exercises are done by the
couple in the privacy of their motel unless there is some
problem which necessitates their asking us if they can do
an assignment in the office. If this occurs, we typically
are not in the room, but available in the next office, and
can be called if there is a problem. This is infrequent, but
it is reassuring to a couple to know we will be available
if needed.

Typically we find most couples have little trouble in
making the transition to the motel.

The amount of time a couple spends in caressing
activities varies. Some couples engage in all kinds of ac-

tivities such as going to Disneyland, Lion Country Safari, Deer Park, The Huntington Library, Museum, Theatre, beach, swimming, tennis, and golf while others spend most of their time in the motel pleasuring each other.

We have found no difference in success rates between the socially active couple and the ones that stay in the motel. This tends to have to do with personalities —as long as both agree on what they will do, we find we get positive results. Where one wants to be active socially, but the other does not want to go anywhere—we encounter basic personality differences that go beyond the sexual problems. We try and have the socially inactive person come up with things they would like to do, while also suggesting that there be a mutual decision by both on how time together will be spent so that if one day it is active socially, the next day may be quiet and restful. Neither partner should feel resentful since they are getting equal opportunity to do what they wish.

Chapter 8

HOMEWORK ASSIGNMENTS

The homework assignments begin the fourth day of the two-week intensive program. They are to be carried out in the motel room occupied by the couple. The first assignment is to wash, comb, or brush their partner's hair. The couple is instructed that each of them is to do this assignment in a way most likely to be a positive and pleasurable experience for their partner; they are asked to give a report of the success or enjoyment of this assignment the next appointment after completion.

The next assignment is to take either a shower or bath together. Washing each other all over with soap can be an enjoyable way to be certain that both partner's bodies will smell clean and fresh, especially where body odors have been a problem in the relationship.

The main purpose of these assignments is to get the couple into touch before the foot, face, body, and sexual caress, which are intermediary steps between the homework assignments and coitus per se. If problems are encountered with these assignments early in the program, then it is best to postpone further assignments until we see warm touch has been established.

Other homework assignments include suggesting to each other activities which they feel both would enjoy. It is important to move toward getting the couple to become innovative and creative in developing touch and pleasuring techniques of their own. This encourages them to "do their own thing," rather than repeating specific assignments given by the therapists or emulating touch or caress techniques they see on video tapes at the Center.

Once successful caressing exercises have been done in the office, they are free to do them in their motel. By successful we mean that both are comfortable with touching each other, are not afraid of what "might" happen in the motel, are able to go slowly and evidence some degree of warmth in the touching activities.

Later, all exercises will be done at the motel. It is important to get the couple functioning away from the office as soon as possible to maximize their ability to function at home.

Once the foot, face, body, and sexual caress are completed, they are given an overnight case containing a variety of lotions, creams, baby oil, non-allergenic emollient oil for the genitalia; the ones they preferred at the Center are included. A tub for the feet is also provided, should they care to repeat the foot bathing and caress in their own motel room. They are told if they run out of creams or lotions, to return the container for a new one.

NON-DEMAND TECHNIQUES

The couple next views a video tape of non-demand coital techniques. (See Chapter 9) They see the stimulation of the male genitalia to erection, and the squeezing of the penis—once successfully and once unsuccessfully. This is especially important in learning to overcome prematurity problems. All of our couples are taught this technique whether or not it is applicable to their particular presenting symptom. The assignment at the motel is that they achieve erection and squeeze a sufficient number of times for the male to have been able to go in protracted vaginal containment for at least 15 minutes. This may mean one or several squeezes, depending upon the couple we are working with. They are reassured that if the man does ejaculate, this is "okay," it does not represent failure. They should continue using this technique until confident of success. Our experience indicates that the majority of couples have no difficulty in learning how to complete this exercise successfully and repeatedly.

For this exercise the man lies with his back flat on the bed with his legs over his partner's legs. His genitalia are in her lap as he has seen depicted in the video tape. The woman sits with her back against the wall or against the headboard of the bed, with her legs underneath her partner's legs. Thus she can easily reach and caress the penis, the testicles, the lower abdomen and up on the chest, (Figure 15). The woman has already learned how to hold the penis for squeezing in the sexological examination so she simply implements that learning. Physicians Formula Emollient Oil[1] is used for pleasuring which is non-allergenic and precludes irritation.

For a man who has impotence problems, it is important to repeat this caressing technique frequently, and long enough so he begins to respond and develop erections in order that intercourse can take place. The assignments vary in length of time. Some couples will take several hours doing them, while others will need much less time. The more comfortable they become holding and touching the penis and having it caressed and touched, the easier future activities become. Some

---

[1] Ibid.

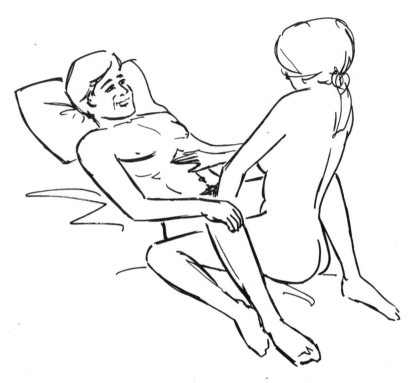

Figure 15.   Female pleasuring male genitalia in non-demand position.

women have never touched a penis before this exercise. They have learned through early socialization to have negative feelings toward any contact with the genitalia. We suggest to such a woman that she caress the penis until she begins to feel uncomfortable, even if it is only for a very brief period of time; then she should stop. The next time, try to extend the duration so that she can build up a longer and longer period of enjoyable pleasuring of him and herself, becoming more and more comfortable touching her partner's genitalia. Sometimes we give the woman a plastic penis to hold until she becomes comfortable with an erect phallus.

The squeeze technique is the most effective treatment for premature ejaculation. Some men are unaware of the arrival of "ejaculatory inevitability." They learn to recognize its approach during the squeeze exercise. Others ejaculate so rapidly that they have never had any opportunity to go more than one or two thrusts, and as soon as erection occurs, it may be necessary to immediately squeeze. The woman is told: "Once you squeeze, hold for about 10 seconds, then release; there will be anywhere from about 20 to 40% loss of erection. Continue to manipulate the genitalia until erection occurs again; then squeeze again for 10 seconds." Becoming aware of the 10 second interval is important in intercourse since an intimate scene need not be interrupted by counting or worrying about how long to squeeze. Either male or female may squeeze. We prefer teaching the woman to do the squeezing so she will be an active partner in coitus. She is instructed to rub the head or shaft of the penis over her labia and clitoris to maintain her own and her partner's arousal during the squeezing procedure—re-inserting after squeezing.

This is only a temporary procedure, and once the male has control of his ejaculation, he rarely needs the squeezing technique. However, it remains part of his repertoire of sexual activity.

The squeeze technique is demonstrated in (Figure 16), where the ball of the thumb is pressed firmly against the frenulum on the underside of the penis. The first two fingers of the squeezing hand are placed on either side of the coronal ridge on the top of the penis. The pressure point is on the underside—the fingers at the top merely make it possible to exert sufficient pressure to reverse the ejaculatory feeling before it reaches the point of inevitability. No harm, damage or trauma to the penis has been reported, and the female client is instructed to squeeze as hard as she can for approximately 10 seconds repeating

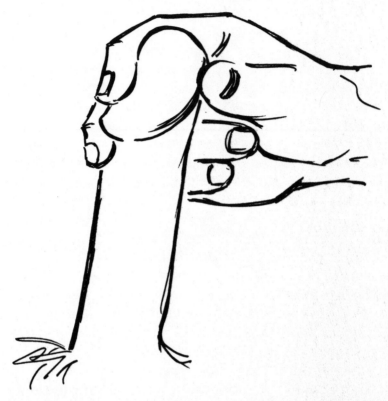

Figure 16. Squeeze technique for ejaculatory control. Must be utilized before point of ejaculatory inevitability is reached.

whenever her partner indicates that he is approaching the point of ejaculatory inevitability.

Some clients must be re-enforced that the pleasuring of the penis is important for a reversal of their symptoms of prematurity. They believe there should be minimal touch in the genital region because they typically say, "As soon as I'm touched on the penis, I ejaculate" or "I get too aroused if I am touched." We have to point out repeatedly to some people that the only way they can be conditioned to having stimulation over an extended period of time, is to experience a great deal of touch.

We also encounter a problem when the man cannot imagine his partner enjoying touching his genitalia, and occasionally we encounter women who do not wish to touch the penis or testicles. The reverse of the no touch is much more common, and they often resent the man doing for them, but not allowing them to do for him. i.e. A woman came in, and was quite upset saying, "It's just not fair—he won't let me caress his penis and testicles." His response was "how can she like to touch them, other women never did?" It becomes necessary to point out that he is not making love to other women, and his wife does enjoy it. Does he enjoy it? He responds, "oh yes, it feels great." So we ask, "what is the problem?"

One female pleasuring technique is done with the male sitting with his back against the head of the bed—she sitting in front of him, her back against his chest between his legs where he has access to the front of her body, approximately from the shoulders to the knees. (Figure 17). The couple is instructed to gently pleasure and caress each other without any demands being placed on the other for sexual arousal or response. Individuals who have deep-seated fears about themselves, their ability to respond or to elicit response in others, are role-trained to be effective sexual partners by being participants in a program where there is no demand for sexual performance and where just an honest emotional and intimate dialogue is the goal of the exercise.

Another non-demand position involves the woman lying on her back on the bed in the same position as that discussed earlier with the male. (Figure 18) Her legs rest on the legs of her partner. He is sitting with his back against the wall with legs stretched out and her legs are open with labia and vagina exposed. This is a very open position for the female, and one that can be beneficial in stimulating areas in the vagina which she has identified

Figure 17.   Male pleasuring female in non-demand position.

as feeling particularly pleasurable, especially the areas at 4 and 8:00 o'clock—approximately two finger joints or 2-2½ inches in depth. The two-finger method can be used—utilizing the first two fingers of either the right or left hand depending on which is easier or the index finger of either hand, in those particular areas where posi-

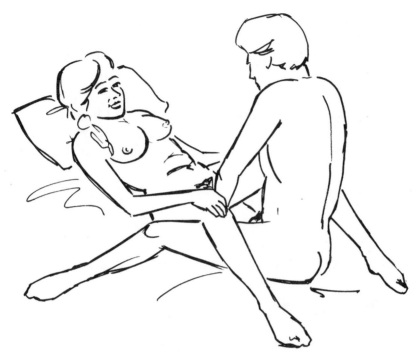

Figure 18.   Male caressing female vagina in non-demand position.

tive feelings were reported in the sexological examination so that development of sexual perception can be
maximized. It is also suggested that if the clitoris is positively responsive, the foreskin of the clitoris may be
gently caressed at the same time the stimulation of the
sexual segments is done, however, care should be taken
since the glans clitoris is often too sensitive for direct
contact.

The movement of the finger or fingers should be
slow and gentle, and should not go over a few minutes
until tolerance is acquired so that the vagina will not become sore and tender. The stimulation of the clitoris will
transfer positive feelings from there into vaginal areas in
a conditioned response pattern of learning to feel more
in the vagina.

Women who report painful intercourse or lack of vaginal perception may be helped appreciably by husbands learning to caress the vagina with information received from the sexological examination. It will be recalled that the husband came into the examining room and stimulated every part of the vagina in a clockwise manner. He thus learned where the best feelings were to be found, and how to stimulate his wife's vagina with the pressure and repetitive motion which the wife reported to be pleasurable. It is this information which the husband is instructed to utilize during the vaginal caress which takes place in the motel as one of the non-demand techniques.

It is particularly important for a woman who has had pain during intercourse or generally negative feelings about her past coital experiences, to be placed in a position of inserting the penis into her vagina at a point in time when she feels positive about the probability of this being a pleasant experience. The dominant and aggressive male in our culture has often forcefully inserted his erect organ and thrust repeatedly to the point of ejaculation. Once the woman has some control and say over the insertion of the penis in her vagina, there is often a critical turning point in her learning to feel positively about penile-vaginal intercourse, sensory perception, and the degree of pleasure which she can experience during this activity. The woman taking this responsibility takes the pressure off of the male. She knows when she is lubricated and ready for penetration, where her vagina is, and she can easily direct his penis into it.

Repeating homework assignments is essential to success in our program. We often suggest doing an assignment again in the motel until the couple can report genuine pleasure and enjoyment in replicating the experience.

QUIET VAGINA

The next assignment will be the quiet vagina. The couple is assigned to insert the erect penis after first doing the caressing activities. It typically comes the day after the first successful pleasuring has taken place. The woman is the one who inserts the penis into the vagina when she feels that she is sufficiently aroused. The couple is asked to lie for 20 or 30 minutes without movement— other than that needed to maintain erection. This is particularly effective for men who have trouble maintaining erections or who are threatened by their inability to perform coitally. It is also useful when the woman is afraid of the penis and feels uncomfortable with coital contact. It is an intermediary step between non-coital and coital functioning. There is no demand expected as far as thrusting or performance is concerned, therefore, there is no pressure involved.

SPONTANEITY

The last assignment is the one on spontaneity. We ask the couple what it is that they can develop that is unique to them? Something that they can do for each other that they both are going to enjoy and find pleasurable, and that they can tell or show us back here at the Center. The couples who are the best able to be original and unique in creating activities that they wish to share, are the ones that are best able to resolve their sexual problems. They are willing to experiment and as a result become freer and more comfortable in their interpersonal relationship, and willing to experiment in lovemaking activities with their partner.

Chapter 9

AUDIO-VISUAL AIDS

The first visual aid used here at the Center is a medical film entitled, "Pathologic Physiology of the Pubococcygeus Muscle in Women." (Kegel Film—for availability of this film see Chapter 5, Footnote 2). It runs approximately 20 minutes, and shows the development of the muscle from infancy to adulthood, and problems that exist due to poor development and/or childbirth trauma. It is important for our work in that it depicts areas of increased sensitivity at 4 and 8:00 o'clock in the vaginal floor about 1 cm. in width between one and two finger joints into the vaginal barrel. (Figure 4, Chapter 5, pg. 8). It also shows the difference between a conditioned and unconditioned muscle—showing the greater contractability and flexibility of a conditioned muscle.

Part of the problems we encounter are a result of the mystery surrounding the female genital area. We have already reported on our work during the fourth day with the sexological examination where the couple have both looked in the vagina with the lighted speculum, and the male has examined the area digitally, the 4 and 8:00 o'clock positions as well as other areas having been identified. Vaginal exercises are taught, they then see the Kegel film showing why the procedures experienced in the sexological are important. We explain the technical terms they are unlikely to know such as "pubococcygeus" and "nullipara." They view the film by themselves in the audio-visual room.

The first video tape a therapy couple views is of caress (Figure 19). The tape presents segments on foot, face, body, sexual caress, and breathing together. The couple have done the foot caress in our presence before they view this tape. This is done so that we may ascertain the extent of warmth in their touching activities before they see suggestions on a tape which may affect their future touching. We have also completed the sensitivity portion of the program before they have done the foot caress which gives further clues about the degree of warmth in these exercises.

Symbolically, the foot caress is very similar to the way a couple engage in sexual intercourse. Males who engage in fast superficial touch are usually premature ejaculators. Having the dysfunctional couple see how slowly and warmly a foot caress can be given helps them set a slower tempo. The research couple on the tape were told to do "their own thing," and the tape indi-cates to the therapy couple various caress techniques the couple use. They see the need for slow gentle strokes and how suggestions may be given by us. This prepares them for our comments and eliminates some of the fears of a performance. Even if their caress is done well, sug-gestions may be made by us to present new or different ways of caressing—encouraging them to experiment.

The second segment of the caress tape shows a re-search couple involved in facial caress. Again the em-phasis here is on slow, warm touch. It is at this point

Figure 19.   Therapeutic couple viewing video tape in audio-visual room.

after the giver has had an opportunity to spend 5 to 10 minutes in facial caress that the receiver is asked to place their hands on the giver's hands and to show how they wish to be touched and caressed. It is this principle of showing the partner what is pleasurable which must be mastered if couples are to learn to function well sexually. While each individual, both gives and receives in every exercise, it is important that the giver of the first exercise be the receiver of the second. This is to establish a giving and taking pattern between the dysfunctional spouses so that neither is allowed to be in the position of the habitual giver, while the other always assumes the role of receiver. Dysfunctional males in particular often have a pattern of only giving, being unwilling to receive. Often one of the individuals is unwilling to receive, since he perceives this as a giving up of power and control in the relationship. The couple are shown through the video tape that it is "as blessed to receive as to give." There are two major reasons for this, first, unless they are willing to receive, they deny their partner the opportunity to give; and second, arousal comes from experiencing warm feelings, particularly by taking in feeling and experiencing pleasure.

The body caress involves the warm touch on both sides of the body—back and front. The exercise always begins with the less threatening back, then the giver is asked to lie down and breath with the receiver, after which they proceed to the front of the body.

The last part of the caress tape shows sexual caress where the couple sees how the back of the neck at the hairline, the lower back about three inches up from the coccyx, the inner thighs, and the genitalia of both male and female may be fondled and caressed in such a way as to produce sexual arousal. Once the couple have viewed this on video tape and have had some direction and suggestions from the therapists, they are asked to become involved in caress activities in the privacy of their motel room.

We next show a one-hour video tape of non-demand pleasuring techniques. The emphasis here is on enjoyment and not on arousal. There is no demand for sexual response or performance. At this point we want them to start the pleasuring exercises while they are concentrating on sensate focus as they are stimulating the genitalia. This is particularly important for a male with a prematurity problem. Both he and his spouse need to learn the squeeze technique. Our tape of the technique teaches both of them how this is done. They can then practice in their motel prior to attempting any coital activities.

The pleasuring tape illustrates a number of points. It shows the insertion of a flacid penis, the breathing together exercise, and a variety of sexual positions. The point of this one-hour tape is to show the couple in therapy how other people touch, relate, pleasure, and function in sexual activities including coitus. We point out that this is not the way things **have** to be done, and that the demonstrations are far from "perfect." Rather, we explain, the tape shows research subjects doing their "own thing" in their own way. We have found such tapes to be helpful in getting couples started on the various assignments.

8 mm. FILMS

Two 8 mm. films of coital positions are shown for instructional purposes. We suggest that they discuss the various positions as they view the film, and decide between them which ones they might like to try when they proceed to coitus in a few days. We suggest that they try as many of these as possible, at least a few times so they can find those positions which they enjoy the most, and which will give variety to their lovemaking activities. The films include only still shots, no movement is taking place which might detract from the learning experience gained in viewing a variety of coital positions.

AUDIO TAPE

The next learning situation concerns an audio tape that is particularly effective when we are working with a non-orgasmic woman. The subject on the tape describes how she became orgasmic, and how she taught other women to function well sexually. The content is reproduced in detail below, even though our non-orgasmic females in therapy listen to it on tape. It is important that the husband hear the tape, as his cooperation is essential.

The couple in therapy will be viewing, in the next few days, both a video tape of intercourse showing this formerly non-orgasmic woman, and also a video tape of the woman she emulated in becoming orgasmic.

The reader will get some understanding of our use of this tape by reading the transcript. The subject is a 30-year old Caucasian female, recently divorced and remarried to a man who is very adept at teaching her to realize her long held desire to be orgasmic during penile-vaginal intercourse.

HOW TO BECOME ORGASMIC

I became orgasmic the morning after I observed a woman who was fully orgasmic have intercourse with her husband. I imitated her breathing and her pelvic movements, the gestures of her head and her hands and her feet, also her breathing. The breathing and the pelvic movements seemed to be the most important. In imitating these things, I put myself in the place of this woman along with her moans and her other verbal expressions, I found myself becoming orgasmic, and the orgasms started coming very fast. I worried a little bit—I didn't know if I would be able to stop them or not. They were very rapid, and one following the other. Since then, I still am able to have them that rapidly, but they last longer and the muscle spasms are stronger in intensity.

Some of the factors other than observing this woman, which I think was very contributory, were that in my sexual relationship with my husband he pointed out to me that I was rather rough in handling his penis and making me aware that my whole attitude toward sex was one of roughness and forcing things and being tense instead of relaxed and flowing and enjoying. Also, he persisted in trying to help me get rid of any feelings of inhibition in different areas; for instance, in mouth

contact—the way he worked on this was just to let me experience whatever I wanted with my mouth on his body or my
own.

I also found that manual stimulation helped things along,
and helped me feel freer and in the beginning of our relationship he did most of the manual stimulation. There was a lot
of stimulation of the clitoris. The stimulation of the clitoris was
done by him. He also inserted his finger in my vagina and
anus. This I found very exciting and then I found that I wanted
to try it also. I had done a little bit of this before, but I felt a
new desire to try it. So I would do it off by myself and then I
found that it was also very pleasurable to do it with him present
until I got to the point where I could freely masturbate myself
to orgasm with him there, either helping or just being a comfortable physical presence. Another thing that was very helpful
was the anal—he helped me somehow overcome any bad feelings that I might have had about—if a man puts a finger in
your anus, you know—does he feel fecal matter, and do I feel
embarrassed about that? He helped me by doing it and sure
enough at times there was a little feces in there, and I inserted
my finger and felt it and really it wasn't all that terrible so that
helped loosen up some inhibitions there.

I now have some very positive feelings because of his total
acceptance of my feces. At one period when I would have orgasms I would sort of lose control and I would pee a little
and this was rather embarrassing at first, but as I strengthened
my muscles (vaginal exercises we recommend)—this went
away. The freedom of acceptance that I got and that there was
nothing nasty or dirty about it was tremendously helpful. As I
became more accepting of all my body functions and secretions and smells, and whatever, I began feeling and having
fantasies that I wanted my partner to massage me internally
with his hand and it was a very loving and intense thing—it
made me feel very much like a woman that was open and
wanted to receive, not only a penis, but the male essence.

Another thing which is peculiarly my situation or problem
is that I have my two front teeth missing and I have a partial
plate, and this—I lost these teeth when I was 9. My partner
also worked with me where he would kiss me without my
partial plate and if you don't think that is a little difficult to
get over. I found that for the first time experiencing a tongue
on the roof of my mouth which I cannot remember ever ex-

periencing and being free enough to be in my really natural state without my partial was tremendously liberating and endeared me even more toward the patience and understanding of my partner.

Now I would like to talk a little bit about what has been happening recently. I find that I do procrastinate a little bit on the pubococcygeus muscle exercises, but I think there are other psychological factors involved here and I'm not too concerned about it because the orgasms are pretty good as they are. Maybe I'm a little frightened to do the exercises because of how much better can they really get. I have experienced some fear of losing control if I really relax and let go and have a big orgasm. I still experience that from time to time and what I do is relax as much as I can, and just let everything flow and I find that the fear goes away and very frequently each time that I lose a little more fear, I have a more intense experience and I feel so much more completely fulfilled and satisfied afterwards—it is a very cleansing thing. It is sort of like I've gone away on a beautiful trip and now I'm back and everything is very nice.

The type of orgasms that I'm having now vary each time and one from the other. I'm having one type of orgasm that is similar to kind of a bearing down feeling at first and then a grasping and a feeling of opening up where I experience that I am heightening my excitement. When I'm on top, my legs may be stretched out on the bed so that I am being a little aggressive and manipulating his penis to my advantage. It becomes very intense and very exciting so that I almost lose control and then I find myself rather spontaneously just moving my knees up and just opening up as far as I can and wanting very, very deep penetration and then the orgasm starts and there is sort of a bearing down or pushing, then a grasping then a sucking in and then a pushing and it sort of undulates and it is very, very pleasurable.

I will leave that area now and talk a little bit about several women that I have helped to become orgasmic. One woman had not experienced any orgasms with her husband, and I told her of my experiences and I gave her the pubococcygeus muscle exercises—how to determine how to do it, and I also told her how to breath and gave her an example of some of the hip movements, and we talked a little bit about some of the resistances she might have—being afraid of losing control or being afraid that if she did become orgasmic, then she would be out screwing everyone and she would lose her husband, home, and health and would end up in the booby hatch or who knows what.

Some of the other things we talked about were how did she feel—that perhaps she was punishing her husband by not giving him orgasms and then we talked about giving orgasms versus having orgasms, and she found that particularly helpful because she felt that she had really been punishing her husband by not having orgasms and she said that she sort of realized that she was cheating herself in this area and really she would have to find some other way to punish him that it wasn't worth deprivation of all that pleasure. I saw her a week later and sure enough she started having orgasms and had a similar experience to mine that once it got started she sort of panicked a little and thought how do I turn it off. This was a married woman with 3 children and she had been married approximately 10 years.

The other one was 18 years old that I happened to meet in a shop and we got to talking and she complained that she loved her boyfriend and really thought he was sexy and just loved to have intercourse with him and wanted to please him, but that she really didn't have orgasms very often and that it was very difficult and she really had to work. We talked over some of the similar things that I talked over with the other girl. With this girl I also talked to her more in detail about working with her boyfriend in the areas of accepting each other's rectums and experimenting with fingers and feces and peeing—I even told her that if they could develop some intimacy they could pee together in the bathroom or play games to become more familiar and comfortable with their bodies and their secretions and eliminations. About a month later I ran into her sister and her sister told me that things were much, much better and that orgasms were easier. I have not see the girl since then.

Several other women that I have talked to, I don't know the outcome except for one older woman which I think she had been having orgasms, but was denying the acceptance of them, and it was very easy. We talked mainly about her feelings toward her husband which seemed to be the problem, and again the thing of feeling that she was punishing him by not having orgasms, and once she found other ways to punish him, but not use that, why she began to open up a little more, but it seemed much harder for her.

The foregoing quotation reflects an open, honest, woman, who by self-exploration physically and emotionally was able to open up and to respond orgasmically. It represents a prototype of willingness to be open and free, which when followed by other non-orgasmic females may provide the same positive sexual response.

Chapter **10**

VIDEO TAPES
OF SEXUAL INTERCOURSE

A minimum of three video tapes of sexual functioning are shown to the couples. The order in which the tapes are presented is contingent upon the couple's existing problems, and their probable reactions to the coital scenes. We feel it is essential that they see at least three different tapes so they can be aware of different types and kinds of sexual functioning. Also they are more likely to view a couple who function similar to their coital pattern or they see how they would like to function.

One video tape we call the "Fun Tape," showing a young couple who are having a lot of fun in their coital activities. The "Romantic Tape" is self-explanatory. For the non-orgasmic woman, we show the couple a tape called "Effective Sexual Functioning." This is a tape of a multi-orgasmic woman who is very verbal in her expression of feelings and emotions. We feel this is beneficial because so many of the couples we work with are afraid that sounds will be heard by family or neighbors. It is also important for them to see that it takes a little work and effort to achieve orgasm and gain for oneself sexual gratification.

EFFECTIVE SEXUAL FUNCTIONING
INTRODUCTION

The idea that there is one coital position or one technique which is miraculous in its results, is misleading. This is one reason we wish to have each of our couples in therapy view at least three different video tapes, each of which is a half hour or more in duration. Our research on coital interaction shows that when applying a number of criteria for determining effective sexual functioning, the longer tapes receive the higher ratings, though length itself is not a criterion. With longer duration there tends to be more warmth and intimacy than found in the shorter tapes, which because of their shortness tend to be mainly physical. Occasionally a useful purpose is served by having a couple see a short tape or one where the couple do not function well. The contrast is immediately apparent and a couple who has never been privileged to see this kind of human interaction before, is able to see the difference between effective and less effective sexual functioning.

We feel it is extremely important to show sexual activities to couples so that they will have something that they can strive for, work toward, or model after. In other areas of education, examples of good functioning like good tennis, golf, and bowling are routinely depicted, but in the area of sexual functioning this has been taboo. As a result, many people are concerned and apprehensive about whether they are a good sex partner, and how they should, can, or will function. If they can see other people functioning, they at least have some idea about what to do and how to do it. They may not function with this competency, but their reaction generally after seeing what we consider good functioning is, "I know that if other people can do it, I can do it, and that I just need some practice to achieve this kind of functioning," or "I don't function too differently from that." Often a couple will tell us that it is reassuring to see that they function like other people, and that what they do is "all right." We do not wish to tell people how to function; we feel that they should function the way they want to function. We simply suggest to them if they see things in the tapes which they would like to try, or they feel might be helpful, or beneficial to them; this may be something that they wish to emulate, incorporating their own mannerisms and styles with whatever behavior patterns they are encountering.

One of the questions received from many of the couples in therapy concerns oral sex. This activity is depicted in most of our video tapes, though we do not feel that this particular technique is essential to effective sexual functioning. We explain that the Kinsey data indicates that the majority of Americans are involved in this type of activity; but we leave them free to determine whether, in regard to their own sexual value systems, they want to include this activity. For couples where one is initially demanding this of the partner, we find that once warm touch and effective penile-vaginal intercourse takes place, the demand for oral sexual stimulation and gratification is often dropped.

Several of the couples have wished to incorporate this kind of activity into their lovemaking, but have been uncertain of how to accomplish it. The tapes show them how other couples function in this type of behavior, and if they wish to try it, they can.

The most useful of our tapes for a non-orgasmic female is titled "Effective Sexual Functioning." It depicts a couple who have been married for thirty years who overcame inhibitions and disagreements about sex in the early years of their marriage. The wife became orgasmic and is now multiply orgasmic in each coital encounter. The husband appears passive compared with his superactive wife, however people work out their own patterns of function which satisfy them. He does show warm use of his hands, and variety in thrusting both in the male supine and superior positions.

We appear on the beginning and end of the video tape on "Effective Sexual Functioning." The purpose of our appearance is to emphasize the main points to be aware of while viewing this tape.

These points are:
1. Preliminaries: Touch — Caress — Arousal — Erection — Relaxation.
2. Emoting — Letting go with sounds, noises, and words.
3. Accentuating the Positive — Always Saying Yes.
4. Maximizing Female Turn-On — Self-Stimulation.
5. Play Function of Sex — Sex Can Be Fun.
6. Oral Stimulation — If Desired and Mutually Agreeable.
7. Sex Flush.
8. Ease of Penetration.
9. Use of Hands.
10. Building Body Tension for Orgasmic Response.
11. Female legs together to counteract tenting or V-shaped vaginal affect.
12. Variation in coital positions and thrusting.
13. Change in Breathing.
14. Ejaculation — Orgasm.
15. Afterglow.

We now discuss the significance of each of these essentials of sexual functioning to better understand the content of the video tape, and our discussion of this material following its presentation.

(1) Preliminaries: Touch — Caress — Arousal — Erection — Relaxation. The beginning of coital activity is usually some kind of touch activity, often using hands to touch and caress various parts of the body. Kissing of lips or other parts of the body is also a step toward couples getting closer in lovemaking activities that may evenuate in intercourse. "May" is a significant word because only in boxing do preliminaries always and inevitably lead to main events.

Throughout the book we have talked about caress; foot, face, body, and sexual. What we have implied here concerns the warm and loving mutually desired fondling of the significant other. This represents the beginning of an intimate dialogue with the option to continue or to stop at any point, being implicit for each of the participants. Much encouragement needs to be given to caressing activities short of coitus per se so that the typical pattern found in dysfunctional couples, where touch or caress always and inevitably leads to and involves coitus will not be the pattern.

When two individuals are touching and caressing, each other, physiological response to this activity develops arousal and relaxation. In our uptight culture it is important that the feelings of uptightness not be part of lovemaking activities. Warm loving feelings develop, and often include some degree of penile erection and possibly some sex flush; nature's blush on various parts of the male and female body.

Muscle tension or tightening of muscles in conscious and unconscious ways leads to enjoyable physiological functioning, but this is not the uptightness that results from dysfunction.

(2) Emoting. When bodies are touched, caressed, and fondled in warm and loving ways, positive feelings are aroused. The usual way for these feelings to be expressed is with some kind of verbal or emotional utterance. Letting each other know what feels good, expressing nonverbally with noises, that which feels good and communicating the same to the partner is an important part of sexual activities. For the unemotive and emotionally noncommital male in our culture, every encouragement should be given for him to attempt to remove as far as possible the cultural restrictions precluding expressing feelings which are positive and enjoyable in lovemaking activities.

(3) Accentuating the Positive—Always Saying Yes. Several years ago while observing a research couple in coitus, the female in the midst of coital activities said to her partner very loudly "stop." Needless to say, the entire lovemaking activities halted. All the enjoyable feelings and the degree of arousal which had been present went "down the drain," and then in a somewhat embarrassing and uncomfortable situation, both partners attempted to continue with their lovemaking activities—never fully recovering the momentum well underway at "stop."

In the video tapes of sexual functioning the couples who seem to function best are the ones who are always saying yes to the lovemaking activities in which they are involved. The implicit suggestion here is that couples encourage their partners, and engage in those activities which they do enjoy, reaffirming by saying yes that they are enjoying the activity. We strongly encourage all our therapeutic couples to lead their partners into positive and pleasurable activities to which they, with complete abandon, can say yes because they are genuinely enjoying those particular activities. A negative response often seriously inhibits further lovemaking efforts and, therefore, should be avoided wherever possible. If something is taking place that one of the couples does not like, we suggest they move their partner on to something they do like. If they are too tired or are not desirous of inter-course at that time, they should make this known, but it should be done in a positive way—possibly suggesting the alternative that intercourse take place in the morning or at some time where it may be more desirable.

(4) Maximizing Female Turn-On—Self-Stimulation. The female in our culture has traditionally laid on her back and supposedly given in to the sexual advances of her husband. This stereotype has now been dramatically changed, with women's liberation's desire for equality between the sexes, and the genuine interests of females in our society to enjoy sexual activity as much as their partners. Both encourage the female to be a more active participant in lovemaking activities.

Women are learning that orgasm is something they give themselves the permission to have for themselves, not something they are giving someone else. To deny oneself orgasm, is to deny oneself pleasure.

She can maximize her turn-on not only by being an active participant, but by freely moving in non-threaten-ing ways to physical positions where movement is pos-sible which will provide the maximum degree of sexual arousal. Sometimes rubbing her labia for example, against her partner's thigh, either in the side by side or in the female superior position will heighten arousal. The male partner must learn to accept the freedom of movement of the female as she attempts to enjoy lovemaking activi-ties, and to elicit as great a degree of physiological re-sponse as possible.

For effective sexual functioning one of the most sig-nificant aspects of female arousal is "letting go." At the peak of arousal, many orgasmic females report a fear of letting go. When questioned in detail as to the worst that might happen if they gave themselves in complete aban-don, we elicited the following replies: "I might urinate" (even though they voided just prior to the beginning of coitus), "I might defecate," "I might break wind"—definitely an unladylike and unfeminine thing to do, "I might loose consciousness," and finally "I am afraid I will die." Effective therapy presumes the realistic meeting of these fears.

In one case the woman occasionally broke wind as she approached orgasm, reporting concern for her husband's reaction. She felt rejection to be a probable response. We worked with her to let herself go and see what his response was, and to accept it without a feeling of personal rejection. In a follow-up interview the husband laughingly reported sex was great, and replied "I have the best air-cooled balls in California." His wife's concern was needless, and his sense of humor lightened our serious deliberations appreciably.

Momentary loss of consciousness accompanies orgasmic response with some women. The responsive female experiences the temporary black-out as an enjoyable part of her trip through orgasmic space. This varies usually due to how they breath during the orgasmic release phase. If they hold their breath or breath rapidly and hyperventilate, they may temporarily black-out. Since no one has ever told them this might happen, they often panic when they get close to this point. The non-responsive female fights arousal, enjoyment, and frequently reports the twin fears of (1) unwillingness to give her partner orgasm (rather than experience it as something she primarily has for herself), and (2) giving the partner too much control over her by letting him bring her to orgasm. Often the coital fear overflows into other areas of the relationship. "If he controls me in sex, he controls me everywhere," is a usual comment. Here ineffective sex is used as her way of exerting pressure on her partner in the ongoing power struggle in virtually all areas of their relationship.

(5) Play Function of Sex—Sex Can Be Fun. A serious mistake made by many dysfunctional couples is taking their lovemaking activities too seriously. There is a happy medium between being serious and making a joke out of a warm and intimate dialogue. Couples who function well obviously enjoy playing with each other, and utilizing many of the pre-coital activities of turn-on and arousal in very playful, yet loving and enjoyable activities. Couples seeking to improve their sexual functioning should be taught and encouraged to play—playing together in and out of lovemaking activities to learn how much fun sex can really be.

(6) Oral Stimulation—If Desired and Mutually Agreeable. In our culture, since the days of the Kinsey Report, it has been understood that a majority of American adults engage in oral-genital stimulation as part of lovemaking activities. There has been a more open and free discussion of this phenomenon. We find this is usually part of the sexual repertoire of our volunteer research couples. It is important, if this activity is to be engaged in, that it is mutually agreeable to both parties. One of the main essentials of effective sexual functioning is some aspect of oral stimulation. It may not involve the genitalia, but often involves breast stimulation, ear nibbling, and kissing as important oral activities which should not be overlooked.

(7) Sex Flush. The preceding activities should produce a reasonably extensive degree of lubrication in the vagina, and possibly a sex flush on both male and female bodies. Until there is a sufficient degree of lubrication present, there should be no consideration of actual intercourse.

(8) Ease of Penetration. With the completion of the preceding steps and adequate lubrication present, there should now be ease of penile penetration of the vagina.

We suggest where a woman has had trouble with lubrication or painful intercourse, she use the female superior position and insert the male penis into her vagina when she is sufficiently aroused and adequately lubricated, making penetration easy. Using the weight of her body to slowly introduce the penis into her vagina gives her control over the situation, and reduces fear of pain or discomfort in intercourse.

(9) Use of Hands. Throughout the coital session, the use of hands is a very significant and essential part of effective sexual functioning. During coitus the hands, for example, can be ruffling or stroking the hair, and caressing and pleasuring of the body. Caressing during coital activities should convey to the female feelings of physical warmth and response, caring, and enjoyment rather than hands being left lying on the bed or locked in some kind of a tight and unyielding embrace.

(10) Building Body Tension for Orgasmic Response. Masters and Johnson in their classical books[1] clearly pointed out that a high degree of myotonia or muscle tension is essential in effective sexual functioning. Individuals consciously and subconsciously contracting gluteal and leg muscles are building a greater sexual tension which will be released in orgasmic response. This activity should be consciously encouraged and the emulating of orgasmic sexual partners, such as seen in the video tapes, part of the training program of sexually dysfunctional individuals.

(11) Female Legs Together to Counteract Tenting or V-Shaped Vagina. Once a high degree of sexual arousal has taken place, there is a tenting affect in the vagina, which

---

[1] William H. Masters and Virginia E. Johnson, *Human Sexual Response,* (Boston, 1966) Little, Brown and Company, and *Human Sexual Inadequacy,* (Boston, 1970) Little, Brown and Company, see references to "myotonia" in each volume.

tends to minimize the penile-vaginal friction and cause difficulty for some females in developing orgasmic response. One of the most effective ways of counteracting the balooning effect of the vagina and in bringing the v-shaped vagina into more direct penile contact is for the female to bring her legs together after the penis has been introduced into the vagina. Often a very slow movement with emphasis on the coronal edge of the penis riding over the sexual segments in the vagina, about two finger joints in depth, produces as much, if not more, response than the traditional fast and deep penile thrusting which has been part of the contemporary myth of what is involved in effective sexual functioning.

(12) Variation in Coital Positions and Thrusting. One significant term for improvement of sexual functioning is variation. There is nothing so deadly as repetition when sexual partners know second by second what exactly is going to transpire. For this reason, we strongly encourage the use of as many coital positions as possible for the couple to develop skill in moving from male superior to side by side to female superior positions without losing the penile-vaginal contact they have. The male should be encouraged to vary his thrusting so that he does not always thrust as rapidly or deeply as is possible, and that he uses circular movements as well as great variation in thrusting to maximize response for his partner.

(13) Changes in Breathing. In observing couples who function well sexually we see variations in their breathing pattern. Some women hold their breath just before achieving orgasm, and others breath rapidly. Couples should be encouraged to experiment in their breathing activities to determine if holding the breath or breathing rapidly will accenuate feelings, sexual tensions, degrees of arousal, and set the stage for orgasmic response.

(14) Ejaculation/Orgasm. The usual termination of sexual activity for the male is ejaculation, and if sufficient stimulation has been part of the activity, orgasm for the female. While these are not always found in effective sexual functioning, they are usually goals which couples would like to achieve in the great majority of their coital opportunities. We suggest that while ejaculation and orgasmic response may be important, they are not necessarily always and inevitably an essential to effective sexual functioning. We prefer to see the goals of real involvement, no one being a spectator in an activity in which both are attempting to be active participants. Intimacy where there is profound emotional feelings which are meaningful expressed in coital activity, is a more reasonable goal to be achieved than ejaculation and orgasm.

(15) Afterglow. What happens when a couple technically finish with coital activities is of the utmost importance in determining the extent to which these activities are enjoyable. The way a couple lie together, continue to touch, kiss and enjoy continued warm contact, after coitus is technically over, is the final essential we think dysfunctional couples should be made aware of. Sometimes coital activities will conclude in sleep, other times particularly during a daytime coital session, they will terminate merely lying together for 5 to 10 minutes after conclusion of coitus, but what a couple learns to do after concluding active intercourse can be a most significant aspect of the extent to which they are effective sexual partners. Each couple is encouraged to develop some kind of spontaneous loving activity mutually agreeable to be engaged in at the end of their coital sessions, like holding or lovingly caressing their partner.

Chapter 11

MISCELLANEOUS TREATMENT TECHNIQUES

HYPNOSIS

For those couples or individuals who still feel "up tight" or are unable to relax or enjoy a sexual encounter after the first week of our program, we suggest the use of hypnosis. It is offered in those cases where it seems to us it may be beneficial. About one-half of all couples in therapy experience hypnosis. While the individual is under hypnosis, appropriate post-hypnotic suggestions are made. Regression is used infrequently to remove blocks. It is more frequently a question of the client giving him or herself permission to experience sexual arousal, pleasure, and response. A firmer and longer lasting erection, for example, in the case of the impotent or premature male; or more arousal, lubrication, feeling, and permission to experience orgasm for the non-responsive female. These post-hypnotic suggestions are effective since so many individuals have been conditioned through some form of socialization, be it religion or family, to feel that sex is bad, nasty, and that only "loose" individuals can enjoy sex. As a result, many are so up-tight they cannot allow themselves to have pleasure, let alone orgasm. They need to be free to suggest to themselves that they can respond.

One specific illustration is a 35-year old woman, married 10 years who came for therapy with her husband because she was non-orgasmic, and detested sex. She reported this to both therapists separately. Because of the trauma and conflict resulting from her non-orgasmic response, a divorce action had already been filed. She had a great fear of and abhorrence of the penis, and would not touch any part of her partner's genitalia. She reported little lubrication during infrequent sexual excitation, and some discomfort during sexual intercourse.

During the second week of therapy the couple was approached as to whether they would consider the use of hypnosis, since she had previously experienced hypnotherapy, and was a likely hypnotic subject. This was agreed upon. Her husband was instructed to do the body caress, and as he did so, the female therapist suggested that there would be more and more feeling throughout her body and more and more feeling and lubrication in her vagina. Further suggestions were that she would be more relaxed, she would give herself permission to experience vaginal feelings, and permission to have orgasm. When it was determined that adequate stimulation had occurred for an effective orgasmic platform to form, she was brought out from the hypnotic state and taken to the examining room where she was examined for vasocongestion and lubrication. During that examination she had a series of violent orgasms. She reported that she had experienced this before, but was unaware that this was what orgasm was. In this case the use of hypnosis proved to be a most effective technique in the achievement of a very positive therapeutic result, for she has been orgasmic in her continuing marriage for the past three years.

Of all the steps in our program, hypnosis is the one which stimulates the greatest request for repeated sessions.

OTHER TECHNIQUES

One specific segment of the video tape of non-demand pleasuring technique shows the insertion of a flaccid penis into a vagina with subsequent coitus. Some men are apprehensive and up-tight about being able to function sexually, and their flaccid penis is simply a protection from failure. When they insert the flaccid penis, they have already overcome that initial fear that they have of putting their penis in a vagina. Some movement can take place once in, and often the man will get an erection and will be able to complete the coital act.

Another method used when dealing with an impotence problem is the holding of the flacid penis in the hand and gently, rhythmically (to the heartbeat) squeezing the penis until he gradually begins to respond and erection occurs. This has been very beneficial for some of our cases of impotence.

Daily discussions occur with the couple in therapy. Content varies widely depending upon the presenting symptoms, and particularly with the dynamics of their relationship as it changes and evolves during the period of treatment. It is common to find role reversals, change in status, or power in the relationship as a result of action therapy.

Several examples of the daily verbal interaction between individuals and the therapists in the course of the therapy are indicated below.

CASE #1

A 40-year old couple who touch and relate well, but have difficulty with actual intercourse. All the positive gains

of a week in the caress exercises appears to go "down
the drain" when the couple reports serious conflict over
the husband's aggressively insisting on intercourse. The
wife refuses intercourse when the husband demands it.
The couple reported that everything was pleasurable until the husband insisted on penetration and maintaining
the wife in the supine position where she had no freedom of movement. If the wife attempts the superior
position, the husband is threatened and feels the entire
coital session is giving her power and control.

Following a discussion of this specific event in the
motel, the female therapist suggests to the husband that
one of the main reasons the wife may not be turning on
is that he has not really given her an opportunity to do
so. The husband requests clarification. The therapist
points out that by allowing his wife to enter into the
lovemaking activities where she can caress, stroke, and
fondle him, she is turning herself on. The wife quickly
agrees. The man was quite surprised saying that this is
a new idea to him—since he was trained that it is the
man's responsibility to be the active aggressor—to turn
the woman on, satisfy her, and expect her to express appreciation for the enjoyment at the termination of the
coital opportunity. The female therapist points out that
his wife cannot agree to be raped by him whenever he
insists on intercourse, and retain her dignity as a person.
She points out further that the wedding license does not
give him authority to rape the wife. Finally she indicates
that for the woman to be able to move freely and turn
herself on is an important part of her arousal before she
is ready for penetration in penile-vaginal intercourse. The
husband responds that this is a very significant point
coming from a woman which he had never considered
before. He was aware that when he stimulates his wife
that it turns him on, and he never realized that it could
affect a woman the same way. He expresses verbal agree-

ment with the proposition that his wife should have the opportunity to turn herself on, and the opportunity to become fully aroused before penetration. Both agree that if there is to be a mutuality in the relationship they are going to have to allow each other freedom to express themselves sexually.

At the termination of the two-week intensive therapy, the husband expresses appreciation for the right of the woman to arouse herself sexually which he had never previously considered. He indicates that he feels that he would have never understood this point from a male therapist, and that his consideration came entirely from the fact that the female therapist as a member of that sex was able to get the point over to him. This particular dialogue which took place in the presence of the female client and male therapist was regarded by the husband to be a significant turning point in achieving the success that was possible during the two weeks of intensive sexual therapy.

CASE #2

This couple reported to the therapists that everything went well until the husband unwittingly failed to follow a role reversal where after the wife had pleasured him, he wished to terminate the caress activities at that point rather than caressing her. The partner felt upset, rejected, and felt that they had made significant progress in moving ahead in treatment of his secondary impotence, but just at the point she was going to be able to receive pleasure from him, he abruptly terminated what should have been in her expectations a role reversal, and his pleasuring of her. In discussing the matter with the therapists, the wife became upset and insisted that her husband leave the room since she did not wish to hurt him and desired to discuss the matter with the therapists. While the husband was out of the room, the wife reported that she could not understand why when pleasuring her husband on several different occasions that he did not always have an erection. We pointed out to her that she could not take responsibility for his erection, his tension, his apprehension, the fact that she was not always responsive to his pleasuring efforts, the fact that he often proceeded to caress the vagina before caressing her body, was something that he would have to learn. She felt that her husband was awkward and inhibited, and we indicated that the only way he would become a more effective lover was for her to lead him in the direction she wished him to go, and give him positive feedback when he did caress her pleasurably. She was relieved to learn that she could not take responsibility realistically for her husband's erections, since her concern about them would flow over to him and cause him concern. To be spontaneous and free-flowing emotionally in responding to his attempts at lovemaking would at least provide opportunities for progress rather than stopping his advances when they were not pleasurable. If he moved directly to the genital area without any pleasuring of other parts of the body, suggest to him that body caress would help her turn on or some other activity that would be mutually pleasurable.

This case illustrates the point that when physical goals such as erection are stated, and when one takes the responsibility for the other's response such as the wife for the husband's erection or the lack thereof, no further progress is made until she is willing to accept the fact that he may not have an erection and that he may be choosing not to have an erection.

In this case when the husband returned to the room and the dynamics of their interaction was explained to him, it was pointed out that they should attempt nothing more than a repeat in the motel of the warm body and sexual caress we had observed in the office.

At the next visit the couple reported satisfactory progress, and enjoyment of the body and sexual caress in the privacy of their motel room and reported that it was more pleasurable than it had been when completed under the direction of the therapists in the office. With this framework and a willingness to accept this as a basic foundation upon which further physical and emotional intimacy could be based, the couple were willing to repeat this exercise on several occasions before proceeding with the quiet vagina and penile-vaginal intercourse. Acceptance of warmth and seeing failure to respond as only part of a total intimacy picture rather than the picture in and of itself is an important responsibility for the therapists to communicate to the couple in treatment as part of their work with them.

CASE #3

This is a case of a successful businessman who was infrequently involved coitally with his partner, and entered the program because of his wife's unresponsiveness. When his wife became responsive to the sexual caresses and his advances, she complained that he never ejaculated. His response was that he would ejaculate if he was able to ejaculate the proper amount. When asked by the therapists what he felt was the proper amount, he said "about one quart of sperm." When he was informed that a tablespoon full or 4 cubic centimeters of fluid was more typical of the average ejaculate, he relaxed and on the next coital opportunity ejaculation occurred. In this case the responsibility of the therapist was merely to communicate an elementary bit of information that one might presume a college-educated man would have. This simple information proved to be a critical turning point, restoring the normal ejaculatory process to this man who had not ejaculated for a number of years because of some wildly, incredibly, and unrealistic view of the actual amount of content in a male ejaculate. Much of our discussion with clients is involved in dispelling such erroneous information and myths related to sexual function.

CASE #4

This couple came in for the initial presenting symptom of non-orgasmic function. The problem was soon identified to be one where the male was also a premature ejaculator with the maximum of four thrusts to his credit.

The vaginal exercise helped her focus on feelings she had in the vagina, and with a reduction of his prematurity problem by the use of the touching exercises which he initially resisted since they both had avoided any kind of contact with each other because he ejaculated so rapidly. It was necessary to re-enforce constantly that they needed to be involved in a great deal of touch to desensitize himself from his rapid response pattern. Once they caressed several days, and used the squeeze technique on a number of occasions they found he did not ejaculate so rapidly. A great deal of touching was then done by both, making up for the 10 years of marriage where touch had been taboo. The quiet vagina exercise was a very pleasurable exercise, and vaginal containment for half an hour was easily accomplished. With her new vaginal awareness, she began having orgasmic response even before active intercourse started. Function has maintained itself on both of their parts, and they report half hour coital sessions with a lot of warmth, pleasuring, and lying with the penis in the vagina as well as thrusting.

CASE #5

A case where the woman was highly frustrated had orgasm through clitoral stimulation, but wanted to have orgasm with her partner in intercourse. The husband was able to go as long as was necessary. We explained that orgasm was orgasm, and that orgasm through clitoral stimulation was an orgasm, and that she should enjoy that. However, she felt frustrated not to be able to achieve orgasm through penile-vaginal intercourse. We explained that we could probably help her if she did not expect immediate results. We needed to examine her to see what the condition of her vagina was before we would know to what extent we might be successful in helping her.

The sexological examination showed extensive tearing from childbirth, and poor surgical repair, although a second doctor had attempted to repair the vagina in a subsequent childbirth, but it still looked as though a "drunken plumber" had made the delivery. The pubococcygeus muscle was completely torn loose on the right side, the vagina was loose and gapping. There was a very low reading on the perineometer, and the ability to contract was almost non-existant. There was no vaginal platform, with the shelf between the vagina and anus paper thin. For a warm, responsive woman in her late twenties, this seemed a tragedy. The probability we could help her seemed slight, and vaginal surgery was discussed, although out of the question financially. Vaginal exercises were given with the information that she should not expect instant results, but if she faithfully did them, she might expect at least minimal results with more perception and feeling in the vagina. Subsequent checks over a year showed marked improvement, and a recent check indicated a reasonably snug vagina, with a great deal of feeling, and the happy announcement that she is consistently orgasmic through penile-vaginal stimulation. Not all women are as persistent as she. Many women forget or do not take the time to do the exercises. She not only did not forget, but faithfully did them.

Another case where the woman was clitorally orgasmic, but not during coitus—resulted in her developing orgasmic response through coitus fairly rapidly because of her determination and persistence in doing her vaginal exercises. She was orgasmic within two months and has remained so.

GOODBYE

We find that working with a couple intensively for two weeks in an emotion-laden area such as sex, brings us close to them even though we may be working with several couples at a time. We felt that just a goodbye was not enough to indicate to them our warm feelings toward them. We decided that we wanted a brief moment that we could share together non-verbally. Our method of saying goodbye involves the interlacing of our arms with the four of us, facing each other in a small circle, and closing our eyes for a few seconds and recalling the sharing of growth and progress with them (Figure 20).

At the goodbye session, we have a discussion of how they can regulate their schedule at home to include time for the possibility that they can be together, being warm and intimate with each other, where pleasuring and caressing can occur, and a time when coitus might take place. Many couples have a hectic life-style of sex only after midnight, and the day's activities, clubs, business, and social life is over, which is one of the least ideal times to function. It then becomes necessary to get them to sit down and talk out how they are going to be able to implement the techniques and methods they have developed here so they can have time for each other—time for caressing, love-making and coital activities to take place.

A telephone date is set for the initial follow-up contact so that we can see how progress is evolving with the couple. It is usually set up for one month from the time we finish with the couple, and with the understanding that if any sexual difficulties arise in the interim that we are to be contacted immediately rather than let some-

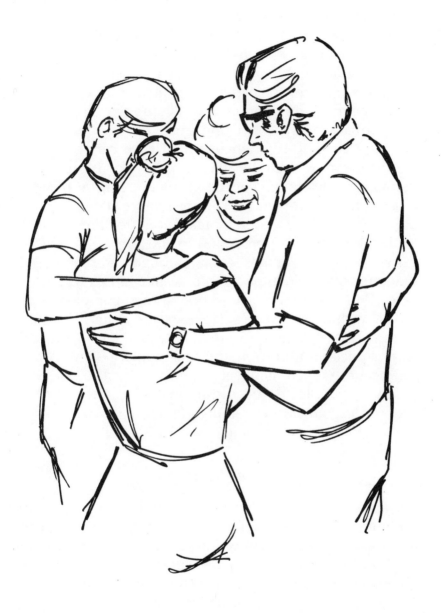

Figure 20. The therapeutic foursome expressing a non-verbal goodbye.

thing build up where it will be more difficult to resolve. If further work is needed, they are given the suggestion that they will have the opportunity to come back and see us. For those who live further away, telephone calls and letters are the usual follow-up. However, we find that if our couples are traveling in this area from other parts of the country they frequently will stop and give us verbal feedback of what is happening.

Our general experience is that if we cannot resolve the problem within the first two weeks of intensive therapy, the likelihood of the problem being resolved at a later date by follow-up is very remote. Penile-vaginal orgasmic response generally takes time for the exercises to develop enough perception in the vagina so that orgasmic response comes easily through intercourse, although some women become orgasmic in this way while here. Primary impotence is not always completely resolved within the two weeks, however, results are sufficient so that a degree of erectibility has developed, and with sufficient improvement taking place—intercourse can occur. As security develops, incapacity decreases and follow-ups indicate successful erections. Orgasmic response through clitoral stimulation, prematurity, and secondary impotence are fairly easily resolved.

RESULTS

We are loath to report statistical "success rates." We are not interested in developing a numbers game where centers such as ours will enter into a kind of spurious competition based on numbers. A center experiencing less-than-optimal success rates may be tempted to alter its definition of success. If a center reports higher success rates than others, the range in which the numbers game is played may be further escalated. The best-known success rates, of course, are those reported by Masters and

Johnson, and their presentation of statistical results was important to establish optimal base lines. We can report, and we can honestly assure candidates for therapy, that at the time of follow-up, couples who have completed our two-week program describe the benefits achieved in approximately the same proportions as are reported by Masters and Johnson.[1]

[1] William H. Masters and Virginia E. Johnson, *Human Sexual Inadequacy*, (Boston, 1970) Little, Brown and Company, p. 367.

Chapter **12**

WHERE DO WE GO FROM HERE?

During the last three years, we have sought to explore ways in which the same basic therapeutic techniques could be applied for a short time to couples in groups. Our "group workshops" are from one to six days in duration with usually 7 to 10 couples. A total of 456 individuals have experienced the group workshop with us. In this situation we are forced timewise, to dispense with the psychological testing, physical examinations, and sex history. A modified version of our body image and sexological examinations are done. The foot, face, body, and sexual caress exercises, and as many video tapes from the intensive two-week program are presented as time permits. The group experience is a mini-version of our two-week intensive therapy program.

The results of our "group workshops" are encouraging. This is particularly true for couples who have been married for a short period of time, and whose problems are not deep seated. The follow-ups on these couples indicate that the great majority are benefitted from this experience, and in some instances we feel that the group experience facilitates greater progress where the participants are encouraged to model themselves on one another. This is to say that in a group situation they are aware of the length of time that others are spending in foot, face, and body caress and that the progress made by the group as such has a positively contagious element to it. There have been no negative experiences in the group situation nor any reason to heed the warnings of some who wonder what happens if sex education or therapy are offered in group situations. Our experience indicated the need for a wider experimentation with group workshops. This we are currently involved in.

Continued requests have necessitated the development of a training program. Beginning in the summer (1972), dual-sex therapy teams were started in a six-week training program. One member of each team must be a licensed professional, and both members must have applied and been accepted as candidates who could profit by the training experience and would likely be effective dual-sex therapy team members.

Along with our clinical program, we have on-going laboratory research which contributes to more effective methods of treating sexual dysfunction. In several of these projects, we have worked in cooperation with other professionals coming from the disciplines of psychology and medicine with specialties in neurology, obstetrics and gynecology, physiology, neuro-endocrinology, biochemistry, and sociology. The research undertaken to date may be summarized briefly as follows.

Contemporary research on "Biofeedback" has produced rather promising results. In collaboration with Zev Wanderer, Ph.D., a psychologist, we sought to determine whether a biofeedback system might be developed for working with a particular subgroup of non-orgasmic women. This was a research sample of 9 women. One reported a lack of feeling of sexual arousal, despite the fact that instrumentation indicated considerable physio-logical arousal to be occurring. The instrumentation used here was a photoplethysmograph which can be used to provide an individual with continuous objective indica-tion of the degree of her sexual arousal. Several biofeed-back research sessions were conducted, and it has proven to be of some value in teaching individuals to be aware of arousal as it takes place.

With Duane Petersen, M.D., eight electromyographic studies were completed where muscle responses among male and female research volunteers were studied as they viewed Danish pornography. Muscle tension was moni-tored and recorded in various regions of the hand and the genitalia during the viewing of films of sexual inter-course. We found male and female responses to be simi-lar in some respects, but dissimilar in others. Responses appeared dependent upon socialization factors in child-hood and adulthood. More study in this area needs to be conducted.

In collaboration with Berry Campbell, Ph.D., a physi-ologist, we recorded sexual responses with a group of 10 female volunteer research subjects who masturbated to orgasm on five separate occasions to obtain base-line readings. This research took place in the laboratory while the physiological parameters of respiration, pulse, vaginal, and anal muscle tension were simultaneously recorded on a four-channel recorder. The most significant finding of this research has been a finger-printing phenomenon re-flecting the wide variation between women's orgasms. It appears that once a woman learns to have orgasm in a particular pattern, she continues habitually to function in a similar manner. Subsequent recordings reflect great similarity to the orgasmic pattern which has been estab-lished as base-line in earlier recordings.

An effort to determine objective criteria of success-ful or effective sexual functioning has been made. This project involved the compilation of specific criteria of what comprises success in human coital encounters. We combined these criteria into twelve steps on a modified Bales Chart,[1] then several teams, including male and female observers, recorded the presence of these criteria at five second intervals as they observed video tapes of coitus of 15 volunteer research couples. In general, the results of these teams were in agreement, but these criteria and evaluations are being further refined, and one other team's observations will be recorded before the data are ready for publication.

Recorded observations of intercourse have been conducted over the last six years with 116 couples, our total coital study population to date. This project is continuing with the majority of currently observed coital sessions now being recorded on video tape.

Several other projects are in initial stages of work, and have been developed for the most part from previous work done here at the Center.

Initial plans have been made to prepare papers for professional journals reporting the findings of the foregoing research projects. These should be available in the next few years.

---

[1] Robert F. Bales, *Interaction Process Analysis,* (Cambridge, Mass., 1950), Addison-Wesley Publishing Company.

APPENDIX

\# _____

INITIAL INTERVIEW_____DATE_____TIME_____

CHECK REFERRING AUTHORITY_____

    NAME_____PHONE_____

    ADDRESS_____CITY_____ZIP CODE_____

TESTS:

    MMPI   HIS_____HERS_____DATE_____TIME_____

    TJTA   HIS_____HERS_____DATE_____TIME_____

    DRAW-A-PERSON   HIS_____HERS_____DATE_____TIME_____

    LUSCHER COLOR   HIS_____HERS_____DATE_____TIME_____

    DRAW-A-SCENE   HIS_____HERS_____DATE_____TIME_____

    OTHER   HIS_____HERS_____DATE_____TIME_____

    SCORING   HIS_____HERS_____DATE_____TIME_____

SEX HISTORY   HERS_____DATE_____TIME_____

                               HIS_____DATE_____TIME_____

HISTORY FOLLOW-UP HIS_____HERS_____DATE_____TIME_____

SWITCH PARTNERS   HIS_____HERS_____DATE_____TIME_____

PHYSICAL EXAM   HIS_____   DATE_____TIME_____

                  HERS_____   DATE_____TIME_____

ROUND TABLE   DATE_____TIME_____

PROGNOSIS_____

SEXOLOGICAL QUESTIONNAIRE   HIS_____.DATE_____TIME_____

                                 HERS_____DATE_____TIME_____

#_____   - 2 -

SEXOLOGICAL EXAM   HIS_____   DATE_____ ·TIME_____

                          HERS_____   DATE_____ TIME_____

    PENIS_____CLITORIS_____KEGEL EXERCISES_____

    TESTICLES_____BREASTS_____BEARING DOWN_____

    PUBOCOCCYGEUS____VAGINA_____· BREATHING_____

                     PUBOCOCCYGEUS_____

KEGEL FILM   DATE_____TIME_____

SELF-CONCEPT:

    BODY IMAGE   MALE_____DATE_____TIME_____

                            FEMALE____DATE_____TIME_____

    SENSITIVITY   ·   DATE_____TIME_____

SUGGESTIONS:

                COMB OR BRUSH HAIR_____

                BATH OR SHOWER_____

                BODY CARESS AT HOME_____

                WASHING HAIR_____

                CLAMPING TECHNIQUE_____

                CLAMPING & PLEASURING_____

                CLAMPING & PLEASURING_____

                QUIET VAGINA_____

                QUIET VAGINA·_____

                INTERCOURSE_____

                INTERCOURSE_____

                INTERCOURSE_____

                CREATIVITY_____

                OTHER_____

\#_____

- 3 -

FOOT BATH CARESS_____DATE_____TIME_____

CARESS TAPE_____DATE_____TIME_____

FACE CARESS_____DATE_____TIME_____

BODY CARESS_____DATE_____TIME_____

SEXUAL CARESS_____DATE_____TIME_____

PLEASURING TAPE_____DATE_____TIME_____

SEXUAL POSITIONS FILM   \#1_____

                         \#2_____

HYPNOSIS_____MALE_____FEMALE_____DATE_____TIME_____

HYPNOSIS_____MALE_____FEMALE_____DATE_____TIME_____

HYPNOSIS_____MALE_____FEMALE_____DATE_____TIME_____

ORGASMIC WOMAN AUDIO TAPE_____DATE_____TIME_____

OTHER_____DATE_____TIME_____

TALK_____DATE_____TIME_____

INTERCOURSE TAPE_____WHICH ONE?_____WHY?_____DATE_____TIME_____

TALK_____DATE_____TIME_____

INTERCOURSE TAPE_____WHICH ONE?_____WHY?_____DATE_____TIME_____

TALK_____DATE_____TIME_____

INTERCOURSE TAPE_____WHICH ONE?_____WHY?_____DATE_____TIME_____

OTHER_____DATE_____TIME_____

\#_____

- 4 -

FOLLOW-UPS: VISIT_____CALL_____LETTER_____DATE_____TIME_____

VISIT_____CALL_____LETTER_____DATE_____TIME_____

VISIT_____·CALL_____LETTER_____DATE_____TIME_____

VISIT_____CALL_____LETTER_____DATE_____TIME_____

VISIT_____CALL_____LETTER_____DATE_____TIME_____

VISIT_____CALL_____LETTER_____DATE_____TIME_____

VISIT_____CALL_____LETTER_____DATE_____TIME_____

VISIT_____CALL_____LETTER_____DATE_____TIME_____

VISIT_____CALL_____LETTER_____DATE_____TIME_____

VISIT_____CALL_____LETTER_____DATE_____TIME_____

VISIT_____CALL_____LETTER_____DATE_____TIME_____

VISIT_____CALL_____LETTER_____DATE_____TIME_____

PHYSICAL EXAMINATION

Temp.___ Pulse___ Res.___ B.P.___ Height___ Weight___ B.S.___

General appearance and nutrition:

_____

_____

Skin:
_____

_____

Head: Eyes
_____

        Nose
_____

        Throat
_____

        Ears
_____

        Teeth
_____

        Mouth
_____

        Tonsils
_____

Neck: Thyroid
_____

Lymphadenopathy
_____

Thorax (shape, breasts)
_____

Lungs
_____

Abdomen
_____

    Heart
_____

    Liver
_____

    Kidneys
_____

Pelvic Exam
_____

Perineometer Reading Unstimulated State
_____

Rectal: (Prostate, masses, induration, etc.)
_____

        Hemroids
_____

Extremities (Deformities, Varicoseties, etc.)
_____

Reflexes
_____

Additional Data
_____

Tentative Diagnosis
_____

Tests:
_____

_____

_____

MEDICAL HISTORY

Name _____ Age _____   □ Single   □ Divorced   Date _____
                                         □ Married   □ Widow(er)

Address _____ Religion _____

Occupation _____ All previous occupations _____

Birth Place _____ List all States or Countries in which you have lived _____

Education: Please encircle the last grade you completed

Grade 5	High School 1 2 3 4	Post Grad. _____ yrs
6 7 8	College 1 2 3 4	Degrees

Date of last physical exam. _____   P.I.   Please do not write in this space.

C.C.   Please list all Symptoms

1. _____
2. _____
3. _____
4. _____
5. _____

Routine check-up — no symptoms □

FAMILY HISTORY

	If Living		If Deceased		Has any blood relative ever had:	Please Encircle (no) or (yes) who
	Age	Health	Age at death	Cause		
Father					Cancer	no yes
Mother					Tuberculosis	no yes
Brother or Sister 1.					Diabetes	no yes
2.					Heart trouble	no yes
3.					High blood pressure	no yes
4.					Stroke	no yes
5.					Epilepsy	no yes
Husband or Wife					Mental illness	no yes
Son or Daughter 1.					Suicide	no yes
2.					Congenital deformities no yes
3.					
4.					
5.					
6.					

NOTE: This is a confidential record of your medical history and will be kept in this office. Information contained here will not be released to any person except when you have authorized us to do so.

PERSONAL HISTORY

ILLNESSES: Have you ever had
Please Encircle all Answers   (no) or (yes)

Measles or German Measles	no	yes
Chicken pox or Mumps	no	yes
Whooping cough	no	yes
Scarlet fever or Scarlatina	no	yes
Pneumonia or Pleurisy	no	yes
Diphtheria or Smallpox	no	yes
Influenza	no	yes
Rheumatic fever or heart disease	no	yes
Arthritis or Rheumatism	no	yes
Any bone or joint disease	no	yes
Neuritis or neuralgia	no	yes
Bursitis, Siatica or Lumbago	no	yes
Polio or Meningitis	no	yes
Bright's disease or Kidney inf.	no	yes

Gonorrhea or Syphilis	no	yes
Anemia or Jaundice	no	yes
Epilepsy	no	yes
Migraine headaches	no	yes
Tuberculosis	no	yes
Diabetes or Cancer	no	yes
High or low blood pressure	no	yes
Nervous breakdown	no	yes
Food, chemical or Drug poisoning	no	yes
Hay fever or Asthma	no	yes
Hives or Eczema	no	yes
Frequent colds or Sore throat	no	yes
Frequent infections or boils	no	yes
Any other disease	no	yes

ALLERGIES: are you allergic to

Penicillin or Sulfa	no	yes
Aspirin, Codeine or Morphine	no	yes

Mycins or other antibiotics	no	yes
Merthiolate or Mercurochrome	no	yes
Any other Drug	no	yes
Any foods	no	yes
Adhesive tape	no	yes
Nail polish or other Cosmetics	no	yes
Tetanus Antitoxin or Serums	no	yes

INJURIES: have you had any

Broken bones	no	yes
Sprains or dislocations	no	yes
Lacerations (Extensive)	no	yes
Concussion, or Head injury	no	yes
Ever been knocked out	no	yes

TRANSFUSIONS: have you ever had
Blood or Plasma transfusion   no   yes
WEIGHT: now _____, one yr ago _____;
Maximum _____, when _____,

Please review the section you have just completed and wherever you answered 'yes' fill in the year (guess if necessary) and also where there is more than one illness to a line encircle the ones you have had.   Example: Chicken pox or (Mumps) _1930_ no (yes)

SURGERY: have you had

Tonsillectomy	no	yes
Appendectomy	no	yes
Any other operation	no	yes

Give details

Have you ever been advised to have any Surgical operation which has not been done. _____   no   yes

Give DETAILS below of all hospitalizations for Surgery or Illness including name and address of Doctor and Hospital.

FORM NO. 325   SUPERIOR PRINTERS, TORRANCE   328-8886

PLEASE TURN PAGE

X-RAYS Have you ever had x-rays of

Chest	no	yes
Stomach or colon	no	yes
Gall bladder	no	yes
Extremities	no	yes
Back	no	yes
Teeth	no	yes
Other	no	yes

EKG: Ever had an electrocardiogram? ___ yes no

IMMUNIZATIONS: Have you had

Smallpox vaccination within last 7 years ___ yes no
Tetanus shots (not antitoxin which lasts only 2 weeks) ___ yes no
Polio shots within last 2 years ___ yes no

SYSTEMS: Do you now have or have you ever had

Any eye disease, injury, impaired sight	no	yes
Any ear disease, injury, impaired hearing	no	yes
Any trouble with nose, sinuses, mouth, throat	no	yes
Fainting spells	no	yes
Loss of consciousness	no	yes
Convulsions	no	yes
Paralysis	no	yes
Dizziness	no	yes
Frequent or severe headaches	no	yes
Depression or anxiety	no	yes
Hallucinations	no	yes
Enlarged glands	no	yes
Enlarged Thyroid or goiter	no	yes
Skin Disease	no	yes
Chronic or frequent cough	no	yes
Chest pain or angina pectoris	no	yes
Spitting up of blood	no	yes
Night sweats	no	yes
Shortness of breath	no	yes
Palpitation or fluttering heart	no	yes
Swelling of hands, feet, or ankles	no	yes
Varicose veins	no	yes
Extreme tiredness or weakness	no	yes
Kidney disease or stones	no	yes
Bladder disease	no	yes
Albumin, sugar, pus, etc. in urine	no	yes
Difficulty in urinating	no	yes
Abnormal thirst	no	yes
Stomach trouble or ulcer	no	yes
Indigestion	no	yes
Appendicitis	no	yes
Liver or gall bladder disease	no	yes
Colitis or other bowel disease	no	yes
Hemorrhoids or rectal bleeding	no	yes
Constipation or Diarrhea	no	yes

Has there been any recent change in —

Your appetite or eating habit	no	yes
Your bowel action or stools	no	yes

HABITS:

Exercise adequately? ___ yes no
How?

Sleep well? ___ yes no
Average 8 hrs.? ___ yes no

Bowels move regularly? ___ yes no
Diet well balanced? ___ yes no

Meat; ___ servings per day
Fruits; ___ servings per day
Vegetables; ___ servings per day
Eggs; ___ per day
Bread; ___ slices per day
Potatoes; ___ servings per day
Cereals; ___ servings per day
Salt; light ☐ moderate ☐ much ☐
Spices, pepper, pickles, etc.; little ☐ moderate ☐ much ☐
Milk; ___ glasses per day
Coffee; ___ cups per day
Tea; ___ cups per day
Soft drinks; ___ per day
Water; ___ glasses per day
Alcoholic beverages; never ☐ rarely ☐ moderate ☐ daily ☐
Have you ever been treated for alcoholism ___ no yes
Tobacco: Cigarettes; ___ packs per day
Cigars ☐ Pipe ☐ Chewing Tobacco ☐ Snuff ☐

Drugs:

Laxatives;	never ☐	occ. ☐	freq. ☐	daily ☐
Vitamins;	never ☐	occ. ☐	freq. ☐	daily ☐
Sedatives;	never ☐	occ. ☐	freq. ☐	daily ☐
Tranquilizers;	never ☐	occ. ☐	freq. ☐	daily ☐
Sleeping pills, etc.;	never ☐	occ. ☐	freq ☐	daily ☐
Aspirin, etc.;	rarely ☐	occ. ☐	freq. ☐	daily ☐
Cortisone, Acth;	never ☐	occ. ☐	freq. ☐	daily ☐

Thyroid; never ☐ yes, in past—none now ☐
now on ___ gr. daily ☐
Appetite depressants; never ☐ occ. ☐ freq. ☐ daily ☐
Have you ever been treated for drug habits ___ no yes
Have you ever taken Insulin, tablets for diabetes,
Hormone shots or tablets ___ no yes

Sex — entirely satisfactory? ___ yes no
Work; ___ hrs. per day — indoors ☐ outdoors ☐
Do you like your work? ___ yes no

Recreation; Do you participate in sports or have any hobbies
which give you relaxation at least 3 hrs. weekly ___ yes no
TV ___ hrs./day
Reading ___ hrs./wk.
Vacations, ___ wks. per year.

WOMEN ONLY

Menstrual History

Age at onset ___
Regular — yes ☐ no ☐
Cycle — ___ days (from start to start)
Usual duration — ___ days
Heavy ☐ medium ☐ light ☐
Pains or cramps — yes ☐ no ☐
Date of last period ___

Pregnancies

How many children born alive ___
How many stillbirths ___
How many prematures ___
How many Cesarean Sections ___
How many miscarriages ___
Any complications with any pregnancy ___ no yes

CENTER FOR MARITAL AND SEXUAL STUDIES
RESEARCH AND THERAPY POPULATION

July 28, 1972

INDIVIDUAL THERAPY SUBJECTS

Consultations Regarding Sexual Problems	196
Sexological and Body Imagery	21
Single Males	9
Couples	112
Workshops 1-5 Day	456

INDIVIDUAL RESEARCH SUBJECTS

Males & Females Individually in Projects	141
Observation of Intercourse (116 Different Couples)	232
TOTAL	1,167
Orgasmic Responses Observed	1,264

Of research couples, 11 have been observed 5 or more times. One couple observed in approximately 75 coital opportunities. Two couples in longer individual study over three years to date. Many research subjects are in several projects, and over a repeated number of sessions.

Total number of different individuals worked with in sexual functioning as of July 28, 1972—1,167.

CASE # _____
DATE _____

FEMALE SEXOLOGICAL FORM
Page 1

Occupation _____ Age _____ Education _____ Number of children born vaginally? _____ Marital status _____ Yrs. Married _____ Number of times married?

Religious background? _____

Surgery which might effect vaginal muscular function? _____

Do you participate in sports activities? _____ If so, what kinds? _____

How long since last pregnancy? _____

How long does menstrual flow usually last? _____

How many days usually between periods? _____

Is menstrual period regular _____ When was last period? _____

Is sexual intercourse ever painful to you? _____

How important to you is clitoral stimulation of your clitoris for sexual satisfaction?
very _____
somewhat _____
not at all _____
don't know _____
Comments _____

Is stimulation of your clitoris necessary for you to achieve orgasm?
always _____
usually _____
sometimes _____
never _____
don't know _____

What position is usually used by you in sexual intercourse?

What position do you prefer in sexual intercourse?

What position is the most sexually satisfying in sexual intercourse for you?

Have you ever had vaginal warts or infections? Frequency?

Do you feel this hampers sexual interest in any way? If so, how?

Do you use any kind of contraceptive? _____ If so, what kind? _____

Do you feel this hampers sexual satisfaction in any way? _____ If so, how? _____

How many different men have you had sexual intercourse with?
Less than 10 _____
10-20 _____
21-30 _____
31-40 _____
41-50 _____
over 50 _____

Do you prefer a male penis which is:
small _____
medium _____
large _____
not important _____
don't know _____
circumcised _____
uncircumcised _____
not important _____
don't know _____

List by number in order of importance the sexual response to the following erogenous areas:
mouth _____
mons _____
breast _____
vagina _____
clitoris _____
ears _____
neck _____
anus _____
other _____

Are you sexually repulsed in any of the following areas by direct contact? _____

Have you ever used any other kinds of contraceptives which you felt hampered sexual satisfaction? _____ If so, what kind _____ In what way or ways did this hamper sexual satisfaction? _____

How would you describe having an orgasm? _____

Are you ever sexually satisfied without orgasm? _____

During sexual intercourse do you usually have simultaneous orgasm with partner? _____

Do you masturbate? _____ If so, how frequently? _____

During sexual intercourse do you ever have multiple orgasm? _____ If so could you approximate the usual number of orgasms that you achieve? _____

When was the last time you had sexual intercourse?
hrs _____
days _____
weeks _____
months _____
years _____
never _____

Do you have orgasm?
always _____
usually _____
sometimes _____
seldom _____
never _____
don't know _____
during sexual intercourse _____

Do you think it is important to achieve orgasm for sexual satisfaction? _____

In your estimation are vaginal muscles useful in achieving orgasm? _____ If so, Why? _____

To what extent are vaginal muscles stimulating to you? _____

Have you ever exercised or made a conscious effort to control vaginal muscles? _____

Do you ever use these muscles to achieve orgasm without sexual intercourse? _____

List any medication you are taking: _____

Do you attain orgasm in other ways beside sexual intercourse? _____ If so, how? _____

Do you ever use these muscles instead of masturbation? _____

How long would you estimate intercourse usually lasts with your partner? _____

MALE SEXOLOGICAL FORM

No.	Date	Age	Marital Status	Education	Yrs. married	No. of times married	No. of children

Religious background

Are you circumcised? _____ uncircumcised? _____

Do you consider your penis? Small _____ Medium _____ Large _____

How often have you experienced different women utilizing muscular contractions during intercourse?
frequently _____
occasionally _____
rarely _____
never _____

Do you consider the use of vaginal muscles during intercourse by the female:
desirable _____
satisfactory _____
undesirable _____
don't know _____
nice but not necessary _____

Have you ever had trouble getting an erection? Yes _____ No _____
Frequency _____

Do you lose your erection during intercourse? Yes _____ No _____
Frequency _____

Do you feel less of a man if your partner does not achieve orgasm?

Do you have difficulty in ejaculating? Yes _____ No _____

Do you have morning erections?
Yes _____ No _____

What position do you prefer in sexual intercourse?

Do you ejaculate without an erection? Yes _____ No _____

Do you have difficulty with prematurity

How long are you able to maintain an erection after insertion in the vagina? Average time _____

What position is most sexually satisfying in sexual intercourse?

How often would you say this occurs?

Are you sexually satisfied if your partner does not achieve orgasm?

During intercourse do you usually have simultaneous orgasm with your partner?

What position is usually used by you in sexual intercourse?

Does your wife use muscular contractions in intercourse? Yes _____ No _____
If she does, do you find this pleasurable?

Have you ever found the use of vaginal muscles to be painful? Yes _____ No _____

Do you masturbate? Yes _____ No _____ Frequency _____

How many women have you experienced who have had unconscious muscular contractions? (estimate) _____ Conscious use? _____

List by number in order of importance those areas you are interested in stimulating in foreplay. (check)
Mouth _____
Mons _____
Breast _____
Vagina _____
Clitoris _____
Ears _____
Neck _____
Anus _____
Other (list) _____

Are you sexually repulsed in any of the following areas by direct contact? (check)
Mouth _____
Mons _____
Breast _____
Vagina _____
Clitoris _____
Ears _____
Neck _____
Anus _____
Other (list) _____

What areas of your body do you find to be the most sexually stimulating to you? (list by # order of importance)
Penis _____
Coronal edge _____
Head of penis _____
Urethra _____
Nipples _____
Scrotum _____
Testicles _____
Mouth _____
Neck _____
Ears _____
Anus _____
Other (list) _____

What areas repulse you by direct contact? (check)

On an experiential basis how would you describe a woman's orgasm? If you have felt it, what did you feel?

When was the last time you had sexual intercourse? (give no.)
Hours _____ Months _____
Days _____ Years _____
Weeks _____ Never _____

How many different women have you had sexual intercourse with?
Less than 10 _____
10-20 _____
21-30 _____
31-40 _____
41-50 _____
over 50 _____

Is sexual intercourse ever painful to you?
Usually _____
Sometimes _____
Seldom _____
Never _____

List any kind of medication you take:

PERINEOMETER

#_____

NAME_____

Reading Unstimulated State_____

Date_____

Dr. comments from physical form:

_____

Breast Response - _____

Erection during stimulation:_____Cold_____Other_____

Nurse Babies:_____Vaginal Feelings_____Orgasm_____

Diastasis_____   Platform_____

Episiotomy_____

Identify Sexual Segments at 4:_____   at 8:_____

Sensory perception in vagina at: Suggested Positions_____

12_____   6_____   _____

1_____   7_____   _____

2_____   8_____   _____

3_____   9_____   _____

4_____   10_____   _____

5_____   11_____   _____

Other Comments:_____

_____

DATE_____   DATE_____   DATE_____
READING_____   READING_____   READING_____
COMMENTS_____   COMMENTS_____   COMMENTS_____

VAGINAL EXERCISES

————Contracting pubococcygeus muscle and holding for three seconds.

————Contracting pubococcygeus muscle rapidly (flicking).

————Breathing deeply, sucking air in and tightening the pubococcygeus muscle as air is inhaled.

————Bear down as if giving birth to a baby or if having a bowel movement. As you relax from bearing down, tighten the pubococcygeus muscle. Especially valuable just prior to intercourse.

All exercises should be done at various intervals throughout the day so the muscles will not become fatigued or tender. If soreness develops, cut down on the number and work up to the prescribed number. If you do the exercises at times you consistently do things, this will act as a reminder. i.e. driving car, washing dishes, talking on the phone, changing diapers, etc. Try and do a few exercises before getting up in the morning so all the weight of the internal organs is not on the muscle.

An easy way to be certain you are using the correct muscles is to sit on the toilet with knees as far apart as possible, and start and stop the flow of urine. Do not be upset if you have difficulty stopping the flow—that may take awhile. Don't expect results immediately. Regular exercises over a period of several months is often necessary before appreciable progress is noted. Once good muscle tone is established, maintenance exercises should be continued throughout your life where 10-25 contractions and flicks a day should be sufficient.

HUMAN SEXUALITY
ANNOTATED BIBLIOGRAPHY

This is a selected annotated bibliography on the subject of 'human sexuality.' Its purpose is to serve those professionals and interested persons who are involved in matters of human sexuality, be it in research, therapy, counseling, etc. This bibliography was compiled and annotated by Dave V. Kusisto at the Center for Marital and Sexual Studies in Long Beach, California.

Abortion—Contraception

Calderone, Mary S., M.D., *Abortion in the United States,* Harper & Row, 1958
   Various papers are presented that show abortion to be a social as well as a legal problem; much statistical evidence is cited although dated.

Calderone, Mary S., M.D., ed., *The Manual of Family Planning and Contraceptive Practice,* Williams & Wilkins Co., 1970
   Comprehensive text for professionals in the field; much on sexual attitudes and family planning behavior.

Cooke, Robert E., M.D., Andre E. Helleghers, M.D., Robert G. Hoyt and Herbert W. Richardson, *The Terrible Choice: The Abortion Dilemma,* Bantam Books, 1968
   The many issues of abortion are discussed without drawing conclusions. The book reports what happened at an International Conference on Abortion in 1967.

Demarest, Robert J. and John J. Sciarra, M.D., *Conception, Birth and Contraception—A Visual Presentation,* McGraw-Hill Book Co., 1969
   61 full color plates about human reproduction.

Fryer, Peter, *The Birth Controllers,* Stein & Day, 1965
   Examines the chief pioneers of birth control through history.

Guttmacher, Alan F., M.D., *Babies by Choice or by Chance,* Doubleday & Co., Inc., 1959
   When is contraception advised, a history of contraception, why sterilization, artificial insemination, etc.

Guttmacher, Alan F., M.D., *Birth Control,* Ballantine Books, 1961
   Medical techniques, the rhythm method, the new pills, contraceptive products, religious endorsements, popular myths.

Guttmacher, Alan F., M.D., ed., *The Case for Legalized Abortion Now,* Diablo Press, 1967
   Articles by various authors in support of legalized abortion.

Guttmacher, Alan F., M.D., Winfield Best and Frederick S. Jaffe, *Birth Control and Love,* The Macmillan Co., 1969
   A revised edition of *The Complete Book of Birth Control* written by officials of Planned Parenthood-World Population.

Lader, Lawrence, *Abortion,* The Bobbs-Merrill Co., Inc., 1966
   Well documented in reviewing abortion in the United States and in the world. Along with covering the religious issues of abortion reforms in the law are also presented.

Maginnis, Patricia and Lana Clark Phelan, *The Abortion Handbook for Responsible Women,* Contact Books, 1969

An outstanding book on abortion that covers the United States, the laws, religious attitudes, modern contraception, abortive methods used, the illegal abortion, rape, incest, etc.

Noonan, John T., *Contraception,* Harvard University Press, 1965

Traces the evolution of Roman Catholic thought on contraception.

Neubardt, Selig, M.D., *A Concept on Contraception,* Trident Press, 1967

A clear presentation of the techniques of contraception.

Peel, John and Malcolm Potts, M.D., *Textbook of Contraceptive Practice,* Cambridge University Press, 1969

An excellent book for the medical student and practicing physician or for other concerned individuals since this book is written in nontechnical language.

Pohlman, Edward, *Psychology of Birth Planning,* Schenkman Publishing Co., 1957

Summarizes the psychological aspects of birth planning, unwanted conceptions, etc.

Rainwater, Lee, *And the Poor get Children,* Quadrangle Books Inc., 1960

An empirical study on family planning among a small sample of the lower socioeconomic white and black couples.

Williams, Glanville, *The Sanctity of Life and the Criminal Law,* Alfred A. Knopf, 1957

A British jurist looks at society in relation to conception, sterilization, artificial insemination, abortion, suicide, and euthanasia.

Wood, H. Curtis, Jr., M.D., *Sex Without Babies,* Whitmore Publishing Co., 1967

A review of voluntary sterilization as a method of birth control.

Aging

Kaufman, M.D., Sherwin A., *The Ageless Woman—Menopause, Hormones and the Quest for Youth,* Prentice-Hall, Inc., 1967

Medical facts about aging with a bibliography of the medical literature.

Peterson, James A., *Married Love in the Middle Years,* Association Press, 1968

Identity crises, sexual problems, etc. in the later years.

Rubin, Isadore, *Sexual Life After Sixty,* Basic Books, 1965
The needs, problems, and attitudes of the elderly emphasizing a need to help the elderly in accepting their sexuality.

Anthologies and Encyclopedias

Beigel, Hugo G., ed., *Advances in Sex Research,* Harper & Row, 1963
A wide array of topics are covered in this anthology from the theoretical as well as the clinical perspective.

Caprio, Frank S., M.D., *Variations in Sexual Behavior,* Grove Press, Inc., 1955
The doctor covers such variations as masturbation, homosexuality, incest, and miscellaneous variations.

Charles, David and R. A. Chez, eds., *Sex on Campus,* Excerpta Medica Foundation, 1969
Based on a seminar that took up such issues as contraception, virginity and unwed pregnancy.

DeMartino, Manfred F., *Sexual Behavior and Personality Characteristics,* Citadel Press, 1963
An anthology of articles by 24 experts dealing with the relationship to sexual behavior and self-esteem.

Ellis, Albert, *Sex Without Guilt,* Borden Publishing Co., 1958
Various articles on sex which advocate a liberal attitude.

Ellis, Albert and Albert Abarbanel, eds., *The Encyclopedia of Sexual Behavior,* Hawthorn Books, Inc., 1961
Book of readings on many sexual topics by these two excellent authorities.

Geddes, Donald, ed., *An Analysis of the Kinsey Reports,* Mentor Books, 1958
16 experts evaluate both the male and the female Kinsey reports in this anthology, also included is the press and the public reaction to each volume.

Himmelhoch, Jerome and Sylvia F. Fava, eds., *Sexual Behavior in American Society,* W. W. Norton & Co., Inc., 1955
39 authorities analyze the Kinsey reports.

Krich, Aron, ed., *The Sexual Revolution, Krafft-Ebing, Ellis, Freud,* volume I, Delta Books, 1964
This volume reviews three of the classic: *Psychopathia Sexualis, Sexual Inversion,* and *Three Contributions to the Theory of Sex.*

Money, John, ed., *Sex Research: New Developments,* Holt, Rinehart and Winston, Inc., 1965

These papers reflect the major research done in the past decade.

Ruitenbeek, Hendrik M., ed., *Sexuality and Identity,* A Delta Book, 1970

A wide ranging exploration of the relationship between the individual's sense of self and his sexual needs.

Schmidt, J. E., M.D., *Libido,* Charles C. Thomas, 1960

A dictionary of slang from a medical lexicographer.

Sexology editors, *Guide to Sexology,* Paperback Library, Inc., 1965

A collection of articles that has appeared in the magazine *Sexology.*

Stiller, Richard, ed., *Illustrated Sex Dictionary,* Health Publications, 1966

A well illustrated dictionary of sex terms.

Winokur, George, M.D., ed., *Determinants of Human Sexual Behavior,* Charles C. Thomas, 1963

Authorities examine five major aspects of human sexuality.

Atlases

Clark, LeMon, M.D., ed., *Illustrated Sex Atlas,* Health Publications, 1963

Charts, diagrams and anatomical artwork on human sexuality.

Dickinson, Robert Latou, M.D., *Atlas of Human Sex Anatomy,* The Williams & Wilkins Co., 1949

A second edition of a pioneer attempt at pictorial statistics. A collection of actual measurements of the up-standing phallus, the form of an axis of re-creation and recreation.

Attitudes, Values and Standards

Allen, Gina, and Clement G. Martin, M.D., *Intimacy,* Cowles Book Co., Inc., 1971

An attempt to tie love and sex together using intimacy as the link. The authors have drawn heavily on methods developed by Encounter Groups, as well as the work of Masters and Johnson. Also, the authors present their own guide for determining one's intimacy potential.

Beach, Frank A., ed., *Sex and Behavior,* John Wiley & Sons, Inc., 1965

Many scholarly papers focusing on a wide variety of aspects of sexual behavior.

Beauvoir, Simone de, *The Second Sex,* Alfred A. Knopf, 1953

A look at the position of women in society; considered to be one of the first books advocating a women's liberation movement.

Bell, Robert R., *Premarital Sex in a Changing Society,* Prentice-Hall, Inc., 1966

Analyzes the changing nature of premarital sex, the forces influencing sexual morality, premarital sexual attitudes, and various marital situations as dependent upon social class, race, and religion.

Bell, Robert R. and Michael Gordon, eds., *The Social Dimension of Human Sexuality,* Little, Brown & Co., 1972

A sociological treatment of sexuality that covers premarital sex, marital sexuality, extramarital sex, female sexuality and the liberated woman, homosexuality, and commercialized sex.

Berne, Eric, M.D., *Sex in Human Loving,* Simon and Schuster, 1970

Looks at: talking about sex, why sex is necessary, the sexual act, exploitation of the sex organs, forms of human relationship, sexual games, and sex and well-being.

Bertocci, Peter A., *Sex, Love and the Person,* Sheed & Ward, 1967

A philosophical discourse that concludes that marriage is the most satisfying sexual relationship.

Chesser, Eustace, Dr., *An Outline of Human Relationships,* Hawthorn Books, Inc., 1960

A general and diversified treatment to provide one with a better understanding of human nature and of oneself.

Chesser, Eustace, *Is Chastity Outmoded?,* James A. Heinemann, Inc., 1960

Considers the arguments for and against premarital intercourse.

Chesser, Eustace, *Unmarried Love,* David McKay Co., Inc., 1965

A sexual code for single people from a leading British psychiatrist who emphasizes honesty rather than chastity.

Comfort, Alex, *Sex in Society,* Citadel Press, 1966

Indicates the type of sexual problems that need to be solved in society and considers the biological, sociological and legal aspects of sex.

Cox, Frank D., *Youth, Marriage and the Seductive Society,* William C. Brown Co., 1968

Deals with dating patterns, premarital sex, and problems of marriage.

Cuber, John F., and Peggy B. Harroff, *Sex and the Significant Americans,* Appleton-Century, 1965
   A study of the sexual behavior and attitudes of upper middle class couples between the ages of 35 and 55.

Dalrymple, Willard, *Human Sexuality and Sexual Responsibility,* McGraw-Hill Book Co., 1969
   Discusses such issues as roles in sex, attaining adult attitudes and behavior, achieving sexual satisfaction, decision making in sex, social problems of sex, family planning, sex education, dating, etc.

Edwards, John N., *Sex and Society,* Markham Publishing Co., 1972
   A sociological study of nonfamilial relationships such as: unmarried heterosexual relations, homosexuality, and prostitution; as well as familial relations: incest, marital sex, and extramarital sex.

Ellis, Havelock, *Studies in the Psychology of Sex,* F. A. Davis Co., 1927
   A classical study by one of the better known writers in the field of human sexuality that covers an array of topics.

Ellis, Albert, *The Art and Science of Love,* Lyle Stuart, 1960
   Provided in easy-to-read pages are the essentials as to physical know-how. A thousand misconceptions about sex are shattered; for its time it was a very liberal attitude toward sex.

Ellis, Albert, *The Folklore of Sex,* Grove Press, 1961
   Contrasting 200 novels to compare sexual attitudes in America from the 1950's to the 1960's.

Ellis, Albert, *The American Sexual Tragedy,* Lyle Stuart, Inc. 1962
   Companion to *The Folklore of Sex,* Ellis traces the change from the 1950's to the 1960's on the American attitudes of love, courtship, marriage, family relations, and divorce.

Fast, Julius, *The New Sexual Fulfillment,* Berkeley Medallion Books, 1972
   The author of *Body Language* discusses the trouble with sex, what we know about sexual response, sexual problems, orgasmic dysfunction, men without partners, etc.

Forel, August, M.D., *The Sexual Question,* Login Brothers, 1929
   A dated philosophical discourse on love, sexual evolution, sexual pathology, religion and sexual life, etc.

Foster, Jeanette H., *Sex Variant Women in Literature,* Vantage Press, Inc., 1956
   An examination through literature of the attitudes over time of lesbian relationships.

Frank, Lawrence, *The Conduct of Sex,* Grove Press, 1963
    The author discusses the need for a new sex ethic and sex education on a broad basis.

Freeman, Lucy and Martin Theodores, eds., *The Why Report,* Arthur Bernard, Inc., 1965
    33 of America's leading doctors and psychologists answer what the causes of frigidity are, whether a parent should appear nude before his children or not, what the meaning of perversion is, if unmarried couples may have sex without guilt or not, why people read marriage and sex manuals, why we have greater difficulty in dealing with our anger and hate than with our love, and many more.

Fromm, Erich, *The Art of Loving,* Harper & Row, 1956
    He explores the nature of love and one's ability to love in a philosophical manner.

Gagnon, John H. and William Simon, eds., *The Sexual Scene,* Transaction Books, 1970
    Articles that cover perspectives on the sexual scene, psychosexual development, how and why our sex standards are changing, hippie morality, our sex laws, abortion laws and their victims, pornography, and more.

Glover, Leland E., *Sex Life of the Modern Adult,* Belmont Books, 1961
    A report based on case histories that covers: premarital sex, impotence, frigidity, the wedding night, sex appeal, homosexuality, adulterous behavior, and after marriage.

Grant, Vernon W., *The Psychology of Sexual Emotion,* Longmans Green & Co., 1957
    A psychologist analyzes sexual love and the factors that come into play in sexual choices.

Grunwald, Henry, ed., *Sex in America,* Bantam Books, 1964
    Articles that deal with today's 'sexual revolution.'

Guyon, Rene, *Sex Life and Sex Ethics,* John Lane The Bodley Head Ltd., London, 1933
    A study of the sexuality in childhood, a study among primitive races, and among more industrialized societies. Guyon comes to some startling conclusions regarding the responsibility, modesty and justifiability of the general taboos affecting human relationships. He makes a penetrating study of many aspects of sex, and proceeds to attribute to our present sexual ethic, the prevalence of unhappiness and neurosis.

Guyon, Rene, *Sexual Freedom*, John Lane the Bodley Head Ltd., London, 1939

Need for and foundation of sexual freedom, practice of sexual freedom; guiding principles, consequences of the guiding principles of sexual freedom, message of sexual freedom, practice of sexual freedom, woman and sexual attitudes, sex relations, psycho-physiology of the erotic life.

Guyon, Rene, *The Ethics of Sexual Acts*, Alfred A. Knopf, 1958

Sexuality, adhesion to Freud's general principles, concordant evidence from primitive sexuality, physiology of sexuality, morality of sexual acts, sexual taboo and its origin, triumph of sexual taboo, the neuroses due to sexual repression, the mechanistic theory of sexuality in its relation to morals, the psycho-physiology of the so-called sexual aberrations, individualized love.

Hartman, William E., Marilyn Fithian, and Donald Johnson, *Nudist Society*, Crown Publishers, Inc., 1970

An authoritative sociological investigation of nudism, as studied at several nudist parks across the country.

Hefner, Hugh, *The Playboy Philosophy*, Parts I-IV, HMH Publishing Co., 1963-1965

Reprinted installments from *Playboy* magazine concerning Hefner's philosophy about sex.

Hofmann, Hans, *Sex Incorporated: A Positive View of the Sexual Revolution*, Beacon Press, 1967

To fully realize one's potentiality sexual experimentation should be utilized is the basic message here.

Hunt, Morton M., *The World of the Formerly Married*, McGraw-Hill Book Co., 1966

A report of what happens to middle class persons after separation or divorce. Combines personal experience with professional literature in the area.

Johnson, Cecil E., ed., *Sex and Human Relationships*, Charles E. Merrill Publishing Co., 1970

11 articles on various sexual topics by such authorities as Margaret Mead, Albert Ellis, Masters and Johnson, James McCary, Allan Fromme, and others.

Kardiner, Abram, M.D., *Sex and Morality*, The Bobbs-Merrill Co., Inc.

Modern sexual practices in America are examined by a psychoanalyst who believes that the changes in sex relations are a result of a general relaxation of sexual morality.

Katchadourian, Herant A., and Donald T. Lunde, *Fundamentals of Human Sexuality,* Holt, Rinehart, and Winston, Inc., 1972

Reviews fundamental questions, the biology of sex, sexual behavior, and culture in relation to sex. A complete and contemporary treatment of human sexuality.

Kirkendall, Lester A., *Premarital Intercourse and Interpersonal Relationships,* Julian Press, 1961

A study of what intercourse means to young men; a suggested framework of values for considering premarital intercourse is forwarded.

Krich, A. M., ed., *Men, The Variety and Meaning of Their Sexual Experience,* Dell Publishing Co., Inc., 1954

Includes the sexual life of man, sexual impulse in childhood, impotence and frigidity, marital complaints from wives, meaning of fatherhood, sex psychology of the unmarried adult, homosexual love, the art of love, etc.

Krich, A. M., ed., *Women, The Variety and Meaning of Their Sexual Experience,* Dell Publishing Co., Inc., 1956

Covers the sexual impulse and the art of love, prepuberty, youth and sex, potency and receptivity, marital complaints from husbands, natural childbirth, motherhood problems, the unmarried, prostitution, menopause, and love.

Lipton, Lawrence, *The Erotic Revolution,* Sherbourne Press, Inc., 1965

The author covers: the vanishing virgin, sex in the parochial schools, premarital sex, monogamy, the office wife, sex and violence, homosexuality, the changing concept of orgasm, etc.

Lowen, Alexander, M.D., *Love and Orgasm,* Signet Books, 1965

A psychiatrist explores the physical and psychic effects of orgasm as he tells why full release is possible only in mature heterosexual love.

Millett, Kate, *Sexual Politics,* Doubleday & Co., Inc., 1970

The author, a radical feminist, examines the relationship between the sexes and finds it essentially to be a political power struggle. She also examines the work of D. H. Lawrence, Norman Mailer, Henry Miller, Sigmund Freud, and Erik Erikson in relation to sexual politics.

Montagu, Ashley, *The Natural Superiority of Women,* The Macmillan Co., 1968

A plea for more love and understanding as well as social equality for the sexes.

Neubeck, Gerhard, *Extramarital Relations,* Prentice-Hall, Inc., 1969
The editor and 9 other contributors discuss the causes, varieties, and results of extramarital relations.

Otto, Herbert A., ed., *The New Sexuality,* Science and Behavior Books, Inc., 1971
Various articles that offer new attitudes on premarital sex, the affair, sex as fun, nudity, sexual life-styles, group marriage, and homosexuality.

Packard, Vance, *The Sexual Wilderness,* David McKay Co., Inc., 1968
The author examines the contemporary upheaval in male and female relationships.

The Playboy Advisor, *Sex Now,* HMH Publishing Co., 1971
Today's sex questions with now answers.

Reich, Wilhelm, *Selected Writings, An Introduction to Orgonomy,* Farrar, Straus and Cudahy, 1960
Includes the orgasm theory, therapy, the discovery of the orgone, orgonomic functionalism, orgone physics, cosmic orgone engineering, the emotional plague.

Reiss, Ira L., *Premarital Sexual Standards in America,* The Free Press of Glencoe, 1960
The sexual nature of man, America's sexual heritage, an objective approach to our sexual standards, the ancient double standard, permissiveness without affection, permissiveness with affection, permissive standards and negative-value consequences, permissive standards and positive-value consequences, our formal single standard of abstinence, future trends in premarital sexual standards.

Reiss, Ira L., *The Social Context of Premarital Sexual Permissiveness,* Holt, Rinehart and Winston, Inc., 1967
The scientific study of human sexuality, premarital sexual permissiveness examined in terms of race and dating, guilt feelings in adolescence, etc.

Roberts, Robert W., *The Unwed Mother,* Harper & Row, 1966
A collection of articles on the subject from various books and scholarly journals.

Russell, Bertrand, *Marriage and Morals,* Bantam Books, 1959
This great thinker's social testament on how marriage does not necessarily have to be a part of one's ethics.

Seward, Georgene H., *Sex and the Social Order,* McGraw-Hill Book Co., Inc., 1946

A psychologist examines sexual activity from primitive times to the present, with particular emphasis on one's sexual role and human sexual development from childhood to adulthood.

Shepard, Martin, M.D., *The Love Treatment,* Peter H. Wyden, Inc., 1971

Sexual intimacy between patients and psychotherapists is reported here in an objective manner.

Sorokin, Pitirim A., *The American Sex Revolution,* Porter Sargent, 1965

A poorly documented argument that a sexual permissiveness will lead to the downfall of our society.

Vincent, Clark E., *Unmarried Mothers,* The Free Press, 1961

A sociological study that breaks down the stereotype of the typical unwed mother coming from the lower social class.

Walker, Kenneth, *The Physiology of Sex,* Penguin Books, 1940

The author treats the topics: sexual differentiation, the sexual impulse, sex and marriage, romantic love, divorce, homosexuality, and sex and education.

Whitely, C. H. and Winifred M., *Sex and Morals,* Basic Books 1967

Discusses generally many of the sexual problems of today.

Young, Leontine, *Out of Wedlock,* McGraw-Hill Book Co., 1963

The author, based on her experience with 1000 women 350 of which were unmarried mothers, defines the major factors in illegitimacy.

Biology and Physiology

Chase, Herman B., *Sex: The Universal Fact,* Dell Books, 1965

Discusses physiology, mating, sex differentiation, and the new role of sex and love in society.

Fisher, Seymour, *Body Experience in Fantasy and Behavior,* Appleton-Century-Crofts, 1970

Significant developments in the study and understanding of body perception, demarcation of one's body limits from the world, body awareness in man, body awareness in woman, sex differences in body awareness and perception, body states in disturbed persons.

Goldman, George D. and Donald S. Milman, eds., *Modern Woman: Her Psychology and Sexuality,* Charles C. Thomas, 1969

A psychoanalytically oriented book that grew out of the post-doctoral program in psychotherapy at Adelphi University.

Greenhill, J. P., *Office Gynecology,* Year Book Medical Publishers, Inc., 1965

Control of conception, etc. One of the particularly relevant chapters is chapter #24, 'Genital Relaxation, Urinary Stress Incontinence and Sexual Dysfunction,' by Arnold H. Kegel, M.D. This is one of the few articles available to the student of human sexuality that deals with the pubococcygeus muscle and its role in sexual functioning in the female.

McCary, James L., *Human Sexuality,* Van Nostrand-Reinhold Books, 1967

A comprehensive textbook on human reproductive and sexual behavior from the aspects of anatomy, physiology, and sociology; detailed anatomical illustrations provided.

Counseling

Basset, William T., *Counseling the Childless Couple,* Fortress Press, 1969

Insightful in relation to the exploration of sexual prejudices, fears and attitudes of many couples who do not have children.

Broderick, Carlfred B. and Jessie Bernard, eds., *The Individual, Sex, and Society: A SIECUS Handbook for Teachers and Counselors,* The Johns Hopkins Press, 1969

A comprehensive volume that deals with sex education, sexuality, and the norms of sexual functioning.

Glassberg, Bert Y., *The Teenage Sex Counselor,* Barron's Educational Series, 1970

Deals with the integration of sex into personality, the differences between the sexes, and the expression of sexual feelings.

K, Mr. and Mrs., *The Couple,* Coward, McCann & Geoghegan, Inc., 1971

An account of a couple that allegedly underwent therapy at the Masters and Johnson sex clinic.

Money, John, *Sex Errors of the Body,* The Johns Hopkins Press, 1968

Such errors are looked into as sex-chromosomal anomalies, gonadal anomalies, fetal hormonal anomalies, internal-organ anomalies, external-organ anomalies, hypothalamic anomalies of sex, anomalies of assignment and rearing, pubertal hormonal anomalies, anomalies of gender identity, and procreative sex impairments.

Osofsky, Howard J., M.D., *The Pregnant Teenager,* Charles C Thomas, 1968

A discussion of the many problems of the pregnant teenager.
Stenchever, Morton A., *Human Sexual Behavior,* The Press of Case
Western Reserve University, 1970
     Designed to be a workbook in reproductive biology for any-
one who needs access to such information for counseling purposes.
Trainer, Joseph B., *Physiologic Foundations for Marriage Counseling,*
The C. V. Mosby Co., 1965
     How marriage looks, what men and women bring to marriage,
sex and the nervous system, physiological aspects of human sexuality, abortion, premarital examinations, man as the best medicine
for man, and the perspective for marriage.
Wahl, Charles Williams, M.D., ed., *Sexual Problems Diagnosis and
Treatment in Medical Practice,* The Free Press, 1967
     A thorough coverage of such areas as the female sex history,
physical symptoms that may reveal sexual conflict, the contributions of psychoanalytic theory, treatment of the homosexual patient, a philosophy of helping the sexual deviate, etc.
Willis, Stanley E., M.D., *Understanding and Counseling the Male
Homosexual,* Little, Brown and Co., 1967
     An excellent objective book for any one who may be involved
in the counseling of homosexuals.

Cross-Cultural

Beach, Frank A., ed., *Sex and Behavior,* John Wiley & Sons, Inc.,
1965
     Some recent studies of the evolution of sexual behavior, sexual
patterns and their regulation in a society of the Southwest Pacific,
sexual behavior in the Rhesus monkey, male dominance and mating behavior in baboons, etc.
Choisy, Maryse, *A Month Among the Girls,* Pyramid Books, 1960
     A famous French woman's documentary of the true life of the
Parisian demi-mode and those who pay her and prey on her.
Choisy, Maryse, *A Month Among the Men,* Pyramid Books, 1962
     There are 8,000 men in the monastic community of Mount
Athos, and for more than 1,000 years not one female has been
allowed to set foot there. Reporter Choisy disguised, extremely
thoroughly, as a man, became the first and only woman to crash
this male sanctuary and spend a month among the men. The result
is a sheer adventure in reporting and a daring glimpse of a man's
world.

Cleaver, Eldridge, *Soul On Ice*, McGraw-Hill, 1968
A recurrent theme throughout the book is the meaning of sex to the black man, and this is one of the few pieces of literature that discusses that topic specifically.

Edwardes, Allen and R. E. L. Masters, *The Cradle of Erotica*, The Judian Press Inc., 1963
    A study of Afro-Asian sexual expression and an analysis of erotic freedom in social relationships.

Epton, Nina, *Love and the French*, The World Publishing Co., 1959
    Examines French love from the Middle Ages through the Renaissance, the Classical Age, the eighteenth, nineteenth, and twentieth centuries.

Epton, Nina, *Love and the English*, Collier Books, 1960
    Examines the development of English love from the Middle Ages up through the centuries to the present.

Epton, Nina, *Love and the Spanish*, The World Publishing Co., 1961
    Similar to the previous two books, Epton historically examines love in Spain.

Ford, Clellan S. and Frank A. Beach, *Patterns of Sexual Behavior*, Harper & Row, Inc., 1951
    Sexual behavior information is presented from biological, cross-cultural and anthropological sources.

Henriques, Fernando, *Love in Action*, Macgibbon & Kee, Ltd., 1959
    Sexual behavior, courtship and marriage in a cross-cultural treatment.

Linner, Birgitta, *Sex and Society in Sweden*, Pantheon Books, 1967
    Describes the Swedish way of life, the national sex education program, and the current debate about sex roles going on in Sweden today. Shows how one country at least has recognized that the facts of sex are not only the individual's concern, but a responsibility that belongs to the whole society.

Marshall, Donald S. and Robert C. Suggs, *Human Sexual Behavior*, Basic Books, Inc., 1971
    A cross-cultural examination of the sexual customs in an Irish folk community, in Cayapa, Turu, Basongye, Mangaia, and the Marquesas.

Mead, Margaret, *Male and Female: A Study of the Sexes in a Changing Society*, William Morrow & Co., Inc., 1949
    An analysis of male and female behavior emphasizing the importance of culture.

Murdock, George P., *Social Structure,* The Free Press, 1965
  250 human societies are studied in terms of sexual and marital structures by this anthropologist.
Suggs, Robert C., *Marquesan Sexual Behavior,* Harcourt, Brace & World, Inc., 1966
  A study of these Polynesian people presently as well as past behavior.

Erotic Art

Brusendorf, Ove and Poul Henningsen, *Love's Picture Book: Love, Lust and Pleasure,* volumes I-IV, Lyle Stuart, 1960
  From the days of classic Greece up to a decade ago, these volumes compile a vast amount of erotic art depicted from several parts of the world.
Kronhausen, Phyllis and Eberhard, Drs., *Erotic Art,* two volumes, Grove Press, Inc., 1970
  A thorough collection of erotic art from several parts of the Western and Eastern world. The work of several artists is depicted.
Surieu, Robert, *Sarv-e Naz,* Nagel Publishers, 1967
  A collection of art work of various sorts on love and the representation of erotic themes from ancient Iran.

For Use With Young People

Anderson, Wayne J., *How to Understand Sex,* T. S. Denison & Co., Inc., 1966
  A frank discussion of sex decisions facing present and future college students, and suggesting guidelines for resolving them.
Anderson, Wayne J., *How to Discuss Sex with Teenagers,* T. S. Denison & Co., Inc., 1969
  Gives practical examples of how to communicate with teenagers.
Anderson, Wayne J., *How to Explain Sex to Children,* T. S. Denison & Co., Inc., 1971
  A handbook that will serve as a guide to parents and teachers as they work together in explaining sex to children.
Andry, Andrew C. and Steven Schepp, *How Babies Are Made,* Time-Life Books, Inc., 1968
  The story of reproduction is told concomitant with color photographs.

Arnstein, Helene, *Your Growing Child and Sex,* The Bobbs-Merrill Co., Inc., 1967

Much useful information for parents, prepared in consultation with the Child Study Association of America.

Bachelor, Evalyn N., Robert J. Ehrlich, Carolyn J. Harris and Robert M. White, eds., *Teen Conflicts: Readings in Family Life and Sex Education,* Diablo Press, 1968

A text for high school students in preparing them for the future.

Beck, Lester F., *Human Growth,* Harcourt, Brace & World, Inc., 1969

The story from mating to birth with cartoon-style drawings. Good for use with children.

The Child Study Association of America, *What to Tell Your Children About Sex,* Duell, Sloan & Pearce, 1964

Sex questions and answers for different age levels are presented.

Dalrymple, Willard, M.D., *Sex is for Real: Human Sexuality and Sexual Responsibility,* McGraw-Hill Book Co., 1969

The stress here is on individual decision-making in regards to one's sexual ethics.

Davis, Maxine, *Sex and the Adolescent,* The Dial Press, 1958

A frank discussion of many areas of sexual interest to the adolescent.

Driver, Heken, ed., *Sex Guidance for your Child,* Monona-Driver Publications, 1961

Sex attitudes of children as seen by a panel of family life authorities.

Duvall, Evelyn M., *Love and the Facts of Life,* Association Press, 1967

Discusses the emotional, social, and physical development of adolescents as based on 25,000 questions asked the author by teenagers.

Duvall, Evelyn M., *Why Wait Till Marriage,* Association Press, 1968

Within a religious framework, that deals one by one with popular arguments for premarital sex.

Eckert, Ralph, *Sex Attitudes in the Home,* Popular Library, 1963

This book covers all ages from infancy to engagement in how a parent may cope with the type of problems in relation to sex that may arise in the home.

Ets, Marie, *The Story of a Baby,* Viking Press, 1968

Designed for younger children on fertilization and gestation processes with clear drawings.

Gordon, Sol, *Facts About Sex for Exceptional Youth,* Charles Brown, Inc., 1969
   A simple book written for handicapped adolescents written on a sixth grade reading comprehension level.

Gottlieb, Bernhardt S., M.D., *What a Boy Should Know About Sex,* The Bobbs-Merrill Co., Inc., 1960
   In a series of casual chats the author discusses the type of issues a boy 11 to 14 years old may ask.

Gottlieb, Bernhardt S., M.D., *What a Girl Should Know About Sex,* The Bobbs-Merrill Co., Inc., 1960
   From case histories the author deals with concerns of girls from 12 to 18 years old.

Group for the Advancement of Psychiatry, *Sex and the College Student,* Atheneum Publishers, 1966
   Psychiatrists suggesting guidelines for college administrators in relation to sexual issues on residential campuses.

Gruenberg, Sidonie M., *The Wonderful Story of How You Were Born,* Doubleday & Co., Inc., 1959
   Explains for young children how life begins.

Gruenberg, Benjamin M. and Sidonie M., *The Wonderful Story of You,* Doubleday & Co., Inc., 1960
   Explains the story of life and human physiological development supported by pictures, diagrams, and charts.

Hatch, Claudia, ed., *What You Should Know About Sex and Sexuality,* Scholastic Book Services, 1969
   Sexual development at adolescence is covered, as is sex before marriage, contraception, pregnancy, VD, and changing morality.

Hegeler, Sten, *Peter and Caroline,* Abelard-Schuman Ltd., 1957
   A book translated from Danish designed for children 4 years old on up as an illustrated story book.

Hettlinger, Richard F., *Living With Sex: The Student's Dilemma,* The Seabury Press, Inc., 1966
   The difficult sexual problems facing college students within a religious framework.

Johnson, Eric W., *Love and Sex in Plain Language,* J. B. Lippincott Co., 1967
   Covers such aspects of youthful concerns as reproduction, masturbation, homosexuality, and contraception.

Lerrigo, Marion O. and Michael A. Cassidy, M.D., *A Doctor Talks to 9 to 12 Year Olds,* Budlong Press, 1964

Tells the story of reproduction along with a 27 page supplement for parents.

LeShan, Eda J., *Sex and Your Teenager,* David McKay Co., Inc., 1969
A guide for parents in dealing with their children.

Levine, Milton I., M.D., and Jean H. Seligmann, *A Baby is Born,* Grossett & Dunlap, Inc., 1964
In picture form it covers conception, the embryo's development, fetus, labor and birth.

Levine, Milton I., M.D., and Jean H. Seligmann, *The Wonder of Life,* Golden Press, 1964
Describes the creation of life and includes clear diagrams of the physiology of human reproduction and a glossary of sexual terms.

Maternity Center Association, *A Baby is Born,* Golden Press, 1962
In picture form the story from conception to birth is covered.

Meilach, Dona Z., and Elias Mandel, M.D., *A Doctor Talks to 5 to 8 Year Olds,* Budlong Press, 1966
An illustrated booklet telling the story of reproduction.

Nilsson, A. Lennart, Axel Ingelman-Sundberg, M.D., and Claes Wirsen, M.D., *A Child Is Born—The Drama of Life Before Birth,* Delacorte Press, 1967
Photographs from conception to birth, including the first ever taken of a live child within the womb.

Pomeroy, Wardell B., *Boys and Sex,* Delacorte Press, 1968
A sexual guide for teenage boys that they can easily understand.

Pomeroy, Wardell B., *Girls and Sex,* Delacorte Press, 1969
The author's views presented in an open way, addressed to the young girl.

Power, Jules, *How Life Begins,* Simon & Schuster, Inc., 1965
The story of reproduction, based from a television program, with photographs and drawings.

Reik, Theodore (introduction), *What Shall I Tell My Child?,* Crown Publishers, Inc., 1966
Sex education material for the Scandinavian countries as prepared by the Royal Board of Sweden in 1957.

Rubin, Isadore and Lester A. Kirkendall, eds., *Sex in the Adolescent Years: New Directions in Guiding and Teaching Youth,* Association Press, 1968
Teenage sex guidance comprehensively treated in 38 articles.

Southard, Helen F., *Sex Before Twenty—New Answers for Youth,* E. P. Dutton Co., 1967
Deals with the sexual concerns of young people in aiding them to discover their sexual role and own sexuality.

Wyden, Peter and Barbara, *Growing Up Straight,* Stein & Day, 1968
What parents can do in preventing their children from becoming homosexual.

General Texts for Physicians and Medical Students

Lloyd, Charles W., M.D., ed., *Human Reproduction and Sexual Behavior,* Lea & Febiger, 1964
Addressed to physicians, a comprehensive handbook.

Maccoby, Eleanor E., ed., *The Development of Sex Differences,* Stanford University Press, 1966
Authorities examine how sex differences develop in young children; it contains a 98 page annotated bibliography and a classified summary of research.

Oliven, John F., M.D., *Sexual Hygiene and Pathology,* J. B. Lippincott Co., 1965
A manual designed for the physician.

Vincent, Clark E., ed., *Human Sexuality in Medical Education and Practice,* Charles C Thomas, 1968
A text for medical schools, health personnel, and practicing physicians.

Wahl, Charles W., M.D., ed., *Sexual Problems,* The Free Press, 1967
A volume for physicians in aiding them to deal with some specific sexual problems their patients may have.

Young, William C., ed., *Sex and Internal Secretions,* Williams & Wilkins Co., 1961
Technical volumes concerned with human sexuality via biology, endocrinology and physiology.

Health Problems

Brenton, Myron, *Sex and Your Heart,* Coward-McCann, Inc., 1968
The problems of sexual activity for the person who has had a heart attack are reviewed.

History

Berrill, N. J., F.R.S., *Sex and the Nature of Things,* Pocket Books, 1953

This book explains the story of sex from earliest times to the present, the mating habits of all creatures, the place of sex in evolution, how the male is expendable in many species, how reproduction can continue without sex, etc.

Bloch, Iwan, Dr., *Marquis de Sade: His Life and Works,* Brittany Press, 1948

The story of his life as well as several excerpts from his most well known works.

Brecher, Edward M., *The Sex Researchers,* Little, Brown and Co., 1969

Describes sex research from the time of Havelock Ellis to the present.

Bullough, Vern L., *The History of Prostitution,* University Books, 1964

Examines prostitution as it has related to ancient societies, the great religions, in Western Europe, the nineteenth and twentieth centuries, and prostitution in a changing world.

Christenson, Cornelia V., *Kinsey, A Biography,* Indiana University Press, 1971

The story of the man who pioneered sex research in the United States and who founded the Institute for Sex Research, as told by one of his associates and friends.

Cleugh, James, *Love Locked Out,* Crown Publishers, Inc., 1964

Sexuality in Europe up to the Middle Ages.

Cole, William G., *Sex in Christianity and Psychoanalysis,* Oxford University Press, 1955

Contrasts the views of Jesus, Paul, Augustine, Calvin and Freud.

Comfort, Alex, *The Anxiety Makers,* Delta Books

A well documented account of how the medical profession has attempted to frighten people away from sexual activity, especially in the last century.

Feldman, David M., *Birth Control in Jewish Law,* New York University Press, 1968

A well documented study of Judaism through history as related to legal-moral teachings, sexual pleasure, contraception, abortion, and masturbation.

Fryer, Peter, *Mrs. Grundy: Studies in English Prudery,* London House, 1964

A study of the verbal taboos, prudery and euphemisms from the English language.

Gulik, Robert Hans van, *Sexual Life in Ancient China,* Humanities Press Inc., 1961
    A survey of Chinese sex and society from 1500 B.C. to the 17th century A.D.

Hays, Hoffman R., *The Dangerous Sex,* G. P. Putnam's Sons, 1964
    A historical analysis of the myth of feminine evil from various societies.

Hunt, Morton M., *The Natural History of Love,* Alfred A. Knopf, 1959
    Dilemma in Greece, bread and circuses, love and games, it is better to marry than to burn, the creation of the romantic ideal, the lady and the witch, the impuritans, the contact of two epidermises, the angel in the house, the age of love.

Kronhausen, Phyllis and Eberhard, Drs., *Erotic Fantasies, A Study of the Sexual Imagination,* Grove Press, Inc., 1969
    Sex fantasies are explored from early erotic literature, from folklore, and covering such topics as homosexuality, transsexualism, bondage, sadomasochism, incest fantasies, and generic bizarre fantasies.

Lewinsohn, Richard, M.D., *History of Sexual Customs,* Fawcett Premier, 1961
    Examines sexual customs from earliest recorded time to the present.

Marcus, Steven, *The Other Victorians,* Basic Books, 1966
    Reports the pornography of Victorian England, analyzing the official views of sexuality along with various examples of the pornography of the period.

Patai, Raphael, *Family, Love and the Bible,* Humanities Press, 1960
    An anthropological treatment of sex and the family in the Middle East.

Pearl, Cyril, *The Girl with the Swans Down Seat,* New American Library, 1956
    Here is an eye-opening tour of the gaudy, bawdy world that flourished beneath the self-rightously proper facade of Victorian England—that wild and raucous place where fashionable harlots rode with Duchesses in Rotten Row, while diplomats and gentry openly negotiated for their favors . . . and sometimes even married them.

Pomeroy, Wardell B., *Dr. Kinsey and the Institute for Sex Research,* Harper & Row, 1972

This is the story of a man who, when he died in 1956 at the age of 62, was one of the most widely known scientists of this century. Many feel that Kinsey ranked with Freud, and yet Kinsey the man was not very well known. This is his story, as told by one of his colleagues at the Institute for Sex Research who also helped author with Kinsey the two landmark studies on the male and the female from that institute.

Sherfey, Mary Jane, M.D., *The Nature and Evolution of Female Sexuality,* Random House, Inc., 1972

Based on her paper from 1966, which culturally and historically investigates the nature of female sexuality and suggests the possibility that female sexuality is literally an insatiable physical drive that has been powerfully repressed for the sake of orderly human relations.

Taylor, G. Rattray, *Sex in History,* Vanguard Press, Inc., 1954

Traces sexual attitudes in Western society and shows how current attitudes are historically related to past notions.

Young, Wayland, *Eros Denied: Sex in Western Society,* Grove Press, 1966

An historical analysis of 2000 years of Western culture and how the human sexual instincts have been suppressed and perverted.

Homosexuality

Bergler, Edmund, M.D., *Homosexuality: Disease or Way of Life,* Collier Books, 1962

An excellent treatment of some of the more crucial issues that concern the homosexual, his role in society, just what his condition is, and his future.

Bieber, Irving, M.D., *Homosexuality,* Basic Books, 1962

A psychoanalytic study of male homosexuals based on treatment programs.

Churchill, Wainwright, *Homosexual Behavior Among Males,* Hawthorn Books, Inc., 1967

The author argues that homosexuality should not be viewed as a crime or as a disease but rather as a merely one more utilization of natural capacities.

Cory, Donald Webster, *Homosexuality: A Cross Cultural Approach,* The Julian Press, Inc., 1956

Explores the subject of homosexuality from the historic world of Plato's Greece to the hard realities of Kinsey's America.

Cory, Donald Webster and John P. LeRoy, *The Homosexual and his Society,* The Citadel Press, 1963

An analysis of the creative homosexual, the body-builder, the male prostitute, the bisexual, and the 'queen.' Such locations are examined as the 'gay' bar, the parks, beaches, coffee houses, steam baths and gymnasiums where homosexual contacts may occur.

Cory, Donald W., *The Lesbian in America,* Citadel Press, Inc., 1964

Delineates some of the differences between lesbianism and male homosexuality and dispels many misconceptions about lesbians.

Ellis, Albert, *Homosexuality, Its Causes and Cure,* Lyle Stuart Inc., 1965

The famed psychotherapist presents a comprehensive study, packed with actual case histories, of the homosexual problem. He offers understanding, and most importantly, hope for a cure, by showing here how he copes with the problem in actual therapy sessions.

Hall, Radclyffe, *The Well of Loneliness,* Covici, Friede Publishers, 1929

One of the first books ever to be written on the subject with a positive and empathetic approach; the book is outstanding in its sincerity in dealing with homosexuality.

Henry, George W., M.D., *Sex Variants,* Harper & Brothers, 1941

A study of homosexual patterns based on case studies of men and women.

Hoffman, Martin, M.D., *The Gay World,* Basic Books, 1968

A social psychiatrist reports the existence of the homosexual in his 'natural milieu.'

Karlen, Arno, *Sexuality and Homosexuality,* W. W. Norton Co., Inc., 1971

A scholarly study of human sexuality, normal and abnormal.

Marmor, Judd, ed., *Sexual Inversion,* Basic Books Inc., 1965

An etiology of homosexuality, cross-cultural anthropological examination of homosexuality, legal and moral aspects, historical and mythological aspects. An examination of bisexuality; clinical treatment and follow up of 19 cases who received psychotherapy.

Robertiello, Richard C., M.D., *Voyage from Lesbos,* The Citadel Press, 1959

The psychoanalysis of a female homosexual.

Ruitenbeek, Hendrik M., *The Problem of Homosexuality in Modern Society,* E. P. Dutton & Co., Inc., 1963

A compilation of several essays that view the enigma of homosexuality by presenting a psychoanalytic discussion of the genesis and treatment of homosexuality from many points of view, and by including several essays which examine the topic purely as a sociological phenomenon.

Schofield, Michael, *Sociological Aspects of Homosexuality,* Little, Brown and Co., 1965

Homosexuals are studied from the prisons, while under treatment, and those not being treated or ever convicted.

Stearn, Jess, *The Sixth Man,* MacFadden Books, 1961

Based on interviews with several people the author forwards the notion that one out of every six males is a homosexual.

Stekel, William, Dr., *The Homosexual Neurosis,* Physicians and Surgeons Book Co., 1933

One of the earliest treatments of this topic, and for this fact alone a very interesting examination of homosexuality.

Weltge, Ralph W., ed., *The Same Sex: An Appraisal of Homosexuality,* United Church Press, 1969

This volume contains several articles, some reprints and some originals, which grew out of a United Church of Christ staff consultation on homosexuality.

West, D. J., M.D., *Homosexuality,* Aldine Publishing Co., 1968

Discusses historical facts about homosexual behavior in past cultures, suggests causes, and treatment and prevention.

Westwood, Gordon, *A Minority,* Longmans, Green and Co., Ltd., 1960

A report on the life of the male homosexual in Great Britain prepared for the British Social Biology Council.

Journals on Sexual Behavior

The Archives of Sexual Behavior, Phenum Publishing Co., 227 W. 17th St., New York, N.Y. 10011

Forum, Forum Press Ltd., 2 Bramber Road, London W14 9PB

The Journal of Sex Research, Society for the Scientific Study of Sex, Inc., 12 East 41st St., New York, N.Y. 10017 c/Robert V. Sherwin, Esq.

Medical Aspects of Human Sexuality, Clinical Communications Inc., 18 East 48th St., New York, N.Y. 10017

Publications Office, 1825 Willow Road, Northfield, Ill. 60093

Sexology, 200 Park Ave. South, New York, N.Y. 10003

Sexual Behavior, Interpersonal Publications, Inc., 299 Park Ave., New York, N.Y. 10017

Journals—Special Issues

The Annals of the American Academy of Political and Social Science, topic: "Sex and the Contemporary American Scene," March 1968, Oxford University Press, 200 Madison Ave., New York, N.Y. 10016

The Journal of Social Issues, topic: "The Sexual Renaissance in America," April 1966, The Heffernan Press Inc., 35 New St., Worcester, Mass.

Psychology Today, special issue: "Human Sexuality," July 1969, Communications/Research/Machines, Inc., 1330 Camino Del Mar, Del Mar, Calif. 92014

Journals—Selected Articles

Comarr, A. E., "Sexual Function Among Patients with Spinal Cord Injury," *Urologia Internationalis,* 25: 134-168 (1970)

Summarizes sexual behavior among 150 spinal cord injury patients.

Comfort, Alex, "Likelihood of Human Pheromones," *Nature*, April 16, 1971

Suggests the need for searching for functional human odors.

Comfort, Alex, "The Strange Role Smell Plays in Sex," *Sexology*, November 1971

An overview that suggests the importance of smell in sex with several examples.

Cooper, Alan J., M.D., "Factors in Male Sexual Inadequacy: A Review," and "Outpatient Treatment of Impotence," *The Journal of Nervous and Mental Disease*, vol. 149, no. 4, 1969

The first article merely reviews the literature; the second reports on 44 patients of a psychiatric outpatient department.

Freyhan, Fritz A., M.D., "Loss of Ejaculation during Mellaril Treatment," *American Journal of Psychiatry*, vol. 118, July 1961

Reports on 3 patients who experienced loss of ejaculation during Mellaril treatment.

Fox, C. A., H. S. Wolff and J. A. Baker, "Measurement of Intra-Vaginal and Intra-Uterine Pressures during Human Coitus by Radio-

Telemetry," *Journal of Reproduction and Fertility,* vol. 22, 1970

A unique and significant study though its population applicability may be questioned.

Fox, C. A., "Reduction in the Rise of Systolic Blood Pressure during Human Coitus by the Adrenergic Blocking Agent, Propranolol," *Journal of Reproduction and Fertility,* vol. 22 1970

Once again, how typical this experiment's results are of the population is not known.

Fox, C. A., A. A. A. Ismail, D. N. Love, K. E. Kirkham, and J. A. Loraine, "Studies on the Relationship between Plasma Testosterone Levels and Human Sexual Activity," *Journal of Reproduction and Fertility,* 1972

Very interesting and unique study.

Harnes, Jack A., M.D., "The Foreskin Saga," *Jama,* August 30, 1971

Raises the issue, but doesn't resolve it, whether or not circumcised men find sexual intercourse with women less pleasurable than do uncircumcised men.

Heath, Robert G., M.D., "Pleasure and Brain Activity in Man," *The Journal of Nervous and Mental Disease,* vol. 154 no. 1, 1972

A highly technical article reporting observations from two patients.

Margolese, M. Sydney, "Homosexuality: A New Endocrine Correlate," *Hormones and Behavior,* vol. 1, no. 2, February 1970

Suggests that homosexuals suffer from a androsterone-etiocholanolone imbalance; the first time this phenomenon has been noted in the literature.

McClintock, Martha K., "Menstrual Synchrony and Suppression," *Nature,* vol. 229, January 22, 1971

Synchrony and suppression among a group of women living together in a college dormitory suggest that social interaction can have a strong effect on the menstrual cycle.

Mosovich, Abraham, "Studies on EEG and Sex Function Orgasm," *Diseases of the Nervous System,* July 1954

A dated study of 3 males and 3 females studied during masturbation.

Nature, "Patterns of Hormone Excretion in Male and Female Homosexuals," vol. 234, December 31, 1971

A highly technical but important article.

Semans, James H., M.D., "Premature Ejaculation: A New Approach," *Southern Medical Journal,* vol. 49, April 1956

The urologist offered this treatment program several years ago now, but its tenets have been basically adapted and utilized by such sex therapist teams as Masters and Johnson, Hartman and Fithian, etc.; a highly significant and original contribution to sex research literature.

Serafetinides, E. A., M.D., "Assessing the Sexual Side Effects of Psychotropic Drugs," *Hospital Physician,* January 1972

The author examines the issues and gives decision-making guidelines.

Smith, Jackson A., M.D., "Psychogenic Factors in Infertility and Frigidity," *Southern Medical Journal,* April 1956

Long standing infertility corrected not infrequently by adoption of a child offers an interesting area of speculation as to psychiatric causes. The interpretation of frigidity in psychiatric terms is on much firmer ground.

Stoller, Robert J., "Etiological Factors in Male Transsexualism," *Transactions of the New York Academy of Sciences,* no. 4 February 1967

A very interesting study yet very short.

Language and Vocabulary

Beigel, Hugo G., *Sex from A to Z,* Frederick Ungar Publishing Co., Inc., 1961

Terms and concepts that relate to sexuality are discussed.

Trimble, John, ed., *5,000 Adult Sex Words and Phrases,* Brandon House, 1966

A compilation of sexual slang terminology.

Sagarin, Edward, *The Anatomy of Dirty Words,* Paperback Library, 1969

A study of the use and effect of taboo language on sexual attitudes.

Law, Pornography, Obscenity, Censorship

Clor, Harry M., *Obscenity and Public Morality,* University of Chicago Press, 1969

Examines censorship in a democracy, and concludes that carefully defined and strictly limited censorship is desirable and possible.

Haney, Robert W., *Comstockery in America: Patterns of Censorship and Control,* Beacon Press, 1960

An analysis of the problem of censorship in a free society.

Hyde, Montgomery H., *History of Pornography,* Farrar, Straus, & Giroux, Inc., 1965

An objective history of pornography.

John-Stevas, Norman St., *Life, Death and the Law,* Indiana University Press, 1961

Law and Christian morals in relation to contraception, artificial insemination, sterilization, homosexuality and other problems.

Kling, Samuel G., *Sexual Behavior and the Law,* Bernard Geis Associates, 1965

A question and answer format in dealing with popular sexual issues.

Kronhausen, Phyllis and Eberhard, *Pornography and the Law,* Ballantine Books, Inc., 1970

From excerpts in various literary works ranging from *Lady Chatterley's Lover* to *Candy,* the authors distinguish 'erotic realism' and 'hard core pornography' in their analysis.

Mueller, Gerhard, *Legal Regulation of Sexual Conduct,* Oceana Publishing, Inc., 1961

Acquaints the layman with the law, discusses reform of 'unenforceable' laws.

Paul, James C. and Murray L. Schwartz, *Federal Censorship: Obscenity in the Mail,* The Free Press, 1961

Two legal experts analyze censorship and offer suggestions for reforms.

Ploscowe, Morris, *Sex and the Law,* Ace Books, Inc., 1962

A judge shows the need for drastic reforms in our laws in regard to those laws that govern marriage, divorce and sexual behavior.

Slovenko, Ralph, ed., *Sexual Behavior and the Law,* Charles C Thomas, 1965

47 authorities discuss issues of sexuality and the law in this comprehensive collection of articles.

Marriage Manuals

Alden, Ray C., *Adult Sex Education,* volumes I and II, Psychosex Library Press, 1972

The first completely authentic, medically and psychologically authoritative, photo illustrated sex education course for adults in book form.

Bardis, Panos D., *The Family in Changing Civilizations*, Simon & Schuster, Inc., 1969
    Scholarly articles on ancient sex and family customs.

Bassett, Marion, *A New Sex Ethic and Marriage Structure*, Foresight Books Inc., 1961
    Material from various social sciences is presented in the form of a dialogue between two sociology teachers exploring the possibilities of a new marriage structure for today.

Clark, LeMon, M.D., *The Enjoyment of Love in Marriage*, The Bobbs-Merrill Co., Inc., 1949
    A frankly written and fully illustrated guide to sex as an expression of love and pleasure.

Collectors Publications, *Intercourse*, Collectors Publications, 1969
    A photo illustrated manual depicting various positions for sexual intercourse.

Comfort, Alex, ed., *The Joy of Sex*, Crown Publishers, Inc., 1972
    A well illustrated manual of sex education that deals with advanced lovemaking, the art of lovemaking, starters, main courses, sauces and pickles, and problems.

Deutsch, Ronald M., *The Key to Feminine Response in Marriage*, Random House, 1968
    A frank treatment of the physical and psychological aspects that control satisfaction in marriage. The book also is illustrated with photographs and line drawings, as well as information and exercises concerning the pubococcygeus muscle based on the work done by the late Dr. Arnold H. Kegel of the University of Southern California Medical School.

Ditzion, Sidney, *Marriage, Morals and Sex in America*, Bookman Associates, 1953
    Sexual attitudes from colonial times to the present.

Eichenlaub, John E., M.D., *The Marriage Art*, Dell Publishing Co., Inc., 1961
    A famed physician's frank, step-by-step guide to sexual joy and fulfillment for married couples.

Garrison, Omar, *Tantra: The Yoga of Sex*, The Julian Press, Inc., 1964
    This book offers, for the first time in the English language, a straightforward and easy-to-read manual of Tantric learning for the academician and general reader alike. Through the 'five disciplines of Tantra' offered in this volume the reader can "change their sex

lives from boredom and maladjustment into the complete, fulfilling and beautiful sacrament it was meant to be."

Harkel, Robert L., *The Picture Book of Sexual Love,* Cybertype Corp., 1969

A well illustrated book that covers the building of sexual power, sexual stimulation, building feminine passion, the dangers of fear, male capacity, and intercourse positions.

Hastings, Donald W., M.D., *A Doctor Speaks on Sexual Expression in Marriage,* Little, Brown and Co., 1966

Expert advice and instruction on achieving a harmonious sexual relationship, that includes an examination of normal sexual development, the background of marriage, the honeymoon, sexual intercourse, contraception, problems of impotence, premature ejaculation, frigidity, and menopause.

Hunt, Morton, *The Affair,* The World Publishing Co., 1969

91 participants in extramarital affairs as reported via questionnaire or in depth interview.

Lindsey, Ben B., and Wainwright Evans, *The Companionate Marriage,* Boni & Liveright, 1927

A classic for its time that emphasized the acceptance of birth control within marriage as well as an acceptance and tolerance towards divorce.

McCary, James Leslie, *Human Sexuality,* D. Van Nostrand Co., Inc., 1967

A contemporary marriage manual that is complete in its coverage of physiological and psychological factors of sexual behavior.

Miles, Herbert J., *Sexual Happiness in Marriage,* Zondervan Book, 1967

A positive approach to the details and techniques one should know to achieve a healthy and satisfying sexual relationship.

Mudd, Emily H., Howard E. Mitchell and Sara B. Taublin, *Success in Family Living,* Association Press, 1965

Based on a study of 100 families to see what factors, including sexual behavior, make for successful functioning in the family.

Neubeck, Gerhard, ed., *Extra-Marital Relations,* Prentice-Hall, Inc., 1969

Several papers on the subject by sociologists and psychologists.

O'Conner, L. R., *The Photographic Manual of Sexual Intercourse,* Pent-R Books, Inc., 1969

150 photographs depicting various coital positions, as well as a commentary on the practicality of these positions, their advantages and disadvantages, etc.

O'Relly, Edward, *Sexercises, Isometric and Isotonic,* Crown Publishers, Inc., 1967

Your amazing sex drive, we have become a race of sex cripples, where sexual relationships go wrong, helpful sex training advice, warm-up and flexibility exercises, the vitally important pelvic thrust, more sex enjoyment with the gluteal squeeze, put thigh action into the sex act, a flabby midregion can ruin your sex life, and special sexometric sexercises.

Rainwater, Lee, *Family Design—Marital Sexuality, Family Size and Contraception,* Aldine Publishing Co., 1965

From 409 interviews, the research offers valuable insight into the difference in sexual attitudes among different social classes and races.

Schulz, Esther D. and Sally R. Williams, *Family Life and Sex Education: Curriculum and Instruction,* Harcourt, Brace & World, Inc., 1968

A useful book in teacher-training and curriculum planning.

Schur, Edwin M., ed., *The Family and the Sexual Revolution,* Indiana University Press, 1964

Readings on changing sex standards, women, and birth control.

Tabori, Paul, *A Pictorial History of Love,* Spring Books, Drury House, 1966

Love among the primitives, gods and mortals, love in the east, love on the Mediterranean, love and Christianity, lists of love, rebirth of Venus, new horizons, from Don Juan to Cassanova, the good old days, between the wars, the endless story, famous lovers.

Terman, Lewis M., *Psychological Factors in Marital Happiness,* McGraw-Hill Book Co., Inc., 1938

Another classic for its time; a thorough empirical investigation with an abundance of statistics and numerations relating to an unveiling of the psychological variables that seemed to make for a successful marriage.

Van De Velde, Th. H., *Ideal Marriage,* Random House, 1957

One of the first marriage manuals to receive the endorsement of the medical profession. The book is very thorough for its time and very clear and easy to follow in the advice that it gives.

Novels

Bannon, Ann, *Journey to a Woman,* Gold Medal Books, 1960
A novel about a woman married for nine years, Beth, who then begins a lesbian relationship with Vega, the woman who could make life worth living.

Malfetti, James L. and Elizabeth M. Eidlitz, *Perspectives on Sexuality,* Holt, Rinehart & Winston, Inc., 1972
A literary collection that reviews a vast amount of material.

M de F, *The Gay Year,* Lancer Books, 1965
The revealing novel of two men and a forbidden passion.

Smith, T. R., ed., *Poetica Erotica,* Crown Publishers, 1949
A collection of rare and curious amatory verse.

Prostitution

Adler, Polly, *A House is not a Home,* Rinehart and Co., Inc., 1953
A personal account of a woman's life as a prostitute.

Choisy, Maryse, *Psychoanalysis of the Prostitute,* Philosophical Library, Inc., 1961
This famous French writer carefully analyzes the biographies and case histories of call girls, street walkers, pimps, and their clientele.

Greenwald, Harold and Aron Krich, *The Prostitute in Literature,* Ballantine Books, 1960
Examines literature from the Biblical world, Egypt, Babylon, Greece, India, Germany, France, London, New York, Vienna, Russia, and Dublin.

Henriques, Fernando, *Prostitution and Society* (I), *Prostitution in Europe and the New World* (II), *Modern Sexuality* (III), Macgibbon & Kee, Ltd.
A sociological survey of prostitution from classical times to the present.

Marlowe, Kenneth, *Mr. Madam, Confession of a Male Madam,* Sherbourne Press, 1964
Marlowe was an active homosexual, a female impersonator, a male whore in an all female cathouse, and the 'madam' of a homosexual whorehouse. This is one of the most startlingly candid homosexual autobiographies ever written.

Current sex concerns are presented in such an ethical framework that the author believes will work for today.

Spitzer, Walter O. and Carlyle L. Saylor, eds., *Birth Control and the Christian*, Tyndale House Publishers, 1969
This comprehensive book grew out of a symposium on The Control of Human Reproduction.

Thielicke, Helmut, *The Ethics of Sex*, Harper & Row, 1964
A Protestant view of sexuality which attempts to combine the theological with the scientific.

Trevett, R. F., *The Church and Sex*, Hawthorn Books, Inc., 1958
A Roman Catholic interpretation of sexuality.

Wilson, John, *Logic and Sexual Morality*, Pelican Books, 1965
Morality and sex education discussed by a former professor of religion.

Wood, Frederic C., Jr., *Sex and the New Morality*, Newman Press, 1968
Sexual morality is discussed in relation to situation ethics by a former college chaplain.

Wynn, John C., ed., *Sex, Family and Society in Theological Focus*, Association Press, 1966
Sex and the family are examined in a religious framework.

Reports of original research, and relating to such reports

Bartell, Gilbert D., *Group Sex*, Peter H. Wyden, Inc., 1971
Based on a three year study by the author and his wife of 280 'swingers.' In using an anthropological approach the book is free of value judgments from their observations. He concludes, and explains why, that swinging is definitely part of our current culture and is not a passing fad.

Belliveau, Fred and Lin Richter, *Understanding Human Sexual Inadequacy*, Little, Brown and Co., 1970
Written in nontechnical language, this book explores the findings reported in the classic Masters and Johnson *Human Sexual Inadequacy*.

Brecher, Ruth and Edward, *An Analysis of Human Sexual Response*, The New American Library, Inc., 1966
In layman's language a critique of the investigations by Masters and Johnson that included the observing under laboratory conditions of 694 men and women who engage in a variety of sexual activities.

Bromley, Dorothy Dunbar, and Florence Haxton Britten, *Youth and Sex,* Harper & Row, 1938
A dated study of 1300 college students.

Byler, Ruth V., ed., *Teach Us What We Want to Know,* Mental Health Materials Center, 1969
From a survey of 5,000 Connecticut school children to discover their interests and problems relating to various areas of health including sex education.

Committee on Homosexual Offenses and Prostitution, *The Wolfenden Report,* Stein and Day, 1963
The Moral Welfare Council in conjunction with the Church of England prepared this report for the British Parliament. The recommendations of the committee, upon examining homosexuality in Britain, amounted to a removal of the criminality aspect of homosexual relationships.

Davis, Katherine Bement, *Factors in the Sex Life of Twenty-Two Hundred Women,* Harper & Brothers, 1929
Even though dated, this study offers an interesting treatment of contraception, marital satisfaction and happiness, auto-erotic practices, and homosexuality.

Ehrmann, Winston, *Premarital Dating Behavior,* Henry Holt and Co., 1959
An authoritative report on the sex behavior of modern American youth with much statistical data.

Fromme, Allan, *Understanding the Sexual Response in Humans,* Pocket Books, 1966
A critical review of the Masters and Johnson research by the author of *Sex and Marriage* and *The Ability to Love.*

Gebhard, Paul H., Wardell Pomeroy, Clyde E. Martin, Cornelia V. Christenson of the Institute for Sex Research, *Pregnancy, Birth and Abortion,* John Wiley & Sons, Inc., 1958
An interview study of 7,000 women concerning pregnancy before, during and after marriage, while separated, divorced, widowed, and the way in which their pregnancy ended. Statistics are presented to show the frequency of such events occuring and in what segment they are more likely to occur.

Gebhard, Paul and John J. Gagnon, Wardell B. Pomeroy, Cornelia V. Christenson of the Institute for Sex Research, *Sex Offenders,* Harper & Row, 1965

Personal interviews of more than 1,500 convicted sex offenders to determine if and how persons imprisoned for various sex offenses differ from those who have not, and how they differ from one another. In addition, the Institute has made use of the sexual histories of two control groups: a normal group, consisting of men never convicted for any offense, and a group of men convicted for various crimes not sexual in nature.

Gebhard, Paul H., Jan Raboch and Hans Giese, *The Sexuality of Women,* Stein and Day, 1970

Various aspects of female sexuality are explored by these behavioral scientists.

Gillete, Paul J., ed., *The Layman's Explanation of Human Sexual Inadequacy,* Award Books, 1970

A close look at the second Masters and Johnson report. It offers the key to eliminating sexual problems, proven successful in 80 per cent of the cases.

Kinsey, Alfred C., Wardell B. Pomeroy and Clyde E. Martin, *Sexual Behavior in the Human Male,* W. B. Saunders Co., 1948

The first of the famous Kinsey reports that pioneered an empirical study of male sexual behavior that reported the gap between actual behavior and officially sanctioned behavior.

Kinsey, Alfred C., Wardell B. Pomeroy, Clyde E. Martin and Paul H. Gebhard, *Sexual Behavior in the Human Female,* W. B. Saunders Co., 1953

This classic volume from the Institute for Sex Research is the companion to the volume on male sexual behavior, and this volume contrasts the results of the two books as well as being more statistically sophisticated.

Kirkendall, Lester A., *Premarital Intercourse and Interpersonal Relationships,* Angora Softback, 1966

A research study of interpersonal relationships based on case histories of 668 premarital intercourse experiences, reported by 200 college level males.

Lehrman, Nat, *Masters and Johnson Explained,* Playboy Press Book, 1970

Offers a clear and concise review of both *Human Sexual Inadequacy* and *Human Sexual Response* by Masters and Johnson.

Lewis, Barbara, *The Sexual Power of Marijuana,* Peter H. Wyden, Inc., 1970

An intimate report of 208 adult middle-class users.

Margolis, Herbert F., and Paul M. Rubenstein, *The Groupsex Tapes,* David McKay Co., Inc., 1971

98 participants who were interviewed about the newest and most revolutionary release of sexual inhibitions. The participants relate what they do, why they do it, and what it reveals about new dimensions in male-female relationships.

Masters, William H., M.D., and Virginia Johnson, *Human Sexual Response,* Little, Brown and Co., 1965

A report of the research and clinical findings of various types of sexual response of men and women during sexual activity, pregnancy, and when aging. The first publication from the Masters and Johnson clinic.

Masters, William H., M.D., and Virginia E. Johnson, *Human Sexual Inadequacy,* Little, Brown, and Co., 1970

The second now classic publication from the Reproductive Biology Research Foundation that reports the therapy team's approach in dealing with the more than five hundred couples who have been sexually dysfunctional that Masters and Johnson have treated in eleven years of clinical work.

Robbins, Jhan and June, *An Analysis of Human Sexual Inadequacy,* Signet Book, 1970

Written in layman's terms and clearing up many of the ambiguities from the original text of the Masters and Johnson volume.

Shiloh, Ailon, *Studies in Human Sexual Behavior: The American· Scene,* Charles C Thomas, 1970

40 articles on sex research. The contributors include those who could be considered members of Who's Who in the area of sex research, mainly from the fields of medicine and sociology, but also from psychology, law, marriage and family life education, anthropology, criminology, public health, and education.

Stoller, Robert J., M.D., *Sex & Gender,* Science House, 1968

This book primarily concerns itself with the development of masculinity and feminity, examining the patients with biological abnormalities, patients without biological abnormalities, and aspects of treatment.

Symonds, Carolyn, *Sexual Mate Swappers,* 1968

Research done on the 'peripheral behavior of sexual mate swappers' as a thesis for the Master of Arts degree at University of California at Riverside. The literature was reviewed as well as questioning mate swappers in this sociological study.

Sex Education

Baruch, Dorothy W., *New Ways in Sex Education,* McGraw-Hill Book Co., 1959

The various stages of growth up to adolescence are examined, emphasizing for one to deal with feelings and not just facts in sex education.

Bohannan, Paul, *Love, Sex and Being Human,* Doubleday & Co., Inc., 1969

This anthropologist believes that human behavior best results from knowledge and not upon fear or superstitution.

Brown, Fred and Rudolf R. Kempton, M.D., *Sex Questions and Answers,* McGraw-Hill Book Co., 1950

Questions of those in the Armed Services are answered, and these issues are typical of general adult groups.

Chicago Museum of Science and the University of Illinois, *The Miracle of Growth,* University of Illinois

Conception, birth, and infancy to adolescence are covered as well as heredity.

Child Study Association of America, *Sex Education and the New Morality,* Columbia University Press, 1967

Papers from the 1966 Annual Conference of the Child Study Association that deal with sexuality and personal identity, social forces, the arts, and the search for a meaningful ethic.

Crawley, Lawrence W., M.D., James Malfetti, Ernest I. Stewart and Nina Vas Dias, *Reproduction, Sex, and Preparation for Marriage,* Prentice-Hall Inc., 1964

Discussion of sex and reproductive problems.

Farber, Seymour M., M.D., and Roger Wilson, M.D., eds., *Sex Education and the Teenager,* Diablo Press, 1967

Non-technical papers from a symposium of the University of California Medical School at San Francisco.

Fast, Julius, *Body Language,* M. Evans and Co., Inc., 1970

This popular book takes up: the body is the message, of animals and territory, how we handle space, the masks men wear, the silent language of love, etc.

Flanagan, Geraldine Lux, *The First Nine Months of Life,* Simon & Schuster, Inc., 1962

What happens between fertilization and birth, with photographs.

Gilderhus, Grant and Elaine M. Larson, eds., *Sex Education: Approach/Program/Resources for the Parish,* Sacred Design, 1968
A guide that churches can use in planning sex education at the upper elementary through adult levels of education.

Hegeler, Inge and Sten, *The XYZ of Love,* Crown Publishers, Inc., 1970
Frank answers to every important question about sex in today's world, by the authors of *ABZ of Love.*

Johnson, Warren R., *Human Sex Education and Sex Education,* Lea & Febiger, 1963
Sex as subject matter, biology and etymology of sex, modern sexual customs in historical perspective, modern marriage, theories of sex education, and more.

Johnson, Warren R., *Human Sexual Behavior and Sex Education,* Lea & Febiger, 1968
Discusses various theories of sex education as well as problems relating to human sexuality.

Jones, Kenneth L., Louis W. Shainberg and Curtis O. Byer, *Sex,* Harper & Row, 1969
Examines before marriage, marriage, deviate sexual behavior, sexual anatomy and physiology, sexual response and technique, fertility control, infertility, pregnancy, heredity, and sex education of children.

Kahn, Fritz, M.D., *Our Sex Life,* Alfred A. Knopf, 1948
Examines the sexual functions, sexual intercourse, the hygiene of sex life, prostitution, juvenile sex life, sex life of unmarried people, etc.

Legman, G., *The Intimate Kiss,* Paperback Library, 1971
The modern classic of oral erotic technique, originally from the hardback *Oragenitalism,* The Julian Press, Inc., 1969

Mazur, Ronald M., *Commonsense Sex,* Beacon Press, 1968
Such subjects are covered as masturbation, petting, mutual masturbation, contraception, pre-marital intercourse, and homosexuality.

McCary, James Leslie, *Sexual Myths and Fallacies,* Van Nostrand Reinhold Co., 1971
Many adult questions are answered ranging over a list of topics that includes sexual physiology and functioning, sex drive, reproduction and birth control, homosexuality, sexual disorders and abnormalities, sex offense, and other fallacies.

Montagu, Ashley, *Touching,* Columbia University Press, 1971
   A unique contribution to human sexuality in this exploration into the human significance of the skin.

Morton, R. S., M.D., *Venereal Diseases,* Penguin Books, 1966
   Treatment discussed as well as the various diseases in a sober and factual manner.

Otto, Herbert A., M.D., and Roberta, *Total Sex,* Peter H. Wyden, Inc., 1972
   This book not only offers new attitudes in relation to human sexuality, but is also a book for doing; the book includes 50 scientifically tested sex experiences and games with reports from hundreds of couples who have learned these techniques and now enjoy total sex.

Parmelee, Maurice, *The Play Function of Sex,* Vantage Press, 1966
   Uninhibited, far-ranging, challenging, its forthright indictment of what the author believes to be Occidental society's failure to deal sanely with a fundamental human need, this is a book whose aim is to clarify the real function of sex, and to offer a modern-day re-evaluation of its importance to the total scheme.

Powers, G. Pat and Wade Baskin, eds., *Sex Education: Issues and Directives,* Philosophical Library, Inc., 1969
   A compilation of articles focusing on sex education.

Reuben, David R., M.D., *Everything You Always Wanted to Know About Sex, But Were Afraid to Ask,* David McKay Co., Inc., 1969
   The intention of the psychiatrist was for the book to be a source of information for the layman, but the book is riddled with a number of errors and an overall weakness in its approach.

Rubin, Isadore and Lester A. Kirkendall, eds., *Sex in the Childhood Years,* Association Press, 1970
   Various reprints of articles are presented by experts in sex education.

SIECUS, eds., *Sexuality and Man,* Charles Scribner's Sons, 1970
   A collection of the first 12 study guides from SIECUS.

Stoller, Robert J., M.D., *Sex and Gender,* Science House Inc., 1968
   A discussion of the development of masculinity and feminity, based on patients with aberrations in this development.

Taylor, Donald L., ed., *Human Sexual Development,* F. A. Davis Co., 1970
   31 contributors discuss such perspectives of sex education as the biological foundations, psychosexual development, sexual problems, and sex education in general.

Wyden, Peter and Barbara, *Inside the Sex Clinic,* World Publishing Co., 1971

The president of the book publishing co. and his wife relate their story of the therapy they received, and the successful results therefrom, at the Masters and Johnson clinic.

Sex Roles

Bernard, Jessie, *The Sex Game,* Prentice-Hall, Inc., 1968

A sociologist examines the communication and the interpersonal relationships that exist between people involved in sex and marriage.

Brenton, Myron, *The American Male,* Coward-McCann, Inc., 1966

A study of the notions the male perceives as necessary in being masculine, re-evaluates these notions, and presents an alternative male image.

DeWit, Gerard, *Symbolism of Masculinity and Feminity,* Springer Publishing Co., 1963

Empirically investigates word associations to test the validity of the Freudian doctrine of sexual symbolism.

Downing, George, *The Massage Book,* Random House, 1972

How to massage all the parts of the body with several illustrations to accompany the directions.

Gunther, Bernard, *Sense Relaxation Below Your Mind,* Collier Books, 1968

Many sensitivity exercises are explained that can be used with a couple as well as in a group. There are several photographs.

Ruitenbeek, Hendrik, *The Male Myth,* Dell Books, 1967

Explores many of the myths concerning the American male in relation to the adult as husband, provider, lover, and father.

Schutz, William C., *Here Comes Everybody,* Harper & Row, Publishers, 1971

By the author of *Joy,* who presents here encounter as a culture by describing such techniques as rolfing and the connections between bodily expression and how we think. This book is everyman's guide and manual to encounter.

Sexual Deviance

Benjamin, Harry, M.D., *Transsexual Phenomenon,* Julian Press, 1966

Analyzes those persons who want to change their sex along with case histories of those who already have.

Breedlove, William and Jerrye, *Swap Clubs,* Sherbourne Press, 1964
    The swinging society, the swinging groups, the swingers, personal observations and opinions of the authors.

Chideckel, Maurice, M.D., *Female Sex Perversion,* Eugenics Publishing Co., 1935
    This dated study investigates: historical perspective, Oedipus complex, castration fear, homosexuality, tribadism, sadism, and masochism, masturbation, kleptomania, fellatio, narcissism, transvestism, frigidity, nymphomania, exhibitionism, prostitution, anal eroticism, bestiality.

Gagnon, John H. and William Simon, eds., *Sexual Deviance,* Harper & Row, 1967
    Most particular attention goes to homosexuality and prostitution in this volume.

Green, Richard, M.D., and John Money, eds., *Transsexualism and Sex Reassignment,* The Johns Hopkins Press, 1969
    Over 30 contributors in this encyclopedic text representing different disciplines.

Guttmacher, Manfred S., M.D., *Sex Offenses,* W. W. Norton & Co., Inc., 1961
    This psychiatrist reviews the problems, causes and prevention of various sex offenses.

Henry, George W., *Society and the Sex Variant,* The Macmillan Co., 1965
    A famous psychiatrist's study of society's attitudes toward sexual maladjustment.

Hirsch, Edwin W., M.D., *Impotence and Frigidity,* The Citadel Press, 1966
    A famous authority describes the causes and treatment of sexual impotence in the male and sexual frigidity in the female.

Hirschfeld, Magnus, M.D., *Sexual Pathology,* Emerson Books, Inc., 1940
    Studies the 'derangements of the sexual instinct' such as hypereroticism, impotence, and many more.

Hopper, Columbus B., *Sex in Prison,* Louisiana State University Press, 1969
    A sociology professor advocates conjugal prison visits based on his evaluation of the program at the Mississippi State Penitentiary at Parchman.

Klein, Leo, *Normal and Abnormal Sex-Ways,* Belmont Books, 1962

From case histories emotional problems are explored that include alcoholism, exhibitionism, fetishism, frigidity, homosexuality, impotence, nymphomania, phobias, prostitution, satyriasis, voyeurism and other deviations.

Krafft-Ebing, Richard von, *Psychopathia Sexualis,* Pioneer Publications, Inc., 1953
One of the best known books on sexual pathology.

Lorand, Sandor, M.D., *Perversions, Psychodynamics and Therapy,* Random House, Inc., 1956
Examines such perversions as homosexuality and sado-masochism as well as discussing therapy programs.

Rickles, Nathan K., *Exhibitionism,* J. B. Lippincott Co., 1950
From clinical evidence a psychiatrist discusses the causes, diagnosis and treatment of this sexual deviance.

Robinson, Marie N., M.D., *The Power of Sexual Surrender,* Signet Book, 1959
The doctor, based on case histories, examines and dispels various long-standing myths concerning women, and shows how frigidity can be turned to fulfillment through self-knowledge and the power of sexual surrender.

Sagarin, Edward and Donal E. J. MacNamara, eds., *Problems of Sex Behavior,* Thomas Y. Crowell Co., 1968
Selections from books discuss such problems as illegitimacy, prostitution, homosexuality, incest, rape, child molestation, and pornography.

Schur, Edwin M., *Crimes Without Victims: Deviant Behavior and Public Policy,* Prentice-Hall, Inc., 1965
A sociological analysis of such areas as drug addiction, abortion, and homosexuality.

Stekel, Wilhelm, M.D., *Sadism and Masochism, The Psychology of Hatred and Cruelty,* Liveright Publishing Corp., 1939
This classic examines the polyphony of thought, the psychology of hatred and cruelty, the theory of the resistance, the definition of sadism and masochism, relation of sadomasochism to homosexuality, sadomasochism and infantilism, sodomy and sadism, and compassion.

Stekel, Wilhelm, M.D., *Bi-Sexual Love,* Emerson Books, Inc., 1946
The doctor's view of homosexuality is offered, as well as discussion of Don Juan and Cassanova, Satyriasis and Nymphomania,

the modern Messalina, the role of infection, and the significance of trauma.

Storr, Anthony, *Sexual Deviation,* Pelican Original, 1964

Reviews that behavior usually thought to be perverted, examining its origins and making a plea for people to be more understanding for those who cannot achieve 'normal' sexual relationships.

Ward, David A. and Gene G. Kassebaum, *Women's Prison: Sex and Social Structure,* Aldine Publishing Co., 1965

Two sociologists explored by questioning inmates and staff the dynamics of prison behavior, and report the large amount of homosexual behavior taking place.

Weinberg, S. Kirson, M.D., *Incest Behavior,* Citadel Press, Inc., 1963

Based on interviews with 200 people who have been involved in incestuous relationships.

Sexual Functioning and Dysfunctioning

Fink, Paul J., M.D., and Van Buren O. Hammett, *Sexual Function and Dysfunction,* F. A. Davis Co., 1969

Papers that were delivered at a psychiatric symposium that include coverage of sexual functioning, sex education and conception.

Hastings, Donald W., M.D., *Impotence and Frigidity,* Dell Publishing Co., Inc., 1963

This book is written for practicing physicians with the hope that it may aid in their understanding of several of the common sexual dysfunctions. Those who counsel people in regards to sexual matters may also find the book beneficial.

Johnson, John, M.D., *Disorders of Sexual Potency in the Male,* Pergamon Press, Inc., 1968

76 patients at the Maudsley Hospital in London were studied who had potency problems.

Marmor, Judd, M.D., ed., *Sexual Inversion,* 17 authorities from the biological, social, medical, and behavioral sciences examine the roots of homosexuality as well as suggesting treatment.

Masters, R. E. L., *Sexual Self-Stimulation,* Sherbourne Press, Inc., 1967

Aspects of masturbation are covered, ranging from modern times to historical and anthropological aspects.

ALPHABETICAL LISTING BY AUTHORS

Page   *Page*

LIST OF PUBLISHERS

Abelard-Schuman Ltd., 257 Park Ave., New York, N.Y. 10010

Ace Books, Inc., 1120 Avenue of the Americas, New York, N.Y. 10036

Aldine Publishing Co., 320 West Adams St., Chicago, Ill. 60606

Apollo Editions, Inc., 201 Park Ave., S., New York, N.Y. 10003

Appleton Century, 250 Park Ave., New York, N.Y. 10017

Association Press, 291 Broadway, New York, N.Y. 10007

Atheneum Publishers, 122 East 42nd St., New York, N.Y. 10017

Avon Books, 959 Eighth Ave., New York, N.Y. 10019

Ballantine Books, Inc., 101 Fifth Ave., New York, N.Y. 10003

Bantam Books, Inc., 271 Madison Ave., New York, N.Y. 10016

Barron's Educational Series, Inc., 113 Crossways Park Dr., Woodbury, N.Y. 11797

Basic Books, Inc., Publishers, 404 Park Ave., S., New York, N.Y. 10016

Beacon Press, 25 Beacon St., Boston, Mass. 02108

Belmont Publishing Co., Belmont, Mass. 02178

Berkeley Press, 14 Bonnie Lane, Berkeley 8, Calif.

The Bobbs-Merrill Co., Inc., 4300 West 62nd St., Indianapolis, Ind. 46206

Bookman Associates, Inc., 31 Union Square, New York, N.Y. 10003

Borden Publishing, 1855 W. Main St., Alhambra, Calif. 91801

Brandon House, 7311 Fulton Ave., N. Hollywood, Calif. 91605

Brown Book Co., 39 Chambers St., New York, N.Y. 10007

William C. Brown Co., Publishers, 135 S. Locust St., Dubuque, Iowa 52001

Budlong Press, 5428 N. Virginia Ave., Chicago, Ill. 60625

Cambridge University Press, 32 East 57th St., New York, N.Y. 10022

Citadel Press, Inc., 222 Park Ave., S., New York, N.Y. 10003

College and University Press, 263 Chapel St., New Haven, Conn. 06513

Columbia University Press, 440 West 110th St., New York, N.Y. 10025

Concordia Publishing House, 3558 Jefferson Ave., St. Louis, Mo. 63118

Coward-McCann, Inc., 200 Madison Ave., New York, N.Y. 10016

Thomas Y. Crowell, 201 Park Ave., S., New York, N.Y. 10033

Crown Publishers, Inc., 419 Park Ave., S., New York, N.Y. 10016

F. A. Davis Co., 1914-16 Cherry St., Philadelphia, Pa. 19103

Delacorte Press, 750 Third Ave., New York, N.Y. 10017

Dell Books, Dell Publishing Co., Inc., 750 Third Ave., New York, N.Y. 10017

Delta Books, 750 Third Ave., New York, N.Y. 10017

T. S. Denison & Co., Inc., 5100 W. 82nd St., Minneapolis, Minn. 55431

Diablo Press, 440 Pacific Ave., San Francisco, Calif. 94133

The Dial Press, Inc., 750 Third Ave., New York, N.Y. 10017

Doubleday & Co., Inc., Garden City, New York 11530

Dover Publications, Inc., 180 Varick St., New York, N.Y. 10014

Duell, Sloan & Pearce, 250 Park Ave., New York, N.Y. 10017

Excerpta Medica Foundation, New York Academy of Medicine, 2 East 103rd St., New York, N.Y. 10029

Farrar, Straus & Giroux, Inc., 19 Union Square West, New York, N.Y. 10003

Fawcett World Library, (Crest, Premier), 67 West 44th St., New York, N.Y. 10036

Foresight Books, Inc., Box 2834, San Raphael, Calif. 94901

Fortress Press, 2900 Queen Lane, Philadelphia, Pa. 19129

The Free Press, 866 Third Ave., New York, N.Y. 10022

Friends Home Service Committee, Friends House, Euston Road, London, NW1, England

Funk & Wagnalls, 380 Madison Ave., New York, N.Y. 10017

Gamut Press, 29 East Tenth St., New York, N.Y. 10003

Garden City Books, 501 Franklin Ave., Garden City, N.Y. 11531

Bernard Geis Associates, 130 East 56th St., New York, N.Y. 10022

Golden Press, Western Publishing Co., Inc., 850 Third Ave., New York, N.Y. 10022

Grosset & Dunlap, Inc., 51 Madison Ave., New York, N.Y. 10010

Group for the Advancement of Psychiatry, 419 Park Ave. S., New York, N.Y. 10016

Grove Press, Inc., 80 University Place, New York, N.Y. 10003

Grune & Stratton, Inc., 381 Park Ave., S., New York, N.Y. 10016

HMH Publishing Co., Inc., Playboy Building, 919 N. Michigan Ave., Chicago, Ill. 60611

Harcourt, Brace & World, Inc., 757 Third Ave., New York, N.Y. 10017

Harper and Row, Publishers, 49 East 33rd St., New York, N.Y. 10016

Harvard University Press, 79 Garden St., Cambridge, Mass. 02138

Hawthorn Books, Inc., 70 Fifth Ave., New York, N.Y. 10011

Health Publications, 154 West 14th St., New York, N.Y. 10011

James H. Heineman, Inc., 60 East 42nd St., New York, N.Y. 10017

Henry Holt & Co., Inc., 383 Madison Ave., New York, N.Y. 10017

Holt, Rinehart & Winston, Inc., 383 Madison Ave., New York, N.Y. 10017

Johns Hopkins Press, Baltimore, Md. 21218

Houghton Mifflin Co., 2 Park St., Boston, Mass. 02107

Humanities Press, Inc., 303 Park Ave. S., New York, N.Y. 10010

Hutchinson Publishing Group, 229 Yorkland Blvd., Agincourt, Ont., Canada

Indiana University Press, Tenth and Morton Sts., Bloomington, Ind. 47401

International Publications Service, 303 Park Ave. S., New York, N.Y. 10010

Julian Press, Inc., 119 Fifth Ave., New York, N.Y. 10003

P. J. Kennedy & Sons, 12 Barclay St., New York, N.Y. 10007

Alfred A. Knopf, Inc., 201 East 50th St., New York, N.Y. 10022

Lawrence, Verry, Inc., Mystic, Conn. 06355

Lea & Febiger, 600 South Washington Square, Philadelphia, Pa. 19106

J. B. Lippincott Co., East Washington Square, Philadelphia, Pa. 19105

Little, Brown and Co., 34 Beacon St., Boston, Mass. 02106

London House & Maxwell, 122 East 55th St., New York, N.Y. 10002

Longmans, Green and Co., 40 Grosvenor St., London W1, England

Louisiana State University Press, Baton Rouge, La. 70803

Lyle Stuart, Inc., 239 Park Ave. S., New York, N.Y. 10003

Macfadden-Bartell Corp., 205 East 42nd St., New York, N.Y. 10017

MacGiggon & Kee, Ltd., 1-3 Upper James St., London W1, England

McGraw-Hill, Inc., 330 West 42nd St., New York, N.Y. 10036

David McKay Co., Inc., 750 Third Ave., New York, N.Y. 10017

Rand McNally & Co., P.O. Box 7600, Chicago, Ill. 60680

The Macmillan Co., 866 Third Ave., New York, N.Y. 10022

Matrix House, Ltd., Publishers, 119 Fifth Ave., New York, N.Y. 10003

Mental Health Materials Center, 419 Park Ave. S., New York, N.Y. 10016

Mentor Books, Publishers, 1301 Avenue of the Americas, New York, N.Y. 10019

Meredith Press, 1716 Locust St., Des Moines, Iowa 50303

Charles E. Merrill Books, Inc., 1300 Alum Creek Dr., Columbus, Ohio 43216

Julian Messner, 1 West 39th St., New York, N.Y. 10018

Modern Library, Inc., 457 Madison Ave., New York, N.Y. 10022

Monona-Driver Publications, P.O. Box 3222, Madison, Wis. 53704

William Morrow & Co., Inc., 425 Park Ave. S., New York, N.Y. 10016

C. V. Mosby Co., 3207 Washington Blvd., St. Louis, Mo. 63103

National Council of Churches, 475 Riverside Dr., New York, N.Y. 10027

The New American Library, Inc., 1301 Avenue of the Americas, New York, N.Y. 10019

New York University Press, 62 Fifth Ave., New York, N.Y. 10011

The Newman Press, 21 Harristown Road, Glen Rock, N.J. 07452

W. W. Norton & Co., Inc., 55 Fifth Ave., New York, N.Y. 10003

Oceana Publications, Inc., Dobbs Ferry, N.Y. 10522

Oxford University Press, Inc., 200 Madison Ave., New York, N.Y. 10016

Pantheon Books, Inc., 437 Madison Ave., New York, N.Y. 10022

Paperback Library, Inc., 315 Park Ave. S., New York, N.Y. 10010

Pelican Books, 7110 Ambassador Road, Baltimore, Md. 21207

Penguin Books, Inc., 7110 Ambassador Road, Baltimore, Md. 21207

Pent-R Books, Inc., 1560 Broadway, New York, N.Y. 10036

Pergamon Press, Inc., 122 East 55th St., New York, N.Y. 10022

Permabooks, 630 Fifth Ave., New York, N.Y. 10020

Philosophical Library, Inc., 15 East 40th St., New York, N.Y. 10016

Pioneer Publications Inc., 1015 W. 22nd St., Kearney, Neb. 68847

Pocket Books, 630 Fifth Ave., New York, N.Y. 10020

Popular Library, 355 Lexington Ave., New York, N.Y. 10017

Prentice-Hall, Inc., Englewood Cliffs, N.J. 07632

G. P. Putnam's Sons, 200 Park Ave., New York, N.Y. 10016

Pyramid Publications, Inc., 444 Madison Ave., New York, N.Y. 10022

Quadrangle Books, Inc., 12 East Delaware Place, Chicago, Ill. 60611

Random House, Inc., 201 East 50th St., New York, N.Y. 10022

Porter Sargent, Publisher, 11 Beacon St., Boston, Mass. 02108

Sacred Design Association, Inc., 840 Colorado Ave. S., Minneapolis, Minn. 55416

W. B. Saunders Co., Inc., 1 Story St., Harvard Square, Philadelphia, Pa. 19105

Schenkman Publishing Co., Inc., Cambridge, Mass. 02138

Schocken Books, Inc., 67 Park Ave., New York, N.Y. 10016

Scholastic Book Services, 50 West 44th St., New York, N.Y. 10036

Science & Behavior Books, Inc., 577 College Ave., Palo Alto, Calif. 94306

Science Editions, Inc., 605 Third Ave., New York, N.Y. 10016

Science House, Inc., 59 Fourth Ave., New York, N.Y. 10003

Charles Scribner's Sons, 597 Fifth Ave., New York, N.Y. 10017

The Seabury Press, Inc., 815 Second Ave., New York, N.Y. 10017

Sheed & Ward, 64 University Place, New York, N.Y. 10003

Sherbourne Press, Inc., 1640 S. La Cienega Blvd., L.A., Calif. 90035

Signet Books, 1301 Avenue of the Americas, New York, N.Y. 10019

Simon & Schuster, Inc., 630 Fifth Ave., New York, N.Y. 10020

Spectrum Books, Englewood Cliffs, N.J. 07631

Springer Publishing Co., 200 Park Ave. S., New York, N.Y. 10003

Stanford University Press, Stanford, Calif. 94305

Stein & Day, Publishers, 7 East 48th St., New York, N.Y. 10017

Tandem Books, 33 Beauchamp Place, London SW3, England

Charles C Thomas, Publisher, 301-27 East Lawrence Ave., Springfield, Ill. 62703

Time-Life Books, Time & Life Bldg., Sixth Ave. at 51st St., New York, N.Y. 10020

Trident Press, 630 Fifth Ave., New York, N.Y. 10020

Tyndale House, Publishers, Wheaton, Ill. 60187

Frederick Ungar Publishing Co., Inc., 250 Park Ave. S., New York, N.Y. 10003

Union of American Hebrew Congregations, 838 Fifth Ave., New York, N.Y. 10021

United Church Press, 1505 Race St., Philadelphia, Pa. 19102

University Books, Inc., 1615 Hillside Ave., New Hyde Park, N.Y. 11041

University of Chicago Press, 5750 Ellis Ave., Chicago, Ill. 60637

University of Illinois Press, Urbana, Ill. 61801

University of North Carolina Press, Chapel Hill, N.C. 27515

Van Nostrand-Rheinhold Co., 300 Pike St., Cincinnati, Ohio 45202

Vanguard Press, Inc., 424 Madison Ave., New York, N.Y. 10017

Vantage Press, Inc., 120 West 31st St., New York, N.Y. 10001

The Viking Press, Inc., 625 Madison Ave., New York, N.Y. 10022

The Westminster Press, Witherspoon Building, Philadelphia, Pa. 19107

John Wiley & Sons, Inc., 605 Third Ave., New York, N.Y. 10016

Whitmore Publishing Co., 1809-11 Callow Hill St., Philadelphia, Pa. 19130

The Williams & Wilkins Co., 428 East Preston St., Baltimore, Md. 21202

Word Books, Publishers, 4800 West Waco Drive, Waco, Texas 76710

The World Publishing Co., 2231 West 110th St., Cleveland, Ohio 44102

INDEX

NOTES

NOTES

NOTES

NOTES

NOTES

NOTES